"Long May Thy Servant
Feed Thy Sheep"

Monographs in Baptist History

VOLUME 37

SERIES EDITOR
Michael A. G. Haykin, The Southern Baptist Theological Seminary

EDITORIAL BOARD
Matthew Barrett, Midwestern Baptist Theological Seminary
Peter Beck, Charleston Southern University
Anthony L. Chute, California Baptist University
Jason G. Duesing, Midwestern Baptist Theological Seminary
Nathan A. Finn, North Greenville University
Crawford Gribben, Queen's University, Belfast
Gordon L. Heath, McMaster Divinity College
Barry Howson, Heritage Theological Seminary
Jason K. Lee, Cedarville University
Thomas J. Nettles, The Southern Baptist Theological Seminary, retired
James A. Patterson, Union University
James M. Renihan, Institute of Reformed Baptist Studies
Jeffrey P. Straub, Independent Scholar
Brian R. Talbot, Broughty Ferry Baptist Church, Scotland
Malcolm B. Yarnell III, Southwestern Baptist Theological Seminary

Ours is a day in which not only the gaze of western culture but also increasingly that of Evangelicals is riveted to the present. The past seems to be nowhere in view and hence it is disparagingly dismissed as being of little value for our rapidly changing world. Such historical amnesia is fatal for any culture, but particularly so for Christian communities whose identity is profoundly bound up with their history. The goal of this new series of monographs, Studies in Baptist History, seeks to provide one of these Christian communities, that of evangelical Baptists, with reasons and resources for remembering the past. The editors are deeply convinced that Baptist history contains rich resources of theological reflection, praxis, and spirituality that can help Baptists, as well as other Christians, live more Christianly in the present. The monographs in this series will therefore aim at illuminating various aspects of the Baptist tradition and in the process provide Baptists with a usable past.

"Perhaps it is time to stop referring to Benjamin Beddome as forgotten. In recent years a slow but steady trickle of articles and books has begun to flow, and after a long dark night of neglect, the long serving Cotswold pastor is once again being thrust into the light of day and his writings examined and discussed afresh. This fine contribution from Yuta Seki breaks new ground by delving into the hitherto neglected question of what can be mined from the Beddome corpus to teach us about the vital matter of pastoral theology. In a robust but very readable and applied manner, an academic and a pastor draws attention to salient lessons on this perennially important subject that will be of interest and benefit to all faithful pastors and to any who seek seriously to serve the Lord Jesus in their own generation. This book is warmly commended. Thank you, Dr. Seki."

—GARY BRADY, Pastor, Childs Hill Baptist Church, London

"Pastors today are facing something of a crisis. Unsure of their identity and role, many are looking to the world of business or entertainment for their models. Seki's study of Benjamin Beddome's pastoral theology provides a refreshing and biblical alternative. Here is one who looked to Christ and his word to shepherd his congregation of fifty-five years. Pastors would do well to remember his example (Heb 13:7) and apply it in their contexts."

—GEOFF CHANG, Assistant Professor of Historical Theology,
Midwestern Baptist Theological Seminary

"In our day of instant gratification, long pastorates that span decades—with the self-denial, patience, and perseverance they demand—are increasingly (and unfortunately) rare. Perhaps the reason why our spiritual forefathers, including such rural pastors as Benjamin Beddome, persevered so faithfully in the ministry was because of their recognition of the dignity, eternal weight, and responsibilities of the pastoral office. Synthesizing Beddome's letters, ordination sermons, hymns, and catechism, Dr. Seki retrieves the pastoral theology of a much-forgotten luminary in the eighteenth-century Particular Baptist movement to provide a compelling account of Beddome's pastoral theology, including his emphasis on the qualifications, duties, gifts, self-examination, spirituality, experiential piety, and preaching of pastors. Here is a goldmine for scholars and pastors alike!"

—JOEL R. BEEKE, Professor of Homiletics and Systematic Theology,
Puritan Reformed Theological Seminary

"I have long encouraged pastors they need two pastoral mentors in their life. They need a living one of which they can sit down, watch, and learn. And they need a dead one they can read, reflect, and consider their example from another age. And after reading the book in your hands, I strongly believe Benjamin Beddome is one of those long gone, faithful pastors, and all modern pastors would immensely benefit from his life and ministry. Yuta Seki has done us a great service by providing this well-written and well-researched account of Beddome's pastoral theology. And the beautiful, insightful account on why Beddome stayed in his smaller country church for his entire ministry, instead of moving to a more predominant, influential church in London is worth the price of the whole book. I commend both Beddome's example and this book to you."

—Brian Croft, Executive Director, Practical Shepherding

"In a world that prizes platform over perseverance and flash over faithfulness even in the pastorate, Benjamin Beddome's life serves as a reminder of a better way. I was deeply convicted and spiritually challenged as Yuta Seki reintroduced me to this Cotswold pastor whose fifty-five years in one congregation yielded a legacy of deep faith, rich preaching, and pastoral steadfastness. This is both a compelling historical portrait and a timeless call for today's pastors to live for the satisfaction of God's pleasure even when in apparent obscurity."

—Hershael W. York, Victor and Louise Lester Professor of Preaching, The Southern Baptist Theological Seminary

"It is in vogue today for evangelical scholars to engage in works of 'retrieval.' Theological retrieval, of course, is only as profitable as what's being retrieved. Dr. Seki has done the church a great service by retrieving Benjamin Beddome, the eighteenth-century English Particular Baptist pastor who ministered for over five decades at Bourton-on-the-Water Baptist Church in rural England. Although his setting might be described as insignificant, Beddome's influence was extraordinary through his catechism, preaching, hymns, and relationship with Bristol Baptist Academy for the training of ministers. Through this thoroughly researched and well-written work, Dr. Seki has accomplished a most worthy service of retrieval. For the good of the church and her ministers, may Beddome's voice resound in our day."

—Michael Pohlman, Associate Professor of Pastoral Theology, The Southern Baptist Theological Seminary

"Long May Thy Servant Feed Thy Sheep"

The Pastoral Theology of Benjamin Beddome

YUTA SEKI

Foreword by Michael A. G. Haykin

☙PICKWICK *Publications* · Eugene, Oregon

LONG MAY THY SERVANT FEED THY SHEEP
The Pastoral Theology of Benjamin Beddome

Monographs in Baptist History 37

Copyright © 2025 Yuta Seki. All rights reserved. Except for brief quotations in critical publications or reviews, no part of this book may be reproduced in any manner without prior written permission from the publisher. Write: Permissions, Wipf and Stock Publishers, 199 W. 8th Ave., Suite 3, Eugene, OR 97401.

Pickwick Publications
An Imprint of Wipf and Stock Publishers
199 W. 8th Ave., Suite 3
Eugene, OR 97401

www.wipfandstock.com

PAPERBACK ISBN: 979-8-3852-4773-8
HARDCOVER ISBN: 979-8-3852-4774-5
EBOOK ISBN: 979-8-3852-4775-2

Cataloguing-in-Publication data:

Names: Seki, Yuta [author]. | Haykin, Michael A. G. [foreword writer].

Title: Long may thy servant feed thy sheep : the pastoral theology of Benjamin Beddome / Yuta Seki. ; with a foreword by Michael A. G. Haykin

Description: Eugene, OR: Pickwick Publications, 2025 | Series: Monographs in Baptist History | Includes bibliographical references.

Identifiers: ISBN 979-8-3852-4773-8 (paperback) | ISBN 979-8-3852-4774-5 (hardcover) | ISBN 979-8-3852-4775-2 (ebook)

Subjects: LCSH: Beddome, Benjamin, 1717–1795. | Pastoral theology—Baptists. | Baptists—History. | Theology.

Classification: BX6495.B4 S455 2025 (print) | BX6495.B4 (ebook)

Where noted, Scripture quotations are from the ESV® Bible (The Holy Bible, English Standard Version®), © 2001 by Crossway, a publishing ministry of Good News Publishers. Used by permission. All rights reserved.

Where noted, Scripture quotations are from the King James Version. The KJV is public domain in the United States.

To my beloved, Alyssa

Table of Contents

Foreword ix
Preface xi
Acknowledgments xv
List of Abbreviations xviii

1. Introduction 1
2. The Pastoral Theology of the English Particular Baptists According to Their Ordination Sermons 18
3. Pastoral Ministry According to Benjamin Beddome's Letters 52
4. Pastoral Ministry According to Benjamin Beddome's Ordination Sermons 105
5. Retrieving Benjamin Beddome's Pastoral Theology for the Contemporary Church 159

Bibliography 185

Foreword

ROBERT HALL JR., ONE of the greatest English preachers during the first half of the nineteenth century, once said of Benjamin Beddome that he was "on many accounts an extraordinary person," for even though "he spent the principal part of a long life in a village retirement, he was eminent for his colloquial powers." "As a preacher," Hall continued, "he was universally admired . . . [and] as a religious poet, his excellence has long been known and acknowledged in dissenting congregations."[1] Yet, like the names of a number of other eminent eighteenth-century Baptists, that of Beddome is known by few Baptists today. He receives mention in three of the standard histories of the Baptist movement in Great Britain that were written in the twentieth century,[2] but the references are all too brief and in at least one instance inaccurate.[3] By contrast, he remained a prominent figure in the British Baptist memory well into the Victorian era, which raises the question as to why he came to be so neglected by Baptists since World War I or so. Possibly it is due to the fact that up until the end of the nineteenth century a goodly number of his hymns were still being sung. In the twentieth and twenty-first centuries, however, his hymns have largely fallen into obscurity, and with them interest in their author.

Beddome does not appear to have left a diary behind to inform any would-be biographer of the details of his life. Nor are many of his personal letters extant. A good number of his sermons exist, and over eight hundred hymns, but they contain little biographical information. The minute books of Bourton-on-the-Water Baptist Church, where he served for fifty-five years, are currently housed in the Angus Library of Regent's Park College,

---

1. Hall, "Recommendatory Preface," v–vii.

2. Whitley, *History*, 224, 260, 308; Underwood, *History*, 140, 142; Brown, *English Baptists*, 84, 93, 121.

3. Underwood places Beddome's death in 1798 (*History*, 140). It actually took place in 1795.

Oxford. They contain copious records of certain aspects of his ministry, for example, records about baptisms, church discipline, and deaths, letters of dismission and correspondence with the Midland Association, but very little about Beddome the person.

Dr. Seki's study of Beddome is therefore most welcome. Through its focus on Beddome's understanding of pastoral leadership, we hear again the wise voice and counsel of one of the most respected English Baptists of the long eighteenth century. And if we wish to be truly wise, we need to pay heed to both his thought and his experience. One may not always agree with him, but in this day of chaotic models of leadership, those in Christian leadership need all the help they can garner so as to rightly guide the people of God.

Michael A. G. Azad Haykin
Dundas, Ontario
March 12, 2025

Preface

It may seem like an oddity to write a book on the pastoral theology of a forgotten Baptist figure who ministered in an obscure village of rural England over two hundred years ago. Benjamin Beddome (1718–1795) was the pastor of the Baptist church in Bourton-on-the-Water from 1743 until his death in 1795. Given that he arrived in Bourton in 1740 as what was called a probationer, he ministered there for fifty-five years. Though he pastored in an insignificant town, this does not entail that his ministry there was insignificant. Rather, quite the opposite was the case. Beddome was well-respected within the Midland Association of churches, the broader Particular Baptist denomination, and beyond. His influence can be demonstrated, for example, in that his catechism was used by the Bristol Baptist Academy, the sole training center for Particular Baptist ministers during the eighteenth century in England. Further, the posthumous publication of his sermons and hymns ensured his legacy endured into the twentieth century. Despite the respect he garnered and the influence he had, Beddome is a forgotten figure amongst evangelicals, even those of the Baptist sort. It is this author's conviction, though, that much can be learned from Beddome. Thus, the goal of this monograph is to retrieve the pastoral theology of Benjamin Beddome for the contemporary church and its pastors.

This book began as a thesis for the doctor of educational ministry program at The Southern Baptist Theological Seminary. The idea for the thesis emerged from the confluence of two factors. First, I wanted to choose a topic that would help me to be a better pastor, and second, I desired to write under the supervision of Michael A. G. Haykin. After some correspondence with Dr. Haykin, it was decided that my topic would be pastoral ministry according to the life and thought of Benjamin Beddome. Though others had written on Beddome in recent years, none had studied his *pastoralia* at any length. Thus, it was a lacuna in eighteenth-century Particular Baptist history. That it was an untapped area of research had a certain appeal to me, as did one other factor: Beddome was an ordinary pastor. Though he was respected by many in his generation, he was not as influential or significant to the Baptist cause as John Gill (1697–1771) or Andrew Fuller (1754–1815), who were both contemporaries of Beddome. Beddome is therefore helpful to the contemporary pastor, because he can be emulated.[1]

A fuller road map of the contents of the book can be found in chapter 1, but I will provide a brief overview to orient the reader. Chapter 1 is a literature review of the key primary and secondary sources on Beddome. The key takeaway is that there has been no sustained work on his pastoral theology. Chapter 2 first provides an explanation of the ordination service, and the ordination sermons preached therein, and the significant role that these sermons played in English Particular Baptist life in the eighteenth century. The remainder of the chapter is an analysis of select Particular Baptist ordination sermons to construct the pastoral theology of this communion. In chapter 3, the letters of Beddome are analyzed to understand his views on pastoral ministry. There are a particular set of letters exchanged between the Baptist churches of Bourton-on-the-Water and Goodman's Fields in London. In them, the two churches were vying for the pastoral services of Beddome—would he remain in Bourton or relocate to London? Much wisdom can be retrieved from these letters. In chapter 4, Beddome's ordination sermons, alongside his catechism and hymns, are analyzed and synthesized to produce his pastoral theology. A particular goal of this chapter is to demonstrate the continuity of Beddome's *pastoralia* with that of his Particular Baptist brethren, and also to show his unique contribution. In the final and fifth chapter, several lessons of wisdom are retrieved from the pastoral theology of Beddome for the contemporary church and its pastors.

It is my desire that this book contributes to Beddome studies as well as to the overall efforts to recover the life and thought of his communion, namely, the English Particular Baptists of the long eighteenth century. Though the book was written originally for academic purposes, the reader will hopefully find it accessible. The work is not laced with technical jargon, and historical practices that are unfamiliar to the modern reader are explained. Further, while the genre of this work is not biography, I have tried to include biographical details in each chapter to retain interest.

At an ordination service of a Particular Baptist pastor, two sermons were prominent—the charge to the ordinand and the sermon to the church. The goal of each was to exhort both parties, the pastor and the church, regarding their respective roles, duties, and motivations. It may be helpful

---

1. For the notion that Beddome can be more easily emulated than other towering figures from church history, see Brady, "Benjamin Beddome (1717–1795)," 145.

for the reader to receive this book in that manner. May ordinary pastors be encouraged toward faithfulness in the station to which God has called them, be sharpened in their understanding of their identity and duties as pastors, and be spurred on to lead their flocks unto greener pastures. Likewise, may ordinary Christians grow in their appreciation for the local church, increase in their esteem for the shepherds appointed to lead them, and be more committed to their responsibilities as members of Christ's flock.

Yuta Seki
Georgetown, Ontario
March 2025

Acknowledgments

I CONCUR WITH THE apostle Paul, who wrote, in his first letter to the Corinthians, "By the grace of God I am what I am" (1 Cor 15:10 ESV). The blessings in my life have been an expression of the undeserved grace and mercy of the God who has, for reasons unbeknownst to me, chosen to redeem me from my sins and adopt me as his son. This book is a further manifestation of his kindness to me, as are all the people and providences that have made the writing of it possible.

At every major writing milestone I cross, I think of my college professor Elaine Phillips, who showed me that writing was both possible and enjoyable. As noted, this book was originally written as a doctoral thesis at The Southern Baptist Theological Seminary. At Southern, Matthew D. Haste helped me in drafting the proposal, and Michael E. Pohlman served on the defense committee as the second reader. Jennifer Stec skillfully edited my work, and Roy M. Paul assisted me in the publication process. Gary Brady was helpful through correspondence, Stephen McKay sent me his master's thesis on a related topic, and Jason C. Montgomery shared with me his photographs of the minute books of the Baptist church in Bourton-on-the-Water. Over the past few years, Michael A. G. Haykin has become my supervisor, mentor, and friend. I am thankful for his guidance during the writing process, with his knowledge and skill as a historian and adept eye at making needed corrections to my work. He has given me a deeper love for church history and a greater appreciation for my roots, not only as an evangelical, Baptist, and Christian, but also as a Canadian and a Fellowship pastor.[1]

When I was growing up, my mother worked tirelessly to provide for my brother and me and to give us opportunities to achieve our goals. The longer I live, the more I have come to appreciate all the sacrifices she has made for me. My wife's parents, Darcy and Sandra Derkson, have always

---

1. Dr. Haykin and I belong to churches that are part of The Fellowship of Evangelical Baptist Churches in Canada.

been kind and generous toward me, even before Alyssa and I were dating. Today, they continue to be a source of support, love, and childcare. My first pastor, Norm Derkson, had an enormous impact on my life, as did my most recent pastor, James Seward. Norm was the pastor of Banff Park Church, at which I was saved, baptized, and discipled as a new believer. James was, until recently, the senior pastor of Maple Avenue Baptist Church (MABC), where I began vocational ministry. Under Norm, I learned the ins-and-outs of being a Christian, and under James, the ins-and-outs of being a pastor. As for friendships, I am thankful for Shaun Martens, a fellow laborer in the gospel and that "friend who sticks closer than a brother" (Prov 18:24 ESV). Caleb Hall and Mitch Hogeveen also deserve mention as close friends. In addition to these three, the Lord has blessed me with many pastoral friendships, and though they could not all be listed here, I am grateful for my brethren in the ministry who labor for the sake of the gospel.

It is a privilege to serve as the senior pastor of MABC. This church welcomed Alyssa and me with open arms when we arrived eight years ago, and they have continued to love our family well since. When our son Noah was diagnosed with leukemia four years ago, the church came alongside us by tangibly serving us and praying for us; God used that trial to knit our hearts closer together. MABC has also given me an environment in which I could grow as a pastor. Furthermore, I am grateful for the fellow elders who diligently care for and lead the flock. With respect to my studies, I am thankful to them and the church for affording me time to be away for classes and periods for coursework and writing. Last, the three men who serve on the pastoral staff of the church, the father-son pair of Terry and Matt Laidlaw, along with Eros Olazabal, have been a constant source of godly encouragement, gospel partnership, and genuine friendship.

Of course, I am grateful for my beloved wife and children. The Lord has blessed Alyssa and me with Noah, Luke, Mark, and four days after defending this thesis, Caleb Benjamin. Though perhaps not always cognizant of it, the older three had to make sacrifices for Daddy to be back in school. I am deeply thankful to be called "Dad" by these gentlemen. They bring much fun, laughter, and volume to our home, and they brighten up my day with their presence. May each of our boys know, love, and serve the Lord Jesus with his whole heart and life. Finally, I want to acknowledge and thank my wife for her consistent support of, and devotion to, her imperfect husband. Even before Alyssa and I were dating, she felt called to be a pastor's wife, and so we truly are in ministry together. Our boys adore her, and she is the one who keeps the ship of our home afloat and sailing. She is a wise counselor, good listener, and kind encourager. Also, since I am a verbal processor, it is often Alyssa who helps me to work through the many thoughts running through my head on any given day, including many conversations about an obscure Baptist pastor who ministered in rural England over two hundred years ago. Both for me to be a pastor and a doctoral student, she has had to sacrifice much. For this, and for one thousand other reasons, I am thankful for Alyssa, my first friend apart from the friend of sinners (Matt 11:19). She is my beloved, and it is difficult to capture in a few sentences my affection and gratitude for the beautiful gift that God has given to me.

Abbreviations

BQ	*Baptist Quarterly*
EQ	*Evangelical Quarterly*
JAFS	*Journal of Andrew Fuller Studies*
MBH	Monographs in Baptist History
NPNF2	*Nicene and Post-Nicene Fathers*, Series 2
POTP	Brooks, Thomas. *Pictures of the Past: The History of the Baptist Church, Bourton-on-the-Water*. London: Judd & Glass, 1861
S&T	Gill, John. *A Collection of Sermons and Tracts*. 2 vols. London: George Keith, 1773
SBHT	Studies in Baptist History and Thought
SBJT	*Southern Baptist Journal of Theology*
SD	Beddome, Benjamin. *Short Discourses, Adapted to Village Worship or the Devotions of the Family*. Vol. 8. London: Samuel Burton; Simpkin and Marshall, 1825
SP	Beddome, Benjamin. *Sermons Printed from the Manuscripts of the Late Rev. Benjamin Beddome, A. M. of Bourton-on-the-Water, Gloucestershire; with a Memoir of the Author*. London: William Ball, 1835
TSD	Beddome, Benjamin. *Twenty Short Discourses*
WAF	Fuller, Andrew. *The Complete Works of the Rev. Andrew Fuller with a Memoir of His Life by Andrew Gunton Fuller*. 3 vols. Edited by Joseph Belcher. Philadelphia: American Baptist Publication Society, 1845

CHAPTER 1

Introduction

MOST EVANGELICALS ARE LARGELY unfamiliar with the story of the English Particular Baptists of the long eighteenth century.[1] The obvious exception, of course, is William Carey (1761–1834), the father of the modern missionary movement. Those who know Carey's story have also heard of his friend, Andrew Fuller (1754–1815), the theological architect behind the Baptist Missionary Society that sent Carey to India.[2] Theological students and pastors may have read the works of John Gill (1697–1771). But what about names like Bernard Foskett (1685–1758), Benjamin Francis (1734–1799), Caleb Evans (1737–1791), or John Ryland Jr. (1753–1825)? Though these men were influential in the Particular Baptist denomination in their time, they are largely unknown today, even among many Baptists who trace their theological and spiritual heritage back to this communion. This paucity of knowledge is regrettable, since the Particular Baptists have much to teach the contemporary church.

There have been recent efforts to fill this lacuna, however. Michael A. G. Haykin, for example, has devoted himself to the recovery of the life and thought of Fuller and his contemporaries. To this end, he publishes the biannual *Journal of Andrew Fuller Studies* and serves as the editor of a critical edition of *The Complete Works of Andrew Fuller*.[3] During his career as a

---

1. Large parts of this chapter, and smaller sections later in this thesis, appeared as Yuta Seki, "A Resurgence of Benjamin Beddome Studies: A Bibliographic Essay," *JAFS* 8 (Spring 2024) 45–60. Used with permission.

2. In addition to Carey, missions-minded evangelicals may have heard of Adoniram Judson (1788–1850) and his wife Ann (1789–1826). The Judsons were *American* Particular Baptist missionaries who took the gospel to Burma, which is modern-day Myanmar. Evangelical awareness of the Judsons has surely been helped by Anderson, *To the Golden Shore*.

3. Fuller, *Works of Andrew Fuller* (2016–). The *Journal of Andrew Fuller Studies*

Baptist historian, Haykin has also done significant work on an earlier and lesser-known figure of the English Particular Baptist movement, Benjamin Beddome (1718–1795), the focus of this book.

For fifty-five years (1740–1795), Beddome ministered in Bourton-on-the-Water in the rural Cotswolds area of south-central England.[4] He was well known in his day and into the nineteenth century for his preaching and hymnody. He also published a catechism that was widely used among English Particular Baptists.[5] During his long pastorate, Beddome had invitations to pastor in Bristol and London—the two largest cities in England at the time—but he chose to remain in the less visible town of Bourton-on-the-Water.[6] Regarding the period in which the Bourton pastor ministered, Haykin said that his was "a ministry between the times—those of Baptist advance in the seventeenth century and those of revival in the final decades of the eighteenth century."[7] Thus, Beddome ministered in an obscure place and did not experience the extraordinarily visible fruitfulness of his Baptist forebears or posterity. Nevertheless, the impact and usefulness of his pastoral ministry, preaching, hymnody, and catechism garnered the respect of his contemporaries and those who would study him generations after his death.

Although Beddome published very few works during his lifetime, he left behind a large body of sermons and hymns that demonstrate his abilities as a preacher and hymnist. These were published in the decades after his death during the nineteenth century, but the Bourton pastor was largely

---

publishes "articles that deal with the life, ministry, and thought of the Baptist pastor-theologian Andrew Fuller . . . as well as essays on his friends, his Particular Baptist community in the long eighteenth century (1680s–1830s), and the global impact of his thought, known as 'Fullerism.'" This note is found in the front matter for the journal, e.g., Haykin, *JAFS* 7 (2023) 3. This resurgence of Fuller studies began in the early 1980s and is captured in Finn, "Renaissance," 44–61.

4. Beddome first went to Bourton-on-the-Water in 1740. For the first three years, he likely divided his time between Bourton and Warwick, but in 1743, he was invited to be the pastor of the Bourton church, where he remained until his death in 1795. Thus, Beddome ministered in Bourton for fifty-five years and was the pastor there for fifty-two. For the information in this paragraph, see Brooks, *POTP*, 25–26, 59; Rippon, "Rev. Benjamin Beddome," 317.

5. For a modern reprint of this catechism, see Beddome, *Scriptural Exposition* (2006).

6. Robert Hall Jr. (1764–1831) said of Beddome's remaining in Bourton, "Though he spent the principal part of a long life in a village retirement, he was eminent for his colloquial powers, in which he displayed the urbanity of the gentleman, and the erudition of the scholar, combined with a more copious vein of attic salt than any person it has been my lot to know." Hall, "Recommendatory Preface," vi. There are two editions of the *Hymns* cited in this thesis; hereafter, the "Recommendatory Preface" and "Editor's Preface" are cited from the 1818 edition.

7. Haykin, "His Hymns," 111.

forgotten in the twentieth. There has been a recent resurgence of Beddome studies, which has brought greater attention to Beddome's life, theology, and hymnody.[8] However, no study has focused on his pastoral theology. This book will examine Beddome's works—his sermons, hymns, catechism, and letters—to explore the nature of pastoral ministry in the life and thought of Benjamin Beddome.

FAMILIARITY WITH THE LITERATURE

This literature review will first survey Beddome's own writings. Then, a historiography of Beddome will be given, noting biographical works and studies conducted throughout the centuries. The third section will review recent works focused on specific aspects of Beddome's thought and hymnody. Last, this survey will list background sources and parallel studies.

Primary Sources

As mentioned, Beddome published few works during his lifetime.[9] Most notably, he published *A Scriptural Exposition of the Baptist Catechism by Way of Question and Answer*.[10] This was an expansion of *The Baptist Catechism* commonly attributed to Benjamin Keach (1640–1704).[11] Following the practice of his forebears, Beddome used *The Baptist Catechism* earlier in his ministry but sensed some lack and so expanded on the original by adding sub-questions and answers to each section. Beddome's catechism was widely

---

8. For the renewed interest in Beddome, see Seki, "Resurgence," 54–59.

9. Daniel S. Ramsey notes that there were only two works produced by Beddome during his lifetime, referring to the catechism and the 1765 circular letter of the Midland Association. Ramsey, "Blessed Spirit," 4. This is corroborated by Brooks who wrote, "Although Mr. Beddome was an indefatigable writer he published but little—his catechism, in 1752, which he employed at Bourton among adults as well as children . . . and the circular letter of 1765, were the only things he thus gave the world." Brooks, *POTP*, 60. Beddome did, however, publish the 1759 circular letter (see n14).

10. Beddome, *Scriptural Exposition* (1752). For a fuller listing of sources on Beddome, see Seki, "Resurgence," 45–60.

11. Haykin says, "Although a pastor by the name of William Collins (d. 1702) was asked to draw it up, many would later know it as *Keach's Catechism*, and it would appear that the prolific Baptist author Benjamin Keach was mainly responsible for it." Haykin, "Benjamin Beddome (1717–1795)" (2018), 4:267. This chapter is a slightly revised version of Haykin, "Benjamin Beddome (1717–1795)" (1998), 1:167–83. See bibliography for full publication details. Unless otherwise indicated, the 2018 version is cited in this book.

circulated, as evidenced by its use in the Bristol Baptist Academy[12]—the principal training center for British Baptists in the eighteenth century—and several printings during his lifetime and into the nineteenth century.[13] Beddome also published the circular letters of the Midland Association in 1759 and 1765.[14] These letters provide helpful information regarding Beddome's association in which he was an active participant and leader. Several circular letters are available, while others have been transcribed into the Bourton church books.[15]

Beddome penned several other letters. There are six letters written to unknown relatives,[16] a letter to Andrew Fuller expressing hesitation concerning the Baptist Missionary Society,[17] and several letters written to Ben-

12. Haykin states, "The Bristol Baptist Academy [was] the sole British Baptist seminary for much of the eighteenth century." Haykin, "Glory to the Three Eternal" (2006), 77. For the history and impact of the Bristol Academy, see Bebbington, "Bristol Baptist College," 149–66; Rippon, *Baptist Academy at Bristol*; Yoo, "Bristol Academy." The institution has been variably titled during its existence. For the first fifty years (1720–70), the school was referred to as an academy, but with the formation of the Bristol Education Society in 1770, the title "Seminary" was used. By 1812, the school was regularly called Bristol Baptist Academy, and in 1841, the printed annual reports called it Bristol Baptist College. For the information regarding the name of the school, see Hayden, "Bristol Baptist Academy."

13. For the details of this paragraph, I am indebted to Haykin, "Benjamin Beddome (1717–1795)," 4:267–68.

14. Beddome, *Circular Letter* (1759); Beddome, *Circular Letter* (1765). William Stokes recorded that Beddome wrote the 1759 circular letter for the Midland Association and that this was "the first *printed* circular letter." Stokes, *Midland Association*, 89. The circular letters of 1753 and 1758 were also penned by Beddome. The 1753 letter, according to Jason C. Montgomery, was transcribed into the church books. Montgomery, "Benjamin Beddome," 143n69, 147. The 1758 letter was also transcribed into the church books and is included in Pickles, *Cotswolds Pastor*, 255–57.

15. E.g., Beddome, *Circular Letter* (1765). The author has found circular letters of the Midland Association from the years 1761, 1763, 1764, 1766–68, 1777, 1772, 1775, 1777–79, and 1789. Regarding the publication of these letters, Montgomery observes, "Beddome transcribed into the church books copies of the Circular Letters from 1751 to 1758. Beginning in 1759, the Circular Letters were published and were no longer inscribed by Beddome into the church books." Montgomery, "Benjamin Beddome," 143n69. There are three volumes of the Bourton-on-the-Water church books, and they are held at the Angus Library and Archive, Regent's Park College, Oxford: *Bourton-on-the-Water Church Book 1719–1802*; *Bourton-on-the-Water Church Book 1745–1773*; *Bourton-on-the-Water Church Book 1765–1920*.

16. These were originally published in the *Evangelical Magazine* 8 (April–September 1800) 156, 197, 229–30, 272–73, 319, 370, and then later reprinted as Beddome, "Extracts from Six Letters," 59–65.

17. Beddome to Fuller, October 2, 1793, in Pickles, *Cotswolds Pastor*, 388–89; the original is at the Angus Library. Montgomery noted that Beddome closed "his letter with a final section in which he [expressed] to Fuller hesitations regarding the formation of the BMS itself." Montgomery, "Benjamin Beddome," 154.

jamin Beddome by his father, John, at important junctures in the younger Beddome's life.[18] There was also a significant correspondence between the Bourton Baptist Church and the Little Prescott Street Baptist Church in Goodman's Fields in London.[19] The London church had recently lost their pastor, Samuel Wilson (1702–1750), and invited Beddome to be his successor. The Bourton church and its pastor, however, refused the persistent appeals of the Goodman's Fields church. An analysis of the seven letters exchanged between Bourton and London, as well as the other correspondence, will be the focus of chapter 3.

As noted, Beddome was a powerful preacher and prolific hymnwriter. He left behind a large collection of sermons and hymns, which were published posthumously.[20] In an introduction to a volume of his sermons, the anonymous memorialist said the discourses were "short sketches of sermons which [were] taken from his manuscripts." Accordingly, the writer reminded his readers, "It must not, however, be forgotten, that they are the mere skeletons and hints, which he filled out in the pulpit, and preserved without the least design of publication."[21] The extant sermons were the notes from his manuscripts and not what he would have preached verbatim to his congregation. The 225 sermons were published in nine volumes. Sixty-seven were in *Sermons Printed from the Manuscripts of the Late Rev. Benjamin Beddome, A.M. of Bourton-on-the-Water, Gloucestershire; with a Brief Memoir of the Author*, which was published in London in 1835 by William Ball.[22] The remaining sermons were published in a collection of eight volumes—the first seven were titled *Twenty Short Discourses, Adapted to Village Worship or the Devotions of the Family* and the eighth, *Short Discourses, Adapted to Village Worship or the Devotions of the Family*.[23] Approximately

---

18. Brooks, POTP, 23–26; these letters also appear in Anonymous, "Memoir," in Beddome, SP, viii–xix.

19. Brooks, POTP, 32–47; these letters also appeared as Brooks, "Ministerial Changes" (July 1859) 425–29; Brooks, "Ministerial Changes" (August 1859) 482–87.

20. Though most of his hymns were published after his death, Haykin notes how Beddome allowed "thirteen of his hymns to be published in a hymnal edited by fellow Baptists John Ash (1724–1779) and Caleb Evans (1737–1791) in 1769, *A Collection of Hymns Adapted to Public Worship*. Twenty or so years later, thirty-six of them appeared in the first edition of John Rippon's *A Selection of Hymns from the Best Authors* (1787)." Haykin, "Bourton-on-the-Water," viii.

21. Anonymous, "Memoir," in Beddome, SP, xxvi.

22. A modern reprint of this work is Beddome, *Sermons of Benjamin Beddome*.

23. Beddome, *Twenty Short Discourses*, 7 vols.; Beddome, *Short Discourses*. There were several publications of these volumes; for more details, see Haykin, "Benjamin Beddome (1717–1795)," 4:273; Montgomery, "Benjamin Beddome," 26n62. The slightly different titling of the eighth volume was because it contained only eighteen discourses,

ten of the sermons have been identified as ordination sermons, and their analysis will be the focus of chapter 4.

Beddome also wrote many hymns. It was the habit of the Bourton pastor to compose a hymn suited to his sermon, which was sung at the close of the service.[24] In 1818, 830 hymns were published by Robert Hall Jr. (1764–1831) in *Hymns Adapted to Public Worship, or Family Devotion: Now First Published, from the Manuscripts of the Late Rev. B. Beddome, A.M.*[25] Several hymns were devoted to the subject of pastoral ministry; these will be explored in chapter 4, alongside his ordination sermons, to establish Beddome's pastoral theology.

A good number of Beddome's letters, sermons, hymns have been preserved for posterity, along with his catechism. Of course, for the Bourton pastor, his main aim in expanding the catechism, penning the letters, crafting the sermons, and composing the hymns was to minister to the Bourton church and those within the Midland Association. That his labors were appreciated even forty years after his death is evident in a passing comment made in an obituary in *The Baptist Magazine*. The memoir is of Boswell Beddome, who was, according to the obituary, the "grandson of the Rev. Benjamin Beddome, whose sermons and hymns are still the admiration of the churches."[26] As for his catechism, it was printed twice during his lifetime, and "reprinted once in the British Isles and twice in the United States" in the nineteenth century, evidencing its popularity and widespread usage.[27] Having cataloged the primary sources of Beddome, the next section will survey the various biographical works on Beddome.

Biographical Sources

Just two years after Beddome's death, John Rippon (1751–1836) wrote an obituary of the Bourton pastor in *The Baptist Annual Register*.[28] In the nine-

---

whereas the others had twenty. Also, a single sermon was published as Rippon, "Sketch of a Sermon," 415–21. This sermon also appeared as Beddome, "Sermon 10," in TSD, 5:81–89.

24. Hall remarked, "During a long-continued and highly useful ministry, he was in the habit of preparing a few verses suited to the subject of his pulpit discourses, and which were sung in his own congregation, more or less frequently, at the close of the public services." Hall, "Editor's Preface," ix.

25. A modern reprint of this work is Beddome, *Hymns* (2020). Haykin says that these were "822 hymns and 8 doxologies." Haykin, "Bourton-on-the-Water," viii.

26. Anonymous, "Mr. Boswell Beddome," 77.

27. Haykin, "His Hymns," 102.

28. Rippon, "Rev. Benjamin Beddome," 314–26. *The Baptist Annual Register*

teenth century, brief sketches of Beddome were included in the prefatory material of publications of his hymns, catechism, and sermons. Hall included two prefaces to his collection of Beddome's hymns, published in 1818.[29] Similarly, J. L. Reynolds affixed an introduction to the 1849 edition of Beddome's catechism, and an anonymously written memoir was affixed to the stand-alone volume of sermons *Sermons Printed from the Manuscripts of the Late Rev. Benjamin Beddome*.[30]

Joseph Ivimey (1773–1834) included a biography of Beddome in *A History of the English Baptists*, which he published in 1830.[31] A few decades later, Thomas Brooks—pastor of the Bourton church in the nineteenth century—published *Pictures of the Past: The History of the Baptist Church, Bourton-on-the-Water*.[32] This history chronicled the period from the church's inception through to the author's own day (1655–1861), and Beddome is the focus of four chapters.[33] Brooks recorded the major events during Beddome's tenure and his pastoral practices. The correspondence between Bourton and Goodman's Fields was reproduced with brief comments, but Brooks did not provide a full analysis.[34] Stephen Albert Swaine wrote a short biography of Beddome in *Faithful Men: Memorials of Bristol College, and Some of Its Most Distinguished Alumni*.[35] Short biographical sketches were also written by Joseph Belcher (1859), G. Hester (1865), and J. M. Cramp (1869).[36]

---

provides background information concerning the English Particular Baptist denomination during a critical period of their history. Ken Manley says, "The thirteen years during which Rippon published his *Register* were among the most significant in the history of the Particular Baptists in both Britain and the United States." Manley, *Redeeming Love Proclaim*, 139. In addition to the register published in 1797 containing the Beddome obituary, Rippon published three other registers: Rippon, *Baptist Annual Register* (1793); Rippon, *Baptist Annual Register* (1801); Rippon, *Baptist Annual Register* (1802).

29. Hall, "Recommendatory Preface," v–viii; Hall, "Editor's Preface," ix–xi.

30. Reynolds, "Introduction," 3–27; Anonymous, "Memoir," in Beddome, *SP*, ix–xxviii.

31. Ivimey, *History*, 4:461–69. The work by Ivimey, though, is largely a reproduction of Rippon's work according to Haykin. Haykin, "Benjamin Beddome (1717–1795)," 4:272.

32. Brooks, *POTP*.

33. Brooks, *POTP*, 21–66.

34. Brooks, *POTP*, 32–49.

35. Swaine, *Faithful Men*, 42–47. Montgomery says that, in Swaine's work, Beddome is "associated with a virtual 'Who's Who' listing of evangelical Calvinistic ministers." Montgomery, "Benjamin Beddome," 5.

36. Belcher, *Historical Sketches of Hymns*, 83–85; Hester, "Baptist Worthies," 441–46; Cramp, *Baptist History*, 519–21.

During the twentieth century, the most important work was Derrick Holmes's "The Early Years (1655–1740) of Bourton-on-the-Water Dissenters Who Later Constituted the Baptist Church, with Special Reference to the Ministry of the Reverend Benjamin Beddome A. M. 1740–1795."[37] The dissertation began with Beddome's early years, education, and call to the Baptist church in Bourton. There was a chapter on the catchment area of the membership, which showed that the church drew people from a twenty-five-mile radius of Bourton-on-the-Water.[38] There were also chapters on the church's practice of discipline, men called to the ministry under Beddome's pastorate, the correspondence between Bourton and Goodman's Fields, Beddome's literary corpus, and his assistant Mr. Wilkins, who was rather discontent in Bourton.[39] Also in the twentieth century, Kenneth Dix wrote an article concerning the exchange between Bourton and Goodman's Fields called "'Thy Will Be Done': A Study in the Life of Benjamin Beddome," and David R. Breed included a section on Beddome in *The History and Use of Hymns and Hymn-Tunes*.[40]

Beginning in the 1990s, there has been a renewed interest in Beddome studies.[41] In 1991, Roger Hayden published his dissertation, "Evangelical Calvinism Among Eighteenth-Century Baptists with Particular Reference to Bernard Foskett, Hugh and Caleb Evans and the Bristol Baptist Academy, 1690–1791."[42] Hayden's dissertation focused on three principals of the Bristol Baptist Academy—Bernard Foskett, Hugh Evans (1712–1781), and Caleb Evans—and their impact upon their denomination, the English Particular Baptists. While Beddome featured significantly in the work, he was not the focus of Hayden's thesis.

The main catalyst for the recent resurgence in Beddome studies has been Michael A. G. Haykin. In 1998, he included a biographical essay,

---

37. Holmes, "Early Years (1655–1740)." Haykin says, "In this century there have been relatively few studies of Beddome. The most important is that of Derrick Holmes." Haykin, "Glory to the Three Eternal" (2006), 82n24.

38. Holmes, "Early Years (1655–1740)," 32–34.

39. Of this study, Ramsey says that Holmes

> has done some important historical research in and around Bourton-on-the-Water. His findings have proven beneficial in understanding the historical context in which Beddome's ministry took place and the physical environment that influenced daily life there. Holmes has also done research into the Bourton church records, which shed further light on Beddome's writings and conclusions. Ramsey, "Blessed Spirit," 3–4.

40. Dix, "Thy Will Be Done," n.p.; Breed, *History and Use*, 149–53.

41. Seki, "Resurgence," 54–59.

42. Hayden, "Evangelical Calvinism"; the dissertation was later published as Hayden, *Continuity and Change*. For a shorter article on Foskett's impact, see Hayden, "Contribution of Bernard Foskett," 189–206.

"Benjamin Beddome (1717–1795)," in his edited work *The British Particular Baptists, 1638–1910*.[43] The essay covered the general contours of Beddome's life with specific incidents included from the minute books of the Bourton church.[44] Haykin also wrote a short biographical sketch, "Benjamin Beddome (1717–1795) of Bourton-on-the-Water," as an introduction to the reprint of *A Scriptural Exposition of the Baptist Catechism*.[45] In 2019, Haykin co-edited, with Roy M. Paul and Jeongmo Yoo, the only monograph on Beddome to date: *Glory to the Three Eternal: Tercentennial Essays on the Life and Writings of Benjamin Beddome*.[46]

Over the past thirty years, other biographical works have appeared. Robert Oliver devoted a chapter to Beddome in *History of the English Calvinistic Baptists, 1771–1892: from John Gill to C. H. Spurgeon*.[47] Luke David wrote a "Biographical Preface: The Life and Times of Benjamin Beddome (1717–1795)," as an introduction to *The Sermons of Benjamin Beddome*.[48] Stephen Pickles has written a full-length biography: *Cotswolds Pastor and Baptist Hymn Writer: The Life and Times of Benjamin Beddome*.[49]

In studying Beddome, the contribution of Gary Brady should not be overlooked. Brady is the pastor of Childs Hill Baptist Church in London and has devoted himself to studying Beddome. Due to his extensive research and writing, Brady is likely the leading expert on the eighteenth-century Bourton pastor.[50] He hosts a website containing hundreds of posts concerning Beddome's sermons, hymns, ministry, correspondence, and pastoral ministry.[51] Brady contributed a chapter, "Being Benjamin Beddome: A Biographical Study," to *Glory to the Three Eternal* and also presented a paper on Beddome at the 2021 Westminster Conference for Theological and Historical Study.[52]

---

43. Haykin, "Benjamin Beddome (1717–1795)" (1998), 1:167–83. A slightly revised version of this chapter was published in 2018; for details, see n11.

44. E.g., the conversion story of Ann Wakefield is reported, as are the events surrounding the church discipline of "Sister Hardiman." Haykin, "Benjamin Beddome (1717–1795)," 4:265–67.

45. Haykin, "Bourton-on-the-Water," i–x. A similar version was published in three parts in *Evangelical Times* as Haykin, "Cloud of Witnesses."

46. Haykin et al., *Glory to the Three Eternal*.

47. Oliver, *English Calvinistic Baptists*, 16–29.

48. David, "Biographical Preface," 1:xi–xxix.

49. Pickles, *Cotswolds Pastor*.

50. Ramsey says that Brady is "one of the most prolific students of Beddome today." Ramsey, "Blessed Spirit," 4.

51. Brady, *Benjamin Beddome 1717–1795* (blog).

52. Brady, "Being Benjamin Beddome," 1–33; Brady, "Benjamin Beddome 1717–1795," 145–64.

The works listed above are biographical. They recount the events of Beddome's life, chronicling his upbringing, family, ministerial training, call to the Bourton church, and pastoral practices. While these works capture Beddome's life and ministry, they do not provide his pastoral theology based on an analysis of his writings.

Hymnody and Theology Sources

During the period of resurgence in Beddome studies, several works on the Bourton pastor's thought emerged. These will be considered under two broad categories: works that deal with his hymnody and those that address the Bourton pastor's theology. First, several pieces were written on Beddome's hymnody. Richard Arnold devoted a chapter to Beddome's hymns in *English Hymns of the Eighteenth Century: An Anthology*, and J. R. Watson included a similar section in *The English Hymn: A Critical and Historical Study*.[53] Anthony R. Cross gave a substantial treatment in *Useful Learning: Neglected Means of Grace in the Reception of the Evangelical Revival Among English Particular Baptists*.[54] Haykin also contributed two articles and a chapter on Beddome's hymnody: "Baptists Reflecting on Adam and Eve in the 'Long' Eighteenth Century," "'Drawn in Crimson Lines': Colour in the Hymnody of Benjamin Beddome," and "Benjamin Beddome (1717–1795): His Life and His Hymns," in *Pulpit and People: Studies in Eighteenth-Century Baptist Life and Thought*.[55]

Second, there were many works published on various aspects of Beddome's theology. Jason C. Montgomery and Daniel S. Ramsey wrote dissertations on the Cotswold divine. Montgomery argued that Beddome was evangelical—namely, that Beddome believed that the gospel was to be freely offered to all people, and they had a duty to believe in Christ, in contrast to the hyper-Calvinism of his day. Montgomery argued that there was a continuity between the stream of evangelical Calvinism—present in the seventeenth-century Particular Baptists and the Bristol Tradition under Foskett and the Evans's—and Beddome.[56] Ramsey's dissertation focused on

---

53. Watson, *English Hymn*, 198–202; Arnold, *English Hymns*, 360–68.

54. Cross, *Useful Learning*, 57–70. Montgomery says of Cross's work that it is "the most comprehensive work to date on the hymnody of Beddome." Montgomery, "Benjamin Beddome," 10.

55. Haykin, "Baptists Reflecting," 92–99; Haykin, "Drawn in Crimson Lines," 60–64; Haykin, "His Hymns," 93–111.

56. Montgomery, "Benjamin Beddome," 7–8. There is a significant connection between Montgomery's work on Beddome and Hayden's dissertation, which focused on three principals of the Bristol Academy—Bernard Foskett, Hugh Evans, and Caleb

the Bourton pastor's pneumatology.⁵⁷ Ramsey demonstrated the continuity of Beddome's pneumatology with that of his Reformed, Puritan, and Baptist forebears.

In addition to the above dissertations, there was a master's thesis by Stephen McKay: "The Trinitarian Theology of Particular Baptists in England (1734–1795): Anne Dutton, Benjamin Beddome, Caleb Evans, and Samuel Stennett."⁵⁸ Addressing a similar topic, Huafang Xu wrote a dissertation on the Trinitarian spirituality of Anne Dutton (1692–1765): "Communion with God and Comfortable Dependence on Him: Anne Dutton's Trinitarian Spirituality." Beddome's catechism and hymns were analyzed in a chapter on the Trinitarian theology of eighteenth-century English Particular Baptists.⁵⁹

Haykin wrote three pieces on Beddome's theology, specifically concerning his trinitarianism, political theology, and bibliology: "'Glory to the Three Eternal': Benjamin Beddome and the Teaching of Trinitarian Theology in the Eighteenth Century," "Benjamin Beddome and the Bible," and "'Nursing Fathers and . . . Nursing Mothers to the Israel of God': Benjamin Beddome on Praying for Godly Rulers."⁶⁰ Haykin also wrote: "'Those Who Plead for Thee': English Particular Baptist Preaching in the Long Eighteenth

---

Evans. Hayden wrote,

> This thesis challenges the commonly received view of eighteenth-century Particular Baptists as obscurantist, ill-educated hyper-Calvinists. From the very beginning Particular Baptists had been evangelical in their Calvinism. In the seventeenth century this was true of all Particular Baptists who shared the 1644 *Confession of Faith* and sought to promulgate it in various parts of the country. At the end of the century this evangelical Calvinism still gripped the minds and hearts of many Particular Baptists in the Western Association, based upon Bristol; and under the leadership of Bernard Foskett in the next century evangelical Calvinism was vigorously continued by those who came into contact with him and the students he trained at the Bristol Academy. (Hayden, *Continuity and Change*, xi)

Though Hayden treats Beddome in his book, with an examination of his life, catechism, and hymns, he is not the principal subject. For the pertinent sections on Beddome, see Hayden, *Continuity and Change*, 80–91, 154–58, 168–72. Regarding the relationship between his thesis and that of Hayden's, Montgomery wrote, "What Hayden's work has done for Foskett and the Evans's, this work hopes to do for Beddome." Montgomery, "Benjamin Beddome," 13.

57. Ramsey, "Blessed Spirit."
58. McKay, "Trinitarian Theology."
59. Xu, "Communion with God," 44–66.
60. Haykin, "Glory to the Three Eternal" (2006); Haykin, "Beddome and the Bible," 12, 15; Haykin, "Nursing Fathers," 65–68.

Century," which is the most pertinent for this book.⁶¹ This article examined the preaching of Beddome and his contemporaries such as Hall and Fuller.

Peter Naylor included a brief section on Beddome's views concerning communion in *Calvinism, Communion and the Baptists: A Study of English Calvinistic Baptists from the Late 1600s to the Early 1800s*, and Brady wrote two articles on the Bourton pastor's understanding of friendship in the *Banner of Truth Magazine*.⁶²

As noted, there is also the monograph edited by Haykin, Paul, and Yoo, *Glory to the Three Eternal*. The first chapter is a biographical sketch by Brady, and the remaining five chapters address an aspect of Beddome's thought: Haykin adapted his article on Beddome's Trinitarian theology; Yoo supplied a chapter on the Cotswold divine's Christology; Ramsey and Montgomery wrote shorter versions of their dissertations—on Beddome's pneumatology and his evangelicalism, respectively; and R. Scott Connell considered his hymnody.⁶³ Written for the tercentennial anniversary of his birth, this collection brings together the fruit of the most important work on Beddome into a single volume. The monograph also illustrates the lacuna this book seeks to fill. In *Glory to the Three Eternal*, there are chapters on the Bourton pastor's life, Trinitarianism, Christology, pneumatology, hymnody, and evangelicalism, yet there is nothing devoted to his pastoral theology.

Historical Context Sources

There are several works that provide further background information pertinent to Beddome's life and ministry. First, there are sources concerning the English Particular Baptists of the long eighteenth century, the denomination to which Beddome belonged. Haykin has written three pieces: "British Particular Baptist Biography," "Particular Baptists," and *From Reformation to Revival: The Story of British Evangelicalism with Particular Attention to the Particular Baptists, 1520s–1830s*.⁶⁴ Raymond Brown's *The English Baptists of the Eighteenth Century* and Stephen L. Copson and Peter J. Morden's

---

61. Haykin, "Those Who Plead," 299–311.

62. Naylor, *Calvinism, Communion*; Brady, "Beddome on Friendship (Part 1)"; Brady, "Beddome on Friendship (Part 2)."

63. Brady, "Being Benjamin Beddome," 1–33; Haykin, "Glory to the Three Eternal" (2018), 34–50; Yoo, "Benjamin Beddome's Christology," 51–88; Ramsey, "Pneumatology of Benjamin Beddome," 89–117; Montgomery, "Modern Question," 142–71; Connell, "Such Wondrous Grace," 118–41.

64. Haykin, "British Particular Baptist Biography," 1:15–19; Haykin, "Particular Baptists," 254–72; Haykin, *From Reformation to Revival*.

Challenge and Change: English Baptist Life in the Eighteenth Century also give glimpses into the Particular Baptists of the eighteenth century.[65]

Second, there are several comparative studies that provide important context for this study. The first is Nigel Wheeler's dissertation: "'Eminent Spirituality and Eminent Usefulness': Andrew Fuller's (1754–1815) Pastoral Theology in His Ordination Sermon," which was later published as *The Pastoral Priorities of 18th Century Baptists: An Examination of Andrew Fuller's Ordination Sermons*.[66] The second is *Being a Pastor: A Conversation with Andrew Fuller*, co-authored by Michael Haykin, Brian Croft, and Ian H. Clary.[67] Both works analyze and construct Fuller's pastoral theology from his ordination sermons. These sources provide helpful background information regarding the role of ordination sermons among the English Particular Baptists and are important comparative studies for this book. In this study, Beddome's ordination sermons will be examined to construct his pastoral theology in a manner similar to Wheeler's study of Fuller's ordination sermons; this analysis, though, will be supplemented by an examination of Beddome's letters, hymns, and catechism.

VOID IN THE LITERATURE

Since Beddome's death in 1795, men have been writing about the eighteenth-century English Particular Baptist pastor. During the nineteenth and twentieth centuries, the works on Beddome were mostly biographical in nature, describing his upbringing, training, ministry, trials, and successes. In the twenty-first century, there have been biographical works, but also studies focused on specific aspects of Beddome's hymnody and theology. Although Beddome's pastoral ministry has been captured biographically, there has been no sustained treatment of his views of pastoral ministry.

This lacuna can perhaps be explained by the lack of familiarity with Beddome. He is not well known even among Baptists, and his works have not received wide distribution since the middle of the nineteenth century.[68] As noted, however, there remains a large corpus of Beddome's works,

---

65. Brown, *English Baptists*; Copson and Morden, *Challenge and Change*.
66. Wheeler, "Eminent Spirituality"; Wheeler, *Pastoral Priorities*.
67. Haykin et al., *Being a Pastor*.
68. Besides the recent reprints of his catechism in 2006, his hymns in 2020, and his sermons in 2022, the last printing of Beddome's work was an American publication of his catechism in 1849. His stand-alone volume of sermons was published in 1835, his eight volumes of sermons was last published in 1824, and his hymns were last printed in 1818. For the publication details listed here, see Haykin, "Benjamin Beddome (1717–1795)," 4:273.

and several sources deal with his *pastoralia*. For example, approximately ten of his ordination sermons are extant; when compared to other figures from the same period, it becomes apparent that this is a significant body of ordination sermons.[69] There are also several of his hymns, and sections in his catechism, that address the subject of pastoral ministry. The extensive correspondence between Bourton and Goodman's Fields is also instructive. It reveals the pastoral theology of Beddome as he was faced with the difficult decision of whether he would remain in the obscure village of Bourton or relocate to the more influential station of London. To date, there has been no work that has examined these works to construct Beddome's pastoral theology.

THESIS STATEMENT

Beddome was a son of the manse. His father, John, was a pastor, having been called to the ministry under the care of Benjamin Keach, who was the minister of the Baptist church in Horselydown, Southwark, in London. The older Beddome then removed to pastor the Baptist church in Alcester, Warwickshire, before settling as the minister over the Pithay church in Bristol. It was during John's ministry in Alcester that Benjamin was born, in Henley-in-Arden on January 23, 1718.[70] Following in the footsteps of his father, the younger Beddome became an eminent and respected minister of the gospel in his generation. The respect he enjoyed among his English Particular Baptist brethren was captured by Rippon, who said, "How acceptable his labours were to the churches, when he could be prevailed on to visit them, has long been known at Abingdon, Bristol, London, and in the circle of the Midland Association."[71] In the same obituary, Rippon said of

---

69. The fullest body of ordination sermons from the English Particular Baptists of the long eighteenth century is that of Fuller's; there are thirty-one of his sermons extant. In an appendix to *Being a Pastor*, Haykin, Croft, and Clary list ordination sermons by eighteenth-century Particular Baptists besides Fuller. Though the list is not exhaustive, only four men have three or more ordination sermons listed: John Gill, Robert Hall Jr., John Ryland Jr., and Beddome. Haykin et al., *Being a Pastor*, 251–56. Cf. Wheeler lists out thirty-two extant published ordination sermons of English Particular Baptists of the long eighteenth century; notably, Beddome's sermons are not listed. Wheeler, "Eminent Spirituality," 13n17. See also Wheeler, *Pastoral Priorities*, 217–23. The reason for Wheeler not listing Beddome's sermons may be that his are not identified as such—that is, Beddome's sermons do not provide the occasion. For an explanation of how some of Beddome's discourses were classified as ordination sermons, see chapter 4.

70. Rippon, "Rev. Benjamin Beddome," 315–16.

71. Rippon, "Rev. Benjamin Beddome," 322.

the father-son pair that they "are names which have given celebrity to the Beddome family."[72]

Another figure that is important in understanding Beddome is Bernard Foskett, who was, according to Robert Strivens, "one of the principal proponents of orthodox Calvinist doctrine among the Baptist churches in the southwest of England in the first half of the eighteenth century."[73] As the principal of the Bristol Baptist Academy, Foskett trained approximately seventy men for ministry, some of these being "the most eminent Baptist ministers of the eighteenth century."[74] Strivens rightly includes Beddome in a list of such "eminent Baptist ministers" who were trained by Foskett.[75] Thus, Beddome embodied and represented the evangelical Calvinism associated with Foskett and his successors, Hugh Evans and his son Caleb.[76] Given that the younger Beddome came from such honorable stock,[77] represented the evangelical Calvinism of the Bristol Tradition, was a respected minister in his own right, and addressed *pastoralia* in several of his extant works, a sustained study of his pastoral theology is needed.

To that end, this book articulates the pastoral theology of Benjamin Beddome according to his own writings. The pastor's significance, qualifications, duties, and motivations are outlined, particularly from his ordination sermons, hymns, and catechism, as well as the duties of the church toward its pastor. Since he was an eighteenth-century Particular Baptist, Beddome's *pastoralia* is considered against the backdrop of this communion. This denominational context shows how the Cotswold divine was in continuity with, and highlights his unique contribution to, the rich pastoral theology of the Particular Baptists.

---

72. Rippon, "Rev. Benjamin Beddome," 314.

73. Strivens, "Bernard Foskett (1658–1758)," 4:87. For further details on the relationship between Foskett and the Beddome family, see the conclusion to chapter 4 in this book.

74. Strivens, "Bernard Foskett (1658–1758)," 4:93.

75. Strivens, "Bernard Foskett (1658–1758)," 4:93–94. On August 26, 1795, Rippon delivered an address concerning the history of the Bristol Baptist Academy, at Broadmead. In that essay, he listed seven "good men" who had trained under Foskett and were still actively ministering; first on that list was Benjamin Beddome. By the time Rippon published his essay, however, Beddome had passed away, on September 3, 1795. Rippon, *Baptist Academy at Bristol*, 21, 22*.

76. Hayden says, "Beddome is a representative of the Foskett tradition who in his own ministry echoed much that Foskett held important." Hayden, *Continuity and Change*, 91.

77. Rippon called John Beddome, "This honoured man." Rippon, "Rev. Benjamin Beddome," 315.

In this chapter, the relevant primary and secondary sources of Beddome have been cataloged, chiefly to show the lacuna of works focused on his pastoral theology. Chapter 2 provides the broader context of Beddome's world. The ordination service, and the ordination sermons preached on such occasions, were an integral part of Particular Baptist ecclesial life. The significance of the ordination sermons, and how they are useful in constructing a pastoral theology, is explained in the first part of the chapter. Then, specific ordination sermons from Beddome's Particular Baptist brethren—such as John Gill, Caleb Evans, Andrew Fuller, and Samuel Pearce (1766–1799)—are examined to develop their understanding of pastoral ministry. In chapter 3, the extant letters connected to Beddome are the focus. A biographical overview of the Bourton pastor is given from the vantage point of his letters. Then, two collections of letters are analyzed. The first collection consists of several letters from John Beddome to his son, Benjamin. These came at critical junctures of the younger Beddome's life; they were letters not only from a father to a son, but from a more experienced minister to a younger minister. The second collection of letters are the seven letters exchanged between the Baptist churches of Bourton-on-the-Water and Goodman's Fields in London. Samuel Wilson, who had been the pastor of the Goodman's Fields church, died, and so the London deacons sought his replacement in Beddome. This exchange provides a picture of *pastoralia* in action, that is, of two churches working out their pastoral theology when faced with the practical challenges of finding a pastoral replacement, in the case of Goodman's Fields, and being asked to release its pastor to another church, in the case of Bourton.

In chapter 4, the pastoral theology of Beddome is constructed from his ordination sermons. The first section of the chapter deals with Beddome's participation in ordination services, his abilities as a preacher, and the publication process of his sermons. Next, an explanation is given of how approximately ten of Beddome's sermons have been identified as those which were probably delivered at an ordination service. In the final and largest section, those ordination sermons are used to construct his pastoral theology, supplemented by his other sermons, hymns, and catechism. In the analysis of the ordination sermons, it should be noted that the structure and headings of chapter 4 mirror those of chapter 2. As part of the analysis of Beddome's sermons, it is demonstrated that though he had his own emphases, the Bourton pastor was consistent with his Particular Baptist brethren with respect to *pastoralia*. Chapter 5 retrieves wisdom from Beddome's pastoral theology for contemporary churches and its pastors.

The research questions that will drive this study are: how did Beddome understand the significance and identity of a pastor? What were the qualifications of a pastor? What were the duties of a pastor? What were the proper motivations of a pastor? Why was Beddome compelled to remain in the same church for over five decades, when there were invitations to more significant stations? What was the church's duty toward its pastor and his ministry? How did Beddome's view of pastoral ministry compare with that of the English Particular Baptists of the long eighteenth century? Last, what can contemporary Christians and pastors learn from this largely forgotten figure from Baptist history? In response to these questions, this study will explore the nature of pastoral ministry according to the life and thought of Benjamin Beddome.

CHAPTER 2

The Pastoral Theology of the English Particular Baptists According to Their Ordination Sermons

AFTER THE DEATH OF Benjamin Beddome, the Baptist church in Bourton-on-the-Water was without a pastor for several years. In the words of Abraham Booth (1734–1806), the pastor of the Little Prescott Street church in Goodman's Fields, the Bourton church was "disappointed in every attempt to procure a successor whose labors would ensure a cordial unanimity, [and thus] they experienced much interruption of their spiritual prosperity. After a long season of trial, they are again favored with a minister, who appears to possess, in an eminent degree, their affectionate esteem."[1] The esteemed minister to whom Booth referred was his assistant, Thomas Coles (1779–1840), who succeeded Beddome at Bourton in 1801, six years after the latter's death.

Coles was familiar to the friends at Bourton since he had been reared in the church. He was the son of William and Mary Coles, but his father died within a year of Thomas's birth. Shortly after, in 1783, his widowed mother moved the family to Bourton-on-the-Water. At the age of eleven, Coles took extended notes of Beddome's sermons, and for the last three years of Beddome's ministry, Coles read his sermon notes to the church at the weekly prayer meetings. Shortly before his sixteenth birthday, and a few weeks before his pastor's passing, Coles was baptized and then received into membership of the Bourton church on August 16, 1795.[2] Soon after, he

---

1. Booth, "Advertisement," 2. For the information in this account, see Booth, "Advertisement," 3–5.

2. For the sake of clarity, his baptism took place on August 9, 1795.

attended the Bristol Baptist Academy, now under the principalship of John Ryland Jr.,[3] though he completed his studies at Marischal College, Aberdeen, earning an MA in April 1800.[4]

A little while earlier, Coles had received invitations from the Cannon Street Baptist Church in Birmingham to be Samuel Pearce's colleague. Such solicitations continued after Pearce's death on October 10, 1799, but due to health challenges, Coles was advised against accepting the call to Birmingham. During that same year, in 1800, Coles also declined an invitation from the Bourton church. Instead, Coles eventually went to serve as an assistant minister to Booth at the Little Prescott Street church in Goodman's Fields in London.[5]

The Bourton church, having been unsettled since Beddome's death six years prior, persisted and wrote to the Goodman's Fields church, requesting Coles's release thus:

> We have lost our pastor, and have long been as sheep without a shepherd [Matt 9:36]. We earnestly wish for the revival of religion amongst us. Our desires and expectations were turned to our brother Coles, now labouring with you. Here he was first awakened to the knowledge of that salvation, which he has devoted his life to extend and promote. He is known and beloved by us all, and we regard him as the person, who, under providence, is the most likely to revive us, to consolidate our affectionate intercourse, and to advance the kingdom of Christ in this place. We entreat you, brethren, to gratify our hopes, by suspending your claims, and allowing our invitation to have its full and free effect, on our brother's mind.[6]

---

3. Dr. John Ryland Jr. (1753–1825) should be distinguished from his father, the Rev. John Collett Ryland (1723–1792). For the sake of clarity, the son will be called Ryland Jr., and his father will be called Collett Ryland.

4. For the details in this paragraph, I am indebted to Brooks, *POTP*, 83–85. For further information on Coles, see 74n121.

5. For the details in this paragraph, I am indebted to Booth, "Advertisement," 3; Brooks, *POTP*, 84–85.

6. Quoted in Booth, "Advertisement," 3–4. For the events and correspondence concerning Coles's call and ordination to the pastorate of the Bourton church, see Brooks, *POTP*, 69–81. In the literature of the Baptists of the long eighteenth century, it was common to italicize words and phrases in a manner that is unconventional for a modern writer. This type of italicization has been removed in this book; therefore, if there is italicization in a quotation, it will be indicated whether it was in the original or added. Similarly, writers of the long eighteenth century used capitalization and punctuation differently than is conventional for modern writers; some instances have been updated in this book.

The London church granted the appeal and responded,

> Moved and resolved, that as we entertain a Christian sympathy for the church at Bourton, under the peculiarly afflictive circumstances which have attended it, and in various respects, yet continue; we will not urge Mr. Coles' connection with us, as a bar to his removal; provided he himself be satisfied, that the leadings of Providence direct him to another situation.[7]

This was an ironic turn of events, considering the exchange that took place between these two churches several decades earlier. On that earlier occasion, the Goodman's Fields church had lost their pastor and sought Beddome's services. Even with persistent invitations coming from London, however, both Beddome and the Bourton church refused the requests for Beddome's removal. Concerning the connection between these two events—though separated by half a century—Brooks wrote,

> It is impossible to forget how fifty years before, the church in London, being greatly distressed, and fearing [lest] they should be "broken to pieces," had applied to that at Bourton, entreating them to leave Mr. Beddome to choose his own course, and how they absolutely refused to "loose him, and let him go." Now the case is reversed, and without insinuating, or even thinking that they were wrong then [i.e., the Bourton church fifty years prior], we must admit that the conduct of the church in London in the present instance does them the greatest credit—reflects upon them the highest honour. Their conduct was disinterested and noble.[8]

Coles's ordination to the Baptist church in Bourton-on-the-Water took place on November 17, 1801.[9] The charge was given by Ryland Jr. from

---

7. Quoted in Booth, "Advertisement," 4.
8. Brooks, *POTP*, 74–75.
9. Brooks sought to capture the experience of Coles on the day of his ordination:
   We know who hath said—"A prophet hath no honour in his own country [Matt 13:57]," and we know also that "there is no rule without an exception." Here we have a happy exception. Very few can fully enter into the feelings of Thomas Coles on that ordination day. Had not the form of Benjamin Beddome been ever in his eye in that ancient house of prayer? And was it not the type of all that was venerable, and sacred, and almost awful? Who does not remember with what peculiar sentiments of awe and reverence he regarded the first minister he ever knew, especially if that minister were an aged man, reverenced by his father and mother? Benjamin Beddome was a big-wigged old gentleman of seventy when Thomas Coles was first taken to chapel, and solemnly assured that he must be a good boy or Mr. Beddome would look at him. And would he not from the pulpit even see that corner, hard by the table-pew, in which he sat and wrote down Mr. Beddome's sermons? Oh, it was a

three texts in 2 Corinthians (2:16; 3:5; 12:9), and James Hinton (1761–1823) addressed the church from Col 1:9–10. The order of service, including the parts played by other pastors, was as follows:

> M. R. Mann, of Morton-in-the-Marsh; read suitable portions of scripture and prayed.
>
> Mr. L. Butterworth, of Evesham, delivered the introductory discourse.
>
> Mr. Smith, of Blockley, asked the usual questions.
>
> The church recognized their free choice of Mr. Coles, who declared his acceptance of the pastoral office, and delivered an avowal of his religious sentiments.
>
> Mr. L. Butterworth, in solemn prayer, commended the minister and people to God.
>
> Dr. Ryland, of Bristol, delivered the charge.
>
> Mr. Hinton, of Oxford, addressed the church.
>
> Suitable hymns were introduced in different parts of the service, which
>
> Mr. Smith, of Shipston, concluded with prayer.
>
> Mr. Page, of Bristol, preached in the evening from 2 Cor 4:18.[10]

---

delicate and arduous task, and his friend, Dr. Ryland, sought to encourage his heart and strengthen his hands by pointing to one who alone could effectually help him. The transition from the pew to the pulpit, in the same sanctuary, is a very affecting one, and yet, it is very pleasing; it is more than a compliment to the individual selected; it is doing him the highest honour, and presenting the best testimonial to his sterling worth. Mr. Coles felt that he was really at home—that he dwelt among his own people. (Brooks, *POTP*, 85–86)

10. See "Order of the Service," in Ryland and Hinton, *Difficulties and Supports* [. . .] *Duties Incumbent*, 6. The sermons preached at the ordination service of an English Particular Baptist pastor were often published together. When citing these works, the first reference (in the book) will include both authors and titles of the charge to the ordinand and sermon to the church, but subsequent references will include only the respective author and respective title.

Charles Boardman Jewson quotes the ordination service of James Freeman Beard to the Baptist church at Worstead in 1794 as illustrative of "the common practice":

> The worship of God began at 10 o'clock in the morning with singing the 2nd part of the 84th Psalm of Dr. Watts's after which Bro. Farmery of Diss engaged in prayer earnestly imploring a blessing upon the important and solemn work of the day. Brother Ridley of Ipswich introduced the work of the day and interrogated the parties particularly interested therein, agreeable to which Brother Shalders, the Senior Deacon, stood up and gave a brief account of the steps the church had taken in her widowhood state, of the particular providences occurring in bringing J. F. Beard among them and their unanimous approbation of him. Then J. F. Beard arose and

The service for Coles followed a typical pattern among Baptists and other dissenting traditions.[11] Though there was variance due to practical concerns, Baptist ordination services featured consistent elements.[12] For example, the ordinations of W. Belsher, Thomas Dunscombe (1748–1811), William Carey, and Robert Fawkner all followed the same general pattern.[13] John Rippon's *The Baptist Annual Register* record of some ninety ordinations reveals a similar outline of the ordination service.[14] Commenting

> gave a brief account relative to his call by grace, his call to the ministry and the leading of Providence his removal from Woodbridge to Worstead &c which being done he gave in a confession of faith relative to the glorious doctrines of the everlasting gospel. The Senior Deacon in the name of the church recognized their call and J. F. Beard his acceptance of the pastoral office amongst them, at the conclusion of which sung 132 Psalm Dr. Watts Long Measure. After which brother Hitchcock of Wattisham gave the charge from 1 Timothy 4 ch. 16 v. Sung 103 Hymn first book Dr. Watts and brother Brown of Yarmouth addressed the church from Eph. 2 ch. 19 v. Sung 132 Psalm from pause, Dr. Watts's Book and brother Kinghorn of Norwich concluded in prayer. (Jewson, *Baptists in Norfolk*, 52)

11. Keith S. Grant gives the account of Andrew Fuller's ordination service from the Soham church books, which was similar to that of Coles. Fuller's ordination service, says Grant, "is illustrative of a pattern that was used consistently among Baptist and Independent churches for the whole of the eighteenth century, giving expression to their congregational ecclesiology." Grant cites the ordinations of Joseph Burroughs (1685–1761) and Collett Ryland—both Baptists—and Philip Doddridge (1702–1751)—a Congregationalist—as examples of ordination services similar to that of Fuller's among Dissenters. Grant, *Andrew Fuller*, 59. Michael A. G. Haykin, Brian Croft, and Ian H. Clary make a similar observation regarding the consistency of ordination sermons in dissenting traditions: "The . . . reflection on ordination sermons from three important, and representative eighteenth-century Nonconformist ministers—[Matthew] Henry, [John] Gill, and [Philip] Doddridge—demonstrates that Andrew Fuller's ordination sermons addresses are firmly in line with this tradition of Dissenting pastoral theology and its concern for ministerial character." Haykin et al., *Being a Pastor*, 40–41.

12. Nigel Wheeler writes,

> There was flexibility in the *modus operandi* of an ordination service due to a variety of mainly pragmatic factors. The accessibility of an appropriate meeting place might affect the number of ministers able to participate, which in turn would influence its length. If time were really short, for example, the address to the Church might be eliminated. Or the number of pastors from other Particular Baptists churches available to conduct the service might be influenced by prior commitments or geographical isolation. Nevertheless, a survey of Rippon's *Register* indicates an homogeny of observance in Particular Baptist ordination ceremonies. (Wheeler, "Eminent Spirituality," 82)

13. Ryland and Pearce, *Duty of Ministers* [. . .] *Duty of Churches*, n.p.; Evans and Evans, *Charge and Sermon*, n.p.; Fuller and Ryland, *Qualifications and Encouragement* [. . .] *Paul's Charge*, n.p.; Rippon, *Baptist Annual Register* (1793), 519. A notable difference between the ordinations is the presence or absence of the evening service; both Coles's and Carey's ordination day included an evening service, whereas the others did not.

14. Rippon recorded ordinations in each of his four registers: Rippon, *Baptist*

on several ordination services among Baptists and independents, Keith S. Grant observes,

> That this pattern of ordination service prevailed until the end of the century, and beyond, is evident from a survey of the descriptions of mainly Particular Baptist ordinations in John Rippon's periodical, *The Baptist Annual Register*. Over ninety ordinations are described in that final decade of the eighteenth century, the summaries usually a paragraph in length, but occasionally occupying several pages.[15]

What, then, were the elements of a typical ordination service in the communion to which the Bourton church belonged? In the following section, the standard elements of an ordination service and the probationary period will be explained. The remainder of the chapter will then focus on two specific elements of the service: the charge to the ordinand and the sermon to the church. For both the charge and the sermon, a general description will be given, followed by an analysis of several ordination sermons by eighteenth-century Particular Baptist pastors. This, of course, situates Beddome in his broader context and provides the background to compare his pastoral theology with that of his Particular Baptist brethren; this will be taken up in chapter 4, when the Cotswold divine's pastoral theology is constructed from his ordination sermons.

THE ELEMENTS OF AN ORDINATION SERVICE

The service generally began with Scripture reading and prayer.[16] Then, the introductory discourse explained the purpose and biblical basis for ordination and provided a defense for their "dissenting principles and ecclesiology."[17] Next, a visiting pastor asked "the usual questions"[18] to the

---

Annual Register (1793), 517–23; Rippon, *Baptist Annual Register* (1797), 117–27, 189–92, 345–49, 479–83; Rippon, *Baptist Annual Register* (1801), 148–55; Rippon, *Baptist Annual Register* (1802), 587–88, 668–69, 773–75, 1110–14.

15. Grant, *Andrew Fuller*, 59–60.

16. The most common texts to commence the day's events included "Ezekiel 3 and 33, Psalm 132 and 133, Ephesians 4, 1 Timothy 3, and Titus 1." Grant, *Andrew Fuller*, 60. For information regarding the elements of the ordination service, I am indebted to Grant, *Andrew Fuller*, 60–61; Wheeler, "Andrew Fuller's Ordination Sermons," 169–70; Wheeler, "Eminent Spirituality," 76–117.

17. Grant, *Andrew Fuller*, 60. Grant calls this an "apologetic: an introductory discourse on the nature of ordination and pastoral ministry, and an apologetic for dissenting principles and ecclesiology." Grant, *Andrew Fuller*, 60.

18. Wheeler, "Eminent Spirituality," 99. To the author's knowledge, there are no

church and the ordinand. The response on behalf of the church was normally given by a deacon who explained the process the church took to procure its pastor. In turn, the ordinand articulated the process of how he was led to this local body of believers, as well as his conversion and call to ministry. After this, the church extended a call to the ordinand, and he accepted that call by a verbal response accompanied by the raising of his right hand.

The ordinand then gave a statement of his religious sentiments, which was examined by the other ministers present.[19] The visiting elders, says Wheeler, "had to be convinced of [the ordinand's] orthodoxy before they could lay hands on him in good conscience."[20] This was followed by the ordination prayer and the laying on of hands by the visiting ministers.[21] While

---

extant records of the questions posed to candidates at a *Baptist* ordination service. There are records, however, in two Congregationalist sources. First, Doddridge elaborated on the content of the questions:

> Pertinent questions are put to [the candidate], relating to the views and purposes with which he undertakes the solemn charge, that he may be brought under the most awful engagements to a suitable behaviour in it; and an express renunciation of the errors and superstitions of the Romish church generally makes a part of these answers, as well as a declaration of his resolution, by divine grace, never to forsake the ministry, whatever inconveniences and sufferings it may draw after it. (Doddridge, "Methods of Ordination Among the Protestant Dissenters," in *Works of the Rev. P. Doddridge*, 3:226)

Second, there were questions posed by William Richards to Thomas Wright at a Congregationalist ordination service: (1) Richards asked Wright to provide a statement of his core beliefs "of the general plan of that excellent and divine religion of Jesus Christ." (2) Wright was asked to state his convictions concerning the Protestant Reformation, against the Roman Catholic Church. (3) Richards asked why the ordinand desired to minister among Dissenters rather than in the established church. (4) The ordinand was asked to state why he desired to enter ministry above other employments. (5) Richards asked Wright concerning his devotion to the ministry and godliness, regardless of the difficulties and discouragement, so that he would be a good and faithful servant of Christ. Richards and Wright, "Questions Proposed [...] Answers Returned," 3-16. In other services—both Baptist and Congregationalist—the ordinand gave his religious sentiments as a separate element during the service. E.g., Evans, "Confession of Faith," 13-45; Wilton and Spilsbury, "Confession of Faith [...] Answers to the Questions," 41-66.

19. On this point, Haykin, Croft, and Clary write, "It is noteworthy that, whereas Presbyterian ordinands would affirm their commitment to the Westminster Standards, Congregationalist (or Independent) and Particular Baptist candidates for pastoral ministry crafted their own confessions of faith." Haykin et al., *Being a Pastor*, 40n17.

20. Wheeler, "Andrew Fuller's Ordination Sermons," 170.

21. Grant says that "the prayer [during the *imposition of hands*] was almost always accompanied by the laying on of hands by the ministers present." Grant, *Andrew Fuller*, 60-61. However, the practice was not universal. A notable exception to the laying on of hands was John Gill; for Gill's views on the imposition of hands, see Arrell, "Laying Aside," 45-64.

Baptist pastors did not think that they were conveying additional gifts or qualifications to the ordinand through the laying on of hands, many viewed it as an important element of ordination.[22]

The final two elements of the service were a pair of sermons—one addressed to the ordinand and the other to the church. Both were typically delivered by a visiting minister, and the sermons highlighted the various aspects of the relationship between the pastor and the church. The charge to the pastor was the most prominent element of the entire service. Nigel Wheeler says, "The main purpose of the charge was to describe the motivations, character, qualifications, duties, and purposes of ministers of the gospel."[23] Similarly, the charge to the church expounded on the church's responsibilities to their newly ordained pastor and toward one another in the context of this covenantal, voluntary relationship.[24] The services also included hymns and prayers interspersed throughout.

Wheeler says that the services began at 10:00 a.m. or 10:30 a.m. and typically took place mid-week, on a Tuesday, Wednesday, or Thursday. The service lasted for three to four hours, though there are good reasons to think they typically went longer.[25] Often, there were additional elements like the ordination of deacons and, as on the day of Coles's ordination, an evening service.

---

22. Wheeler says, "The laying on of hands was defended as a continuing practice, but they stressed that it conveyed no extraordinary gifts." Wheeler, "Eminent Spirituality," 98.

23. Wheeler, "Eminent Spirituality," 110. Wheeler here was leaning on Gill who preached the charge to John Davis (1731–1795) at his ordination to the pastorate of the Baptist church at Waltham Abbey. In that sermon, the London divine drew his discourse from Ezek 10:20, "This is the living creature, that I saw under the God of Israel, by the river of Chebar; and I knew that they were the cherubim." He conceded that such a text was strange for an ordination, but it would be from this text that Gill purposed "to lay before [Davis] the qualifications, duties, work, and usefulness of the ministers of the gospel." Gill, "Doctrine of the Cherubim," in S&T, 2:30–31. Grant notes that "the most regularly repeated texts for the charge included Acts 20:28, Colossians 4:7, and 1 Timothy 4:16." Grant, *Andrew Fuller*, 61.

24. Grant observed that common texts for the address to the church "included Deuteronomy 1:38, Ephesians 5:2, and 1 Thessalonians 5:12–13." Grant, *Andrew Fuller*, 61; Wheeler, "Eminent Spirituality," 111. For the voluntary nature of the relationship between the pastor and the church, see Grant, *Andrew Fuller*, 53–72.

25. Wheeler, "Eminent Spirituality," 86. Wheeler bases his claim regarding the length of the service on Thomas Hunt's recollection of his ordination and Rippon's editorial comments concerning it. Wheeler, "Eminent Spirituality," 86–87.

THE PROBATIONARY PERIOD

The probationary period was the time between a man's call to the ministry and his ordination. Beddome, Coles's predecessor, was put forward in the Goodman's Fields church to preach on January 9 and February 28, 1740. Beddome had been baptized several months prior, in September or October of 1739. After preaching on these two occasions, the church called him to ministry.[26] Upon the death of their pastor, Thomas Flower Sr., the Bourton church invited Beddome to come and preach. He arrived in July 1740 and, over the next three years, likely divided his time between Warwick and Bourton. Three years later, in July 1743, the Bourton church called him to be their pastor, and Beddome was ordained on September 23 of that same year. At the ordination, Bernard Foskett gave the charge to his former student from 1 Tim 4:12, and Joseph Stennett Jr. (1692–1758) gave the address to the church from Heb 13:17.[27] The probation period was the time between Beddome's arrival in Bourton and his ordination to the pastorate of the church.

Another scenario, recounted by Wheeler, is that of Samuel Rushton.[28] Baptist churches often looked internally for potential pastoral candidates. Thus, if a man seemed to possess the requisite moral qualities and ministerial gifting, he was called to demonstrate his gifts before the church.[29] In the case of Rushton, he was asked to preach on a Sunday evening, as was customary in these situations. He was initially approved but continued to preach for another six or seven weeks so that all the members could hear him and form a better judgment. The whole church then gathered for a day of fasting and prayer, which was accompanied by a sermon from the pastor. The church at Hamsterly unanimously agreed to call Rushton to the ministry, which he accepted. There was an official service that took place on November 8, 1795, to call him to the ministry, two months after he started preaching.[30] Wheeler adds, "The actual ordination procedure usually came even later."[31]

---

26. Brooks, *POTP*, 23.

27. Brooks, *POTP*, 25–26; Rippon, "Rev. Benjamin Beddome," 317.

28. For the information in this paragraph, I am indebted to Wheeler, "Eminent Spirituality," 83. For the original account of Rushton's call to the ministry, see Rippon, *Baptist Annual Register* (1797), 483.

29. Wheeler, "Eminent Spirituality," 83.

30. According to Rippon, the purpose of the service was "the churches [sic] call of him to the ministry, to preach the word and baptize those who were proper subjects, under the direction of the church, and as eligible to the pastoral office." Rippon, *Baptist Annual Register* (1797), 483.

31. Wheeler, "Eminent Spirituality," 83.

Thus, the period between November 8 and Rushton's ordination service was his probationary period.³²

THE CHARGE TO THE ORDINAND

As noted, the charge to the ordinand was the most prominent element of the ordination service. It instructed and exhorted the candidate in his duties as the newly ordained pastor of the church.³³ Furthermore, while preaching was integral among all Christian traditions in England, the ordination sermon was particularly valued among Particular Baptists; thus, they were printed and disseminated.³⁴ Also, while the Particular Baptists had a systematic expression of pastoral theology, such as in John Gill's *Practical Divinity*, the ordination sermons were more practically oriented.³⁵

The reason for this, of course, was the setting in which these sermons were delivered: at a church meeting wherein the members of a church called a man to be their pastor, and he accepted their invitation. As already noted, the typical ordination service consisted of four addresses (including the ordinand's religious sentiments), the laying on of hands, prayers, and hymns. Visiting ministers typically led the services and preached the ordination sermons. As such, the charge to the ordinand was given by a pastor to another pastor.³⁶

Wheeler, summarizing the nature and purpose of the charge to the ordinand, says,

> A unique feature of the charge was that it represented an admonition from one pastor to another pastor on how the office of elder should function effectively and successfully. This [is]

32. For further examples of the probation period for English Particular Baptist pastors, see Wheeler, "Eminent Spirituality," 83–84.

33. Wheeler says, "The charge represents the address of a visiting pastor to the newly ordained pastor outlining his duties and responsibilities as a minister of the church." Wheeler, "Eminent Spirituality," 79n22.

34. Wheeler comments, "Sermons covered a broad spectrum of thought including religion, politics, ethics, and science. But among Particular Baptists, ordination sermons were regarded as uniquely important and were frequently published." Wheeler, "Eminent Spirituality," 78.

35. Wheeler, "Andrew Fuller's Ordination Sermons," 170. Gill had sections in his *Practical Divinity* that addressed the subject of pastors, deacons, the duties of church members to one another and to their pastors, and the public aspects of worship. Gill, *Body of Practical and Doctrinal Divinity* (1810), 514–94.

36. Wheeler says, "The charge which contained the pastoral advice of a more senior minister is central to understanding what was important to them concerning the ministry." Wheeler, "Andrew Fuller's Ordination Sermons," 117.

what makes this corpus of material so valuable. These sermons embody a uniquely personal and practical exposition of the execution of the pastoral office, for beyond just a systematic exposition of a Particular Baptist pastoral theology, they contain an elucidation of pastoral theology purified in the crucible of practiced ministry. Pastors who had learned to implement their inherited Particular Baptist theological convictions in their own unique context strove to transmit what they had learned to a new generation of pastoral leadership. This direct and accountable advice served inimitably to further shorten the gap between orthodoxy and orthopraxy—between a written practical theology and a practiced theology. For example, although John Gill's *Practical Divinity* clearly articulates a more pragmatic theology beyond his systematic works, and was written by a practicing pastor, ordination sermons were delivered by active practitioners who were directly addressing other practicing pastors with the fervor of a shared special interest in a divine cause.[37]

Thus, the charge to the ordinand gives modern readers a sense of what was important to English Particular Baptist pastors in sermonic form.[38] The major themes in these charges will be examined under the headings of the significance, qualifications, duties, preaching, and motivations of a pastor.[39]

---

37. Wheeler, "Andrew Fuller's Ordination Sermons," 170.

38. Commenting on the paucity of studies on ordination sermons in eighteenth-century England, Haykin, Croft, and Clary say, "Such a lacuna is strange because this homiletical genre provides a wealth of information about the way that Dissenters understood pastoral ministry. Ordination sermons regularly describe the ideals of pastoral ministry, addressed from one pastor to another as well as charges given to the congregation that the ordinand would pastor." Haykin et al., *Being a Pastor*, 38–39.

39. The most significant work done on the ordination sermons of the English Particular Baptists of the long eighteenth century is Wheeler's 2009 dissertation, "Eminent Spirituality," which has since been published as Wheeler, *Pastoral Priorities*. Wheeler examines the thirty-two extant published sermons from the period and compares them with the thirty-one extant ordination sermons of Fuller. His conclusion is helpful for our purposes here:

> An evaluation of the available published Particular Baptists ordination sermons beginning in the long eighteenth century with Nehemiah Coxe's sermon of 1681 to George Sample's ordination in 1818 as compared with Andrew Fuller's published ordination sermons of the late eighteenth century manifests a palpable theological continuity within the larger Particular Baptists ordination history. (Wheeler, "Eminent Spirituality," 213)

He also says,

> Fuller's emphasis on eminent spirituality and eminent usefulness was more closely mirrored by his contemporaries as the revival took hold. Especially in sermons from Caleb Evans in the West Counties there was a predominance of evangelical language

The Significance of a Pastor

John Gill pastored the Baptist church in Horselydown, London, for fifty-one years. Though he is better known today for his contribution as a systematic theologian and biblical expositor, Gill also participated in many ordination services, and four of his ordination sermons are extant.[40] On one occasion, Gill gave the charge at the ordination of his nephew and four other ordinands. In that sermon, "The Work of a Gospel-Minister Recommended to Consideration," the London pastor argued that the weightiness of the ministry came from Christ's association with it. He exhorted the five ordinands that Christ was concerned about the ministry and was the essence of it; Christ called, qualified, and assisted those engaged in ministry; and when ministry was properly discharged, he was glorified.[41] The ordinands were urged to work to the point of exhaustion since ministry was "a laborious work" and would test even the strongest of men.[42] Gill encouraged the candidates by reminding them that ministers were engaged in an honorable work as ambassadors for Christ, the work itself was respectable among men, and God labored alongside ministers.[43]

A consistent theme in the ordination sermons of the English Particular Baptists was the pastor as a gift of Christ to the church. They drew on this idea from the apostle Paul, who said, "He led captivity captive, and gave

---

and exhortations for enhanced ministerial usefulness through personal holiness. But there remained a strong continuity with the Particular Baptists of the earlier part of the century even when compared with those affected by high Calvinism. This close continuity does not argue in favour of a radical redefinition of pastoral theology transformed by the so called rise of evangelicalism. The main difference in terms of renewal centered on a return to biblical precedent of offering the gospel freely to all. (Wheeler, "Eminent Spirituality," 239)

Some of the points of discontinuity will be mentioned in the footnotes of this chapter; for a fuller discussion on the continuity and discontinuity between the pastoral theology of the English Particular Baptists of the eighteenth century and that of Fuller's, see Wheeler, "Eminent Spirituality," 213–42.

In addition to Wheeler's dissertation and monograph, for studies on Fuller's ordination sermons, see Haykin et al., *Being a Pastor*; Sanchez, *Spirituality of Love*; Sanchez, "'Love the Souls,'" 85–99; Wheeler, "Andrew Fuller's Ordination Sermons."

40. There are four ordination sermons of Gill; see Gill, "Duty of a Pastor," in *S&T*, 2:1–13; Gill, "Gospel-Minister," in *S&T*, 2:14–29; Gill, "Doctrine of the Cherubim," in *S&T*, 2:30–48; Gill, "Form of Sound Words," in *S&T*, 2:49–64. For a study on the ordination sermons of Gill, see Arrell, "Laying Aside." For a biographical sketch of Gill, see Oliver, "John Gill (1697–1771)," 7–50; Rippon, *Rev. John Gill*. The works of Gill alluded to are Gill, *Body of Doctrinal and Practical Divinity*; Gill, *Exposition*, 9 vols.

41. Gill, "Gospel-Minister," in *S&T*, 2:15.

42. Gill, "Gospel-Minister," in *S&T*, 2:15–16.

43. Gill, "Gospel-Minister," in *S&T*, 2:16.

gifts unto men. . . . And he gave some, apostles; and some, prophets; and some, evangelists; and some, pastors and teachers" (Eph 4:8, 11 KJV). Andrew Fuller preached to the Moulton church, at the ordination of William Carey, a message entitled "Importance of Christian Ministers Considered as the Gift of Christ." Fuller explained that Christ had led captive the spiritual enemies of Satan and death, obtained victory, and divided the spoils. These spoils, or gifts, included ministers of the gospel. The church had to acknowledge their minister as Christ's gift to them and receive his ministry—not owing to anything in the minister, but to the grace of Christ.[44]

Preaching from that same passage at the ordination of Belsher to the pastorate to the Baptist church in Worcester, Samuel Pearce proclaimed that the giving of ministers to the church demonstrated "the care which the blessed redeemer exercises over his church upon earth."[45] In a similar vein, Fuller preached in a different sermon that Christ appointed loving pastors to feed his church, which was a demonstration of his love for the sheep. "There is a close connection" said Fuller, "between his having died for them and his desire to have them fed."[46] Thus, the significance of the pastor was demonstrated in that the nature of his work was divine,[47] and his appointment to a church was an expression of Christ's love for his people.

The Qualifications of a Pastor

The English Particular Baptists were also insistent on the godly character of pastors. Due to the nature of ministry, certain traits were necessary in those who were engaged in pastoring. These characteristics, according to Wheeler, were derived from the biblical texts that list the qualifications of elders in 1 Tim 3:1–7 and Titus 1:5–7.[48] Wheeler adds,

---

44. Fuller, "Importance of Christian Ministers," in *WAF*, 1:521–22.

45. Pearce, *Duty of Churches*, 42.

46. Fuller, "Pastors Required to Feed," in *WAF*, 1:477.

47. Ryland Jr. spoke of the nature of the pastoral charge as "real and divine." Ryland, *Duty of Ministers*, 19.

48. Wheeler writes, "The church recognized the call of God on an elder based on evidence of certain qualifications manifest in him. These scripturally defined qualifications, found mainly in the biblical texts, 1 Timothy 3:1–7, and Titus 1:5–7, reveal the essential moral standards that the church required." Wheeler, "Eminent Spirituality," 129. Wheeler observes that while ordination sermons of the earlier part of the eighteenth century specified the biblical qualifications in the Pastoral Epistles, Fuller "used broader descriptors such as piety and holiness as the necessary qualities of an elder. . . . Perhaps he used these more general categories for the pragmatic purpose of conserving time as there is evidence that there was pressure to shorten the length of the services as the century advanced. Many later ordinations reflect this same trend." Wheeler, "Eminent Spirituality," 217.

> The most important preliminary characteristic for the office of elder was evidence that his heart had been renewed by grace so that he both knew and felt the gospel. "Knowing the gospel," referred to an understanding and adherence of biblical precepts expressed through a Reformed, baptistic orthodoxy as articulated, for example, in Baptist confessions of faith, while "feeling the gospel" implied an emotional attachment to those truths. They were looking for signs that he had become a new creature in Christ no longer governed by the old nature. This did not mean he was perfect or free from the influence of sin, but that his life was generally consistent with the gospel.[49]

Wheeler is drawing from the introductory address, delivered by G. Osborn, at Belsher's ordination. Later in that ordination service, Ryland Jr. delivered the charge to the ordinand in which he elaborated on the "principal requisites" of the ministry.[50] Ryland listed these prerequisites in pairs: "knowledge and judgment [referring to knowledge of God and the Scriptures], ... wisdom and prudence, ... assiduity and diligence, ... fidelity and a sense of responsibility, ... tenderness and affection, ... patience and meekness, ... self-denial and resolution, ... [and] faith and confidence in God."[51] There was an overlap of these traits with the qualifications for elders found in the Pastoral Epistles, but Ryland went beyond them. This is not to suggest that Ryland was adding his own qualifications to 1 Timothy and Titus, but rather he drew additional characteristics from other scriptural texts and inferred traits from what was required of the pastoral task. Thus, the godliness of a pastor was important to the Particular Baptists and considered by them as a predominant qualification for ministers of the gospel.

In what follows, further qualifications of a pastor will be considered, including the requisite ministerial gifting, the necessity to watch one's life and doctrine, the propriety of love in the minister since he represented the Great Shepherd, and the principle that God tended to grant usefulness to those ministers who were devoted to godliness.

The Gifting of a Pastor

In the sermon to his nephew and four other ordinands, Gill defined the gift that was necessary for pastoral ministry. He said that the requisite pastoral

---

49. Wheeler, "Eminent Spirituality," 130. Wheeler is drawing from the phrase "They knew and felt the evidences of the gospel," in Osborn, "Introductory Address," 6.

50. Ryland, *Duty of Ministers*, 24.

51. Ryland, *Duty of Ministers*, 24–33.

qualification was not necessarily the grace of God, human learning, or natural abilities.[52] According to Gill, the qualification for ministry was "a peculiar gift, fitting and qualifying him for this important work."[53] This gift was present to a greater or lesser degree in different ministers, and it consisted of two parts: (1) a knowledge of the Scriptures with an ability to interpret them for the edification of his hearers, and spiritual judgment to make known what was necessary for salvation; and (2) an ability to teach and instruct others in a way that promoted edification.[54]

Gill exhorted the ordinands to regularly exercise the pastoral gift so that they were useful. Initially, a man had to be called by a church for him to exercise his gift.[55] For those who possessed the gift, Gill said they needed to improve their gifts through diligent and industrious use. Otherwise, a failure to exercise the pastoral gift would result in its decline and, after a long period of neglect, its eventual loss.[56] In another sermon, preached at the ordination of George Braithwaite (1681–1748) to the pastorate of the Devonshire-square church in London, Gill provided two sources of temptation to neglect the gift: a lack of success in ministry, and contempt and persecutions on account of one's ministry.[57] Instead, a pastor needed to resist such temptations and exercise his gift; this usage would result in its improvement, and Gill likened this process to metal armor: "Through disuse, [they] grow rusty,[58] but the more they are worn the brighter they are."[59] A pastor could improve his gift, Gill added, through "prayer, meditation, and reading."[60] While the London pastor acknowledged that improvement of the pastoral gift was divinely given, God was pleased to work through

---

52. Regarding the grace of God, Gill observed that was the possession of all believers; however, not all were called to the ministry. Concerning learning and natural abilities, while both were serviceable to the pastoral task, they neither qualified nor disqualified a man based on his possession of them or lack thereof. Gill, "Gospel-Minister," in S&T, 22–23.

53. Gill, "Gospel-Minister," in S&T, 2:23.

54. Gill, "Gospel-Minister," in S&T, 2:23.

55. Gill, "Gospel-Minister," in S&T, 2:24.

56. Gill, "Gospel-Minister," in S&T, 2:24.

57. Gill, "Duty of a Pastor," in S&T, 2:1–13. The service took place on March 28, 1734; Samuel Wilson preached the sermon to the church. For details of this service, see Ivimey, History, 3:355. Both Gill's and Wilson's sermons were published as Gill and Wilson, Mutual Duty. Note that while Ivimey said that Wilson preached from Heb 13:17, the text at the top of the respective sermon in Mutual Duty is 1 Tim 5:17.

58. There was a footnote in the original pointing the reader to Matt 25:29, 30.

59. Gill, "Duty of a Pastor," in S&T, 2:4.

60. Gill, "Duty of a Pastor," in S&T, 2:4.

"the diligent use of means" in order "to give to his servants greater abilities, more light and knowledge."[61]

"Take Heed unto Thyself"

In his charge to Braithwaite, Gill preached from 1 Tim 4:16, "Take heed unto thyself, and unto thy doctrine; for in doing this, thou shalt both save thyself, and them that hear."[62] Having exhorted the ordinand to take heed to the gifts that qualified him for ministry, Gill proceeded to urge Braithwaite to diligently watch other aspects of his life and ministry. Specifically, the ordinand needed to pay careful attention to his time and the proper use of it. He was to ensure that his doctrine remained pure and unmixed with error and heterodoxy.[63] Gill exhorted the ordinand to keep watch on his temper and passions so that he was not governed by them, and on his life and conversations so that he was an example to his people. The ordinand was also charged to take heed to the church now under his care.[64]

Spiritual Light and Holy Love

In his sermon "Pastors Required to Feed the Flock of Christ," Fuller made a connection between Christ's love for the church and the necessity of under-shepherds to love the flock.[65] Preaching from John 21:16, "Feed my sheep,"

---

61. Gill, "Duty of a Pastor," in *S&T*, 2:5.

62. Gill, "Duty of a Pastor," in *S&T*, 2:1. The text was incorrectly cited as 2 Tim 4:16 by Gill. Unless otherwise noted, all Bible quotations are from the sermons or letters under consideration; thus, this quotation is from Gill, "Duty of a Pastor, in *S&T*, 2:1.

63. Gill, "Duty of a Pastor," in *S&T*, 2:6. At this point in the sermon, Gill was warning Braithwaite of the danger of error and heresy infiltrating the mind of the minister since his downfall in this regard would have a far-reaching impact. This warning was included in his first heading, where he exhorted Braithwaite "to take heed to himself." In the second heading, Gill exhorted the ordinand "to take heed to his doctrine," which was broader than watching for error and heresy. The London pastor summarized the instruction to watch his doctrine, stating that when a minister was diligent to take heed to his doctrine, it would "be according to the scriptures, agreeable to the doctrine of Christ and his apostles; that it be according to godliness, and makes for the use of edifying; that it be sound and incorrupt, pure and unmixed, and consistent with itself, and that it be expressed in the best manner, and to the best advantage." Gill, "Duty of a Pastor," in *S&T*, 2:10.

64. Gill, "Duty of a Pastor," in *S&T*, 2:3–8.

65. Paul A. Sanchez, commenting on this sermon, says, "Christ modeled a love beyond parallel when he laid down his life for his sheep. Pastors must recognize that these are the very sheep entrusted to them." Sanchez, *Spirituality of Love*, 12.

Fuller said love was a qualification required of under-shepherds of Christ.[66] Such love included divesting oneself of a selfish spirit and being conversant with the gospel. For the ordinand to have "the character necessary . . . to thrive under the word," Fuller wisely counseled that he had to be a sheep who found rich pasture in the gospel of Christ.[67]

A similar theme appeared in Fuller's sermon "Spiritual Knowledge and Love Necessary for the Ministry," which he preached from John 5:35, "He was a burning and shining light." In Fuller's mind, the work of God was accomplished through two ordinary means of "enlightening the minds and affecting the hearts of the people," and so a minister had to "be under their influence," that is, a minister needed to be "a burning and a shining light."[68] For Fuller, a preacher who was popular but had inadequate spiritual light or a minister who was zealous but lacked love for God were both ineffective in transforming hearts. After those introductory remarks, Fuller stated that the minister needed "to be made up of pure intellect—to be all light."[69] Further, a minister needed a firm understanding of "the holy character of God" and Christ as the mediator between men and God; he also had to have a grasp of human nature in its various aspects as created, depraved, and sanctified by the Spirit.[70] Before proceeding, Fuller returned to his earlier exhortation, namely, that mere knowledge was insufficient and the ordinand would also need "a heart *warmed* with divine things" or he would never be "a burning and shining light."[71] A pastor who preached and found no inner satisfaction was compared to a millstone that could prepare food for others but could not enjoy the fruit of its own labor.[72] A minister could cultivate this spiritual light and holy love by: reading the lives of good men, studying and praying over the Word of God, studying human nature, living as a Christian

---

66. Fuller, "Pastors Required to Feed," in *WAF*, 1:477–78.

67. Fuller, "Pastors Required to Feed," in *WAF*, 1:478. In another sermon, Fuller said, "We must mediate on these things *as Christians*, first feeding our own souls upon them, and then imparting that which we have believed and felt to others." Fuller, "Preaching Christ," in *WAF*, 1:501 (emphasis original).

68. Fuller, "Spiritual Knowledge and Love," in *WAF*, 1:479.

69. Fuller, "Spiritual Knowledge and Love," in *WAF*, 1:479.

70. Fuller, "Spiritual Knowledge and Love," in *WAF*, 1:479–80. Wheeler, commenting on this sermon, says, "Just as a doctor is required to know the anatomy of a body, the minister must be intimate with the anatomy of the human soul." Wheeler, "Eminent Spirituality," 183.

71. Fuller, "Spiritual Knowledge and Love," in *WAF*, 1:480 (emphasis original).

72. Fuller, "Spiritual Knowledge and Love," in *WAF*, 1:480.

(and not merely as a minister), communing privately with God, and holding forth the light by a holy life.[73]

"Eminent Spirituality and Eminent Usefulness"

On October 31, 1787, Fuller addressed Robert Fawkner at his ordination in a sermon entitled "The Qualifications and Encouragement of a Faithful Minister Illustrated by the Character and Success of Barnabas."[74] In it, Fuller held forth Barnabas as a model minister and outlined the sermon according to the three phrases in Acts 6:24: "He was a good man, and full of the Holy Spirit, and of faith."[75]

First, Fawkner was exhorted to pursue eminent goodness in his family life, private life, public ministry, and general demeanor; he was to value godliness above worldly greatness and even ministerial gifts.[76] Second, Fuller spoke of the need to be full of the Holy Spirit. By this, he did not mean the miraculous gifts but the ordinary gifts of the Spirit for Christian life and ministry; though the latter was less impressive, it was of greater value. To underscore this truth, Fuller proclaimed, "To be able to surmount a difficulty by Christian patience is a greater thing in the sight of God than to remove a mountain."[77] This greater gift, according to Fuller, was "an unction from the Holy One," and it affected the various aspects of a pastor's ministry. This unction preserved the minister from destructive heresies; it gave a spiritual tenor to his preaching and conversations; it caused the doctrines he preached to seem fitting when coming from his lips; and it instructed the minister in how he ought to conduct himself in every situation.[78] Third, Fawkner was to be full of faith, with his mind full of "divine sentiment," fully persuaded of the truth of the gospel, and exercising faith in that gospel as a Christian.[79]

The minister's commitment to this kind of spirituality was often what resulted in an effective ministry. Fuller said, "I think it may be laid down as a rule, which both Scripture and experience will confirm, that *eminent*

---

73. Fuller, "Spiritual Knowledge and Love," in *WAF*, 1:481–82.
74. Fuller, "Qualifications and Encouragement," in *WAF*, 1:135. For a treatment of this sermon, see Auld, "Eminent Spirituality," 33–43.
75. Fuller, "Qualifications and Encouragement," in *WAF*, 1:135.
76. Fuller, "Qualifications and Encouragement," in *WAF*, 1:136–38.
77. Fuller, "Qualifications and Encouragement," in *WAF*, 1:138.
78. Fuller, "Qualifications and Encouragement," in *WAF*, 1:139–41.
79. Fuller, "Qualifications and Encouragement," in *WAF*, 1:141–42.

spirituality in a minister is usually attended with eminent usefulness."[80] He carefully qualified that a minister could not effect results, and usefulness was not always proportionate to the spirituality of a minister. This notwithstanding, Fuller asserted that God usually worked through his prescribed means. Thus, often, the explanation behind an ineffective ministry was not a lack of talent but a lack of spirituality.[81] Fuller then listed three results of this spirituality, or "eminency in grace": it gave the minister a love for Christ and souls; it directed his aims "to the glory of God, and the welfare of men's souls"; and it allowed him to experience success in "ministry without being lifted up with it," that is, without becoming prideful.[82]

This connection between a minister's spirituality and his effectiveness was a vital point in Fuller's pastoral theology. Wheeler says, "These sermons clearly reveal that running through every published ordination sermon and sketch of Fuller is the common, prominent, and central thread of thought captured in the phrase, 'eminent spirituality leads to eminent usefulness.'"[83] For Fuller, godliness was important since it pleased God, but it was also significant for the pastor's ministerial effectiveness. Fuller captured this principle in two other sermons. First, in "Spiritual Knowledge and Love Necessary for the Ministry," he showed how spiritual light and holy love were useful in the pastoral duties of preaching, presiding over the church, and visitation.[84] Second, in "The Influence of the Presence of Christ on a Minister," Fuller connected the blessing of Christ's presence upon a minister and his effective preaching and profitable visitations.[85]

The Duties of a Pastor

The ordination sermons conveyed the significance of a pastor, the qualifications of a pastor, as well as the duties of a pastor. The duties appeared in many of the ordination sermons of the English Particular Baptists of the long eighteenth century. Three representative sermons will be considered below.

At the ordination service of Thomas Dunscombe, Caleb Evans[86] preached the sermon from Col 4:17, "Say to Archippus, take heed to the

---

80. Fuller, "Qualifications and Encouragement," in *WAF*, 1:143 (emphasis original).
81. Fuller, "Qualifications and Encouragement," in *WAF*, 1:143.
82. Fuller, "Qualifications and Encouragement," in *WAF*, 1:143–44.
83. Wheeler, "Eminent Spirituality," 211.
84. Fuller, "Spiritual Knowledge and Love," in *WAF*, 1:479–81.
85. Fuller, "Influence," in *WAF*, 1:505.
86. Caleb Evans should be distinguished from his father, Hugh Evans; if the person in view is not clear from the context, the first name will be given.

ministry which thou hast received in the Lord, that thou fulfill it." In his charge, Evans exhorted Dunscombe regarding the "several branches of that ministry or service which [he had] received in the Lord."[87] The six branches, or duties, of pastoral ministry were: preaching the Word, praying publicly, presiding over the singing of psalms or hymns,[88] administering the ordinances, presiding in the government of the church, and visiting the people and teaching them from house to house.[89] Gill gave a similar—though shorter—list of duties in the ordination charge to his nephew and four other men: ministration of the Word, administration of the ordinances, discipline of the church (including ruling and governing it), and visitation of members for spiritual care.[90]

Finally, at the ordination of Abraham Booth to pastorate of the Little Prescott Street church in Goodman's Fields, Benjamin Wallin (1710–1782)[91] listed several branches of the ministry. The branches of the ministry, according to Wallin, were preaching the Word, praying publicly and privately, knowing the state of the flock through "a welcome access to your person, and share in your pastoral visits," administering the ordinances, gathering the church (a reference to church meetings for the purpose of discipline), and seeking the increase of the flock through conversions.[92] Before he ex-

87. Evans, *Charge*, 4.

88. Wheeler observes that this duty of presiding over and regulating the singing is "mentioned very infrequently in the extant published ordination sermons." In his dissertation, he only cites Evans's charge to Dunscombe in the section on presiding over singing. Wheeler, "Eminent Spirituality," 154–55.

89. Evans, *Charge*, 4–14.

90. Gill, "Gospel-Minister," in *S&T*, 2:16–22.

91. There is some discussion concerning Wallin's year of birth; for details, see Cook, "Benjamin Wallin," 14n1; McKay, "Trinitarian Theology," 176n209.

92. Wallin and Stennett, *Charge and Sermon*, 35–42. Of the above-cited works, only Wallin explicitly mentioned evangelism. However, according to Wallin, this evangelistic work was to be done through preaching ("to testify . . . is to exhort and plead with our hearers") and visitation ("this attempt for increasing the flock is likewise to be made, by taking occasion in private to put even the youngest of the rising generation, who are capable of being taught, on prayer, and a concern about their eternal welfare"). Wallin, *Charge*, 42. Thus, there was probably an assumption that some aspect of a pastor's preaching and visitation would be evangelistic in nature. E.g., Evans said that "ministers should not overlook little children [and] they should be ready to gather them with their arm, and carry them in their bosom." Evans, *Charge*, 14. Arrell said of Gill that he emphasized "the evangelistic responsibilities of the pastor, arguing that this should include personal visitation." Arrell, "Laying Aside," 59. Fuller also related the importance of evangelism for the minister in a section concerning the necessary duties for a faithful discharge of the ministry: "Without considering you as evangelists in the full import of the term, there is a portion of the work pertaining to that office which is common to us all as ministers. Wherever Providence may station you, my dear young men, be concerned to evangelize your neighbourhood." Fuller, "Young Minister Exhorted," in *WAF*, 1:519.

plained each of the duties, Wallin introduced the pastor's responsibilities in this way:

> The branches of this sacred ministry are for substance invariably the same, to be applied according to the different situation and condition of the flock. They are clearly laid out in the New Testament, particularly in the epistles to Timothy and Titus, with which you are not unacquainted: yet give me leave on this occasion to rehearse those which are essential, with some hints, as proposed, by way of advice.[93]

Wallin's comment that the duties of the pastor had their source in the Pastoral Epistles elucidates the substantial consistency between him, Gill, and Evans on this matter. According to the English Particular Baptists, a pastor needed to devote himself to these responsibilities if he was to faithfully discharge the duties of his ministry.[94] The chief duty of a pastor was preaching, to which we will now turn.

The Preaching of a Pastor

Fuller addressed both the ordinand and the church in his sermon "Ministers and Churches Exhorted to Serve One Another in Love." In the address,

---

93. Wallin, *Charge*, 35.

94. Stennett gave a similar list of pastoral duties in his charge to Caleb Evans at his ordination to the pastorate of the Broadmead Church: (1) to preach the Word, (2) to administer the ordinances, (3) to preside over the house of God, and (4) to privately instruct the people through visitation. Stennett and Thomas, *Charge and Sermon*, 58–62. The list of pastoral duties was somewhat flexible. Stennett did not list private and public prayer as a separate duty, but he included them in his section on preaching the Word. Thus, while the specific enumeration of duties varied, there was great consistency in the core duties of the pastor according to English Particular Baptists of the eighteenth century.

Likewise, Fuller provided a list of duties in an ordination charge given to a young minister: (1) preaching the gospel, (2) presiding over the church, and (3) privately visiting the people. Fuller, "Spiritual Knowledge and Love," in *WAF*, 1:479–81. This sermon illustrates well that these were the core duties of the pastor for Fuller. In the sermon, he was not enumerating the branches of the ministerial work (as Caleb Evans, Gill, and Wallin were), but rather demonstrating the necessity of spiritual light and holy love in the different aspects of a pastor's work. Concerning the issue of the administration of baptism and the Lord's Supper, Wheeler observes that "somewhat surprisingly, Fuller rarely stresses the ordinances in terms of a specific duty of a minister." Wheeler supposes this was because Fuller did not want to place emphasis on what may have been a potentially controversial and distracting issue on such joyful occasions, knowing there was disagreement among Baptists. Similarly, Wheeler notes that Fuller did not emphasize public prayer as a core pastoral duty. Wheeler, "Eminent Spirituality," 218, 220.

Fuller exhorted the minister, "You must serve the church of God, by feeding them with the word of life—*This is the leading duty of a minister.*"[95] The pastor was called to spiritually nourish God's people by preaching the gospel and the Word of God during their corporate gatherings.[96] The pastor, according to the English Particular Baptists, was chiefly a preacher, a "public herald"[97] of the gospel of Jesus Christ. It was for this reason that preaching always appeared first in the above lists of pastoral duties.

The Content of Preaching

If preaching was the chief duty of the pastor, Christ was to be the chief subject of his preaching.[98] This was made clear in the sections concerning preaching in the ordination sermons.[99] Caleb Evans urged Dunscombe at his ordination to preach Christ, whether he was preaching the law, or the gospel, or expounding on doctrine or more practical matters. Dunscombe was exhorted to preach Christ regardless of the genre of Scripture. If he was preaching the historical sections, he was to show how "they ultimately referred to Christ"; if the prophetic portions, how Christ was "the great object regarded in them"; if the types and ceremonies of the Law, how they were

---

95. Fuller, "Ministers and Churches Exhorted," in *WAF*, 1:544 (emphasis added).

96. Fuller stated, "I would advise that one service of every sabbath consist of a well-digested exposition, that your hearers may become Bible Christians." Fuller, "Ministers and Churches Exhorted," in *WAF*, 1:544.

97. Evans, *Charge*, 5.

98. Fuller said, "We preach 'Christ Jesus the Lord.' This is the grand theme of the Christian ministry." Fuller, "Preaching Christ," in *WAF*, 1:503.

99. E.g., Gill said, "It is the gospel that is to be preached, the good news and glad tidings of peace, pardon, righteousness, and salvation by Christ; it is the gospel, which is given in commission to preach; it is the glorious gospel of the blessed God, which ministers are entrusted with [1 Tim 1:11]; and there is a wo upon them, if they preach it not [1 Cor 9:16]." Gill, "Gospel-Minister," in *S&T*, 2:17. Similarly, Caleb Evans said,

> The ministers of Christ are to be preachers, public heralds; and the subject of their preaching or heraldry, if I may be allowed the expression, is to be the word, the gospel, the word of life and salvation. . . . Preach then, my dear brother, the pure gospel of Jesus Christ. Preach to your people as the apostles and primitive ministers did to those amongst whom they labored, preach Jesus to them, preach Christ and him crucified [1 Cor 2:2]. (Evans, *Charge*, 5)

Also, Wallin said, "It is our business to testify the gospel of the grace of God. You need not be told that preaching the gospel is preaching the cross; and we are glad to find that there is so much reason to conclude, that you come hither determined, as the apostle, to know nothing among us save Jesus Christ and him crucified [1 Cor 2:2]." Wallin, *Charge*, 36.

but shadows of Christ; and if the promises of the Old Testament, how they were all yes and amen in Christ (2 Cor 1:20).[100]

In his sermon "Preaching Christ," Fuller said that if a man committed to the gospel, he would never run out of preaching material since all the attributes of God were reflected in Christ and all the teachings of Scripture were intricately connected to him.[101] In that sermon, Fuller showed how the preaching of Christ could be succinctly proclaimed in four simple points.[102] The gospel message could also be expanded into a ten-point summary of the Christian faith, as was done by Gill in his ordination charge to John Reynolds (1730–1792) to the pastorate of the Baptist church in Cripplegate in London, in a sermon entitled "The Form of Sound Words to Be Held Fast."[103]

In the sermon to the five ordinands, Gill said these doctrines of Scripture were to be preached "because that is the food with which the flock and church of God is to be fed, by those who are the pastors and overseers of

---

100. Evans, *Charge*, 6–7.

101. Fuller, "Preaching Christ," in *WAF*, 1:503.

102. Fuller put forward the following tenets: (1) the divinity and glorious character of Christ, (2) the atonement and mediation of Christ as the only grounds of a sinner's hope, (3) the blessings of salvation for those who accept it, and (4) Christ is the Lord of his church. Fuller, "Preaching Christ," in *WAF*, 1:503.

103. Gill, "Form of Sound Words," in *S&T*, 2:53–62. The John Reynolds in question had been a member of the Baptist church in Bourton-on-the-Water. He was one of the men who drafted the letters from the Bourton church in response to the Little Prescott Street church in Goodman's Fields; this correspondence will be the focus of chapter 3. Later, Reynolds was released by the Bourton church to the Cripplegate church. For the information regarding Reynolds and his ordination, see Brooks, *POTP*, 37, 42; Rippon, "Rev. John Reynolds," 41. Concerning Gill's sermon, see Arrell, "Laying Aside," 58. John Brine (1703–1765) provides a similarly long list of seven doctrines in Brine, *Solemn Charge*, 7–21. Wheeler's observation about the discontinuity between Gill and Fuller's pastoral theology is helpful here:

> The main difference between Fuller and Gill was not in the primary objective of the spirituality of the heart. The main difference was in the method. Gill was reluctant to offer the gospel to all, his style was more didactic, and he didn't plead with sinners in the same way Fuller did. Rather Gill believed that it was through teaching doctrine truthfully and carefully that this warm spirituality was achieved. Whereas both Gill and Fuller knew that true spirituality came through the head and heart, at times Gill emphasised a more rational appropriation of holiness. (Wheeler, "Eminent Spirituality," 235)

Similarly, concerning Brine, Wheeler says, "His main emphasis in the charge usually took the form of detailed doctrinal expositions explicating the necessity of the Doctrines of Grace understood from a high-Calvinist perspective. He differs somewhat from Gill in that he did not believe it was the duty of sinners to put their trust in Christ, but like Gill was reticent to offer the gospel to all people." Wheeler, "Eminent Spirituality," 235–36.

it."[104] The conviction that these doctrines needed to be scriptural was nearly assumed by the English Particular Baptist community and made plain by Gill's comment: "Yea, every truth that is contained in the Scriptures, and is agreeable to them, is to be preached; for all Scripture is profitable for doctrine."[105]

The faithful minister was also to preach, to borrow the words of the apostle Paul, "all the counsel of God" (Acts 20:27 KJV). In his sermon "Preaching Christ," Fuller warned the ordinand not to preach for the applause of others. This was a "subtle poison" and could lead a minister to proclaim "flattering doctrine, dwelling on what are known to be favourite topics, and avoiding those which are otherwise."[106] Similarly, in his charge to Booth, Wallin urged ministers to guard against "a partial and confined ministration of the word."[107] By this, Wallin meant that a minister needed to preach all the doctrines of the Bible since that would build the congregation's knowledge of divine truth and hold their attention. One safeguard in this respect was to preach the doctrine that naturally flowed from the text.[108] Gill also cautioned his nephew and four ordinands that the minister was to preach the whole gospel and not shrink from declaring certain doctrines, even though it might offend some.[109] Last, Caleb Evans urged Dunscombe,

> Upon the whole, keep back no part of the counsel of God [Acts 20:7], explain, illustrate, and by every powerful argument endeavor, in a humble dependence upon the Spirit's aid, to enforce the whole of the mind and will of God made known in his word. Suit your discourses to the young and to the old, the rich and the poor, the weak and the strong, to such as are babes in Christ, to such as are young men, and to such as are fathers [1 John 2:12–14]. Preach to saints and sinners, to men of every class and character; giving milk to babes, and strong meat to them that are strong [see 1 Cor 3:2; Heb 5:12–13];—but in all your preaching see to it that you preach Christ.[110]

---

104. Gill, "Gospel-Minister," in *S&T*, 2:18.

105. Gill, "Gospel-Minister," in *S&T*, 2:18. There was a footnote in the original pointing the reader to 2 Tim 3:16.

106. Fuller, "Preaching Christ" in *WAF*, 1:502.

107. Wallin, *Charge*, 36.

108. Wallin, *Charge*, 37.

109. Gill, "Gospel-Minister," in *S&T*, 2:17.

110. Evans, *Charge*, 7.

Evans connected preaching the whole counsel of God with the reality that the minister needed to proclaim Christ to all kinds of people from different walks of life and in varying spiritual conditions.

The Manner of Preaching

The preaching was to be constructed in a methodical manner. In his sermon "The Solemn Charge of a Christian Minister Considered," John Brine (1703–1765) exhorted the ordinand to prove a single principle, then another principle which followed from the first principle, and so forth. The preacher also needed to answer any objections and prove their doctrines from the "clear testimonies of Scripture."[111] Brine helpfully distinguished between concepts and formulations of those concepts. His point here was that a doctrine might be taught by Scripture even if the wording of a particular doctrine was not found therein.[112]

Caleb Evans, in his charge to Dunscombe, exhorted the ordinand with respect to the construction of his sermons. An effective sermon was of substance and not superficial; clear rather than obscure; methodical rather than confused; "plain, easy and natural" rather than full of impressive language; and, with respect to the delivery, animated and passionate rather than dry and formal.[113] Wheeler comments that this "emphasis on simplicity and plainness was at least partly a reaction to a widespread trend in the eighteenth-century for ministers to deliver eloquent discourses designed to impress congregations with their erudition and elocution."[114] In order to compose and preach such discourses, Dunscombe needed to study diligently as a workman "that need not be ashamed, rightly, skillfully dividing the word of truth [2 Tim 2:15]," and to meditate on the subjects of their sermons.[115]

Then, in "Ministers Should Be Concerned Not to Be Despised," Fuller gave several cautions so that a minister's preaching would not lead to his being despised. The ordinand was warned against delivering his sermons to impress others, seeking the applause of others (more than the gospel's reception), using vulgarity and silly joking in the pulpit, making assertions

---

111. Brine, *Solemn Charge*, 22–23.

112. Two examples he cited were the triunity of God and justification by imputed righteousness. Brine, *Solemn Charge*, 23.

113. Evans, *Charge*, 8.

114. Wheeler, "Eminent Spirituality," 145.

115. Evans, *Charge*, 8.

without scriptural proof, preaching "an unfelt gospel," avoiding difficult topics due to a fear of man, and making personal rebukes through the sermon.[116]

The Motivations of a Pastor

After he exhorted Dunscombe regarding the branches of the ministry, Caleb Evans anticipated the ordinand sensing his own inadequacy. He preached, "But perhaps your heart melts within you, and with a sorrowful accent you are ready to say—who is sufficient for these things? [2 Cor 2:16]."[117] As was typical of ordination sermons from this period, encouragements were given to motivate the ordinand for the task. Evans gave five encouragements to Dunscombe.

First, he told Dunscombe that he had been placed, gifted, and providentially called to the ministry by the Lord who saved him. Second, Dunscombe was reminded of the great importance of pastoral work, namely, that he was to watch over souls. The minister was engaged in "the best cause in the world," and he served a "great master"; thus, he was to give himself willingly and cheerfully to the work.[118] Another motivation for the ministry was the divine assistance that Christ gave to his ministers.[119] Similarly, in a different sermon, Fuller encouraged an ordinand that since he was a fellow laborer with God, he would receive heavenly assistance in both his private and public labors.[120]

Fourth, the time left to serve Christ on earth was short, and the pastor would soon need to give an account of how he had stewarded his life and ministry.[121] Last, though the Christian minister was but an unprofitable servant, there were great rewards that awaited him in the future due to the grace of his master. While the ministry may have posed "difficulties and discouragements," the Chief Shepherd would appear shortly, and the faithful minister would receive the unfading crown of glory (1 Pet 5:4).[122] In agreement with Evans, Fuller exhorted an ordinand to seek the approbation

---

116. Fuller, "Ministers Should Be Concerned," in *WAF*, 1:489–90.

117. Evans, *Charge*, 16. Wheeler says, "The vast majority of all Particular Baptists sermons at one time or another pose the question, 'Who is sufficient for these things?' [2 Cor 2:16]." Wheeler, "Eminent Spirituality," 215.

118. Evans, *Charge*, 17–18.

119. Evans, *Charge*, 18.

120. Fuller, "Ministers Fellow Labourers," in *WAF*, 1:493–94.

121. Evans, *Charge*, 18.

122. Evans, *Charge*, 18–19.

of the Lord on the last day in "The Work and Encouragements of the Christian Minister." What was most important for the faithful minister was not to hear "Well done" from others in this life but to hear "Well done" from the Lord in the life to come (Matt 25:21, 23). Fuller taught that faithfulness in this life would lead to greater rewards in the world to come, though he was reticent to claim with certainty what those rewards would be.[123]

Another motivation for the ministry came from Paul's first letter to Timothy, which was the basis for Gill's charge to Braithwaite: "Take heed unto thyself and unto thy doctrine; for in doing this, thou shalt both save thyself, and them that hear thee" (1 Tim 4:16).[124] Gill explained that the sense in which a minister could save himself was not that he was the "efficient and procuring cause" of his own salvation. Rather, a minister could save himself by taking heed to himself and thereby preserving himself from the pollutions of the world and unsound doctrine and heresies. Also, by proclaiming the gospel to the righteous and the wicked, he would save himself in that their blood would not be required at his hand.[125] Regarding how a "minister's self-watch"[126]—to borrow the words of Charles H. Spurgeon (1834–1892)—resulted in the salvation of his hearers, Gill gave two possibilities: (1) by their example "in word and conversation," a minister would be used in the lives of his hearers to protect them from doctrinal error and ungodly living, or (2) a minister would be the instrumental cause of his hearers' eternal salvation.[127] For the sake of his own soul and the souls of his hearers, the pastor had sufficient motivation to give himself wholly to the work of ministry.

THE SERMON TO THE CHURCH

At an ordination service of an English Particular Baptist pastor, visiting ministers often delivered the charge to the ordinand and the sermon to the church. The significant involvement of ministers from other churches may

---

123. Fuller, "Work and Encouragements," in *WAF*, 1:499–500.

124. Gill, "Duty of a Pastor," in *S&T*, 2:1. The text was incorrectly cited as 2 Tim 4:16 by Gill.

125. Gill, "Duty of a Pastor," in *S&T*, 2:12–13. Fuller also recognized this latter interpretation: "The expression may also have reference to that particular kind of salvation which consists in being delivered from the blood of souls." Fuller, "Habitual Devotedness," in *WAF*, 1:508.

126. In an address to ministerial students at his pastor's college, Spurgeon gave a lecture based on 1 Tim 4:16; that chapter was called "The Minister's Self-Watch." Spurgeon, *Lectures to My Students*, 1–17.

127. Gill, "Duty of a Pastor," in *S&T*, 2:13.

give the impression that they, and not the church, possessed the right to select and appoint a pastor. This, however, is a mistaken understanding of Baptist polity, which asserted that the local church had final authority over its own affairs. Grant says, "The act of ordaining, and the pastoral ministry and authority derived from it, was conceived to belong to the local church by its voluntary choice, rather than finding its authority from without."[128] Ordination in a Baptist church was the appointment of a pastor by its membership rather than by an external authority. Wheeler notes that though the visiting pastors played an important role in the service since only they could lay hands on another elder, their authority was granted to them by the church.[129] Therefore, the sermon to the church should be seen in light of this voluntary and covenantal context.[130]

The sermon to the church consisted of two primary themes: the church's responsibility to their newly appointed pastor and their responsibilities toward one another as members of the church.[131] Regarding the church's responsibility to the pastor, they needed to respect him, not because of his worthiness, but due to a high regard for the office. The church was exhorted to love their pastor, overlook his faults, and speak well of him so long as he continued to reflect the gospel in his life and ministry. Since the minister was responsible for building up the church through his preaching and visitation, it was advisable for members to attend services, particularly the Lord's Supper, and receive his ministry. The church could also help the pastor by providing for his temporal needs, helping to protect his time, and praying for him regularly.

The members were to express the same love to one another, though it would manifest differently than in their care for the pastor. The members were to bear one another's burdens, strive for peace within the body, pray for each other, and share the peaks and valleys of life with one another. In the following section, the addresses to the church will be discussed in greater detail.

---

128. Grant, *Andrew Fuller*, 65–66.

129. Wheeler, "Eminent Spirituality," 109. Arrell summarizes the matter well (leaning on Wheeler): "As all of the above confessions make clear, Particular Baptists held that the church alone selected its officers. Nevertheless, they also generally believed it was the visiting ministers who had the right to lay hands on an ordinand. Although it was acknowledged that ultimately this authority was given to them by the church through the invitation from the congregation to ordain the pastor." Arrell, "Laying Aside," 55n53.

130. Wheeler, "Eminent Spirituality," 111. See Grant, *Andrew Fuller*, 53–75.

131. For the information in this paragraph, I am indebted to Wheeler, "Eminent Spirituality," 111–17.

The Duties of a Church

The Connection Between a Church's Duties and a Pastor's Duties

A study of the ordination sermons of the English Particular Baptists reveals a correspondence between the duties of the church and those of the pastor. This is illustrated by two of Fuller's sermons. First, in "The Obedience of Churches to Their Pastors Explained and Enforced," Fuller addressed the Baptist Church at Cannon Street, Birmingham, at the ordination of Thomas Morgan (1776–1857).[132] He began by saying that if no one, or everyone, sought to rule and oversee the flock, the church would not mature. The pastor's authority in the church was legitimate if three factors were present: the church voluntarily chose their pastor, the pastor was teaching according to the will of Christ, and the pastor subjected himself to the same commands he placed upon the church. Fuller then laid out four ways in which the church ought to submit to their pastor with respect to his preaching, private visitation and counsel, presiding over church meetings, and private admonitions.[133] These duties of the church mirrored the duties of a pastor already discussed. In other words, there was a definite correlation between the duties of the church and those of its pastor. God intended for the church to be built up as the pastor faithfully discharged his duties and the people engaged with and received his ministry.

Second, in "Christian Churches Fellow Helpers with Their Pastors to the Truth," Fuller addressed an unnamed congregation. The text he expounded (3 John 8) addressed missionaries, but Fuller was convinced that its principles also applied to settled pastors. In the previous sermon, Fuller simply laid out the church's responsibility to submit to their pastor's ministry. Now, Fuller demonstrated how members of the church were helpers, or partners, in the pastor's ministry of propagating the truth. Fuller structured his address to the church around the three core duties of the pastor—preaching, visitation, and presiding over the church—and showed the church how they could be fellow helpers to the minister with respect to each of his duties.[134] A church could be a helper to its pastor with respect to his preaching by praying for him, attending and receiving his preaching, supporting him financially, and pursuing godliness so that he may point to his people as evidence of "the holy effects of religion."[135] With respect to visitations, a church could be helpers to their pastor by receiving him and

---

132. Fuller, "Obedience of Churches," in *WAF*, 1:196.
133. Fuller, "Obedience of Churches," in *WAF*, 1:196–99.
134. Fuller, "Christian Churches Fellow Helpers," in *WAF*, 1:526–27.
135. Fuller, "Christian Churches Fellow Helpers," in *WAF*, 1:526.

speaking honorably of him to their children and servants, and ministering to others in their midst, particularly those who were inquiring, poor, timid, and sick. Regarding the minister's presiding over the church, Fuller exhorted the people, particularly the deacons, to stand with the pastor on matters of church discipline and called for the pastor and deacons to consult about the business of the church regularly.[136] Thus, it was the church's godliness that rendered them effective helpers to their pastor.

The Godliness of the Church

Even as a pastor was required to have certain characteristics befitting a Christian minister, a church needed to pursue godliness which was suitable to their profession. In *The Duties Incumbent on a Christian Church*, Hinton reminded the Bourton church at Coles's ordination that they were "called to sustain a sacred and exalted character." This godly character was to be maintained both individually and corporately.[137] According to Hinton, the members of the Bourton church were to aim all their conduct to the glory of God.[138]

At the ordination of Carey, Fuller preached "Importance of Christian Ministers Considered as the Gift of Christ." In the sermon, he exhorted the members to seek after godliness by pursuing peace and avoiding that which provoked the Lord if they desired his presence and blessing among them.[139] In another sermon, "Nature and Importance of Christian Love," Fuller instructed the people to cherish Christian love in their midst by avoiding things that stifled it and being spiritually minded.[140] In his address "Christian Steadfastness," Fuller said that a godly people afforded the pastor the opportunity to point to his members as "letters of recommendation [2 Cor 3:1–2]."[141] Fuller went on to exhort the church that the success and

---

136. Fuller, "Christian Churches Fellow Helpers," in *WAF*, 1:526.
137. Hinton, *Duties Incumbent*, 36–39.
138. Hinton, *Duties Incumbent*, 39.
139. Fuller, "Importance of Christian Ministers," in *WAF*, 1:522.
140. Fuller, "Nature and Importance," in *WAF*, 1:524.
141. Fuller, "Christian Steadfastness," in *WAF*, 1:529. In another sermon, Fuller exhorted the congregation to

> "hold forth the word of life [Phil 2:16]" by recommending it in your spirit and practice.... This is a powerful way of preaching the gospel. It speaks louder than words—louder than thunder. Your ministers may assure those who are strangers to religion that religion is a matter of infinite importance, and you may say so too; but if they see you light and frothy in your conversation, indifferent and negligent in your duties, do you think they will believe you? (Fuller, "Churches Should Exhibit," in *WAF*, 1:533)

happiness of their pastor depended on the members' ministry to one another and their involvement in service.[142]

The effectiveness of a pastor's ministry and the godliness of his people were vitally connected. The church's godliness and duties were intertwined, to some degree, with the success of their pastor's ministry. Therefore, the church was to receive his ministry toward them and honor him as a minister sent by Christ. This reception of the pastor by his people—according to Hugh Evans's sermon to the church at the ordination of Dunscombe—benefited the pastor, the church, and Christ.[143] One could add that a church's reception of their pastor's ministry was also beneficial to the world, given Fuller's earlier emphasis that Christians were fellow laborers with God.[144] What were the ways that a church could honor its pastor and receive his ministry? Several exhortations emerge from these addresses.

The Duties of a Church Outlined

Pearce's address at the ordination of Belsher, *The Duty of Churches to Regard Ministers as the Gift of Christ*, gave a basic outline of the church's duties. Pearce instructed the church on how it could improve the gift of pastors so that they were being effectively used "for the purposes that Christ intended."[145] The Birmingham pastor provided several ways in which the church could promote the usefulness of their minister. A church was to pray regularly for their pastor, provide for him so that he was not anxious about temporal concerns, promote habits of diligent study by not intruding on his time, attend the ordinances and engage in worship during public services, and embrace the truth and reproofs delivered by the pastor.[146]

The reader can get a sense of the *pathos* with which Pearce delivered this portion of the address. He proclaimed,

> Give me the preacher who opens the folds of my heart; who accuses me, convicts me, and condemns me before God; who loves my soul too well to suffer me to go on in sin, unreproved, through fear of giving me offence; . . . who gives me no rest until he sees me, with unfeigned penitence, trembling at the feet of

---

142. Fuller, "Christian Steadfastness," in *WAF*, 1:529.

143. Evans, *Sermon*, 34–37.

144. Fuller made a similar point in another sermon; when churches are walking in the truth, it "greatly assists a minister in his public work—it recommends his preaching to the world." Fuller, "Churches Walking," in *WAF*, 1:531.

145. Pearce, *Duty of Churches*, 47.

146. Pearce, *Duty of Churches*, 47–59.

Jesus; and then, and not till then, soothes my anguish, wipes away my tears, and comforts me with the cordials of grace.[147]

Pearce went on, "Brethren, if Christ have given you such a man as this, receive him as an angel from heaven; and prize such a pastor as one of the most valuable gifts that can be imparted to the church."[148] Conversely, the church was to guard against "unbecoming sentiments of your minister" and to disapprove of such in other members since this would be a poison in the church.[149] A final way a church could improve the gift of a pastor was to support him to be extensively useful for building up the church[150] by ministering to the "unawakened, the careless, [and] the prophane" among their families and neighbors, and encourage their pastor's ministry in other places, such as in village preaching.[151]

The Motivations of a Church

In their sermons to the church, English Particular Baptist pastors held forth motivations to encourage the people to fulfill their duties as a church. In his sermon "Churches Walking in the Truth the Joy of Ministers," Fuller preached from 3 John 4, "I have no greater joy than to hear that my children walk in truth."[152] Since a pastor and his people were in a voluntary relationship, they had to maintain brotherly love for the sake of holiness and happiness. As the church walked in truth, it promoted joy and happiness in the minister.[153] Since the goal of a minister's life was to see his people conformed to Christ, Fuller said to the church, "Your sanctification and salvation are his great reward."[154] Fuller made a similar point in a sermon to the Baptist church at Cannon Street, Birmingham, at the ordination of Morgan. He said, "Finally, if you be a spiritual, affectionate, and peaceable people, your pastor will perform his work with joy; but if you be carnal and contentious . . . he may preach, but it will be with a heavy heart."[155] Thus, the conduct of his people would lead either to the minister's joy or grief. Lest the

---

147. Pearce, *Duty of Churches*, 56.
148. Pearce, *Duty of Churches*, 56.
149. Pearce, *Duty of Churches*, 57.
150. I.e., building up the church beyond the local church.
151. Pearce, *Duty of Churches*, 59–61.
152. Fuller, "Churches Walking," in *WAF*, 1:529.
153. Fuller, "Churches Walking," in *WAF*, 1:529–31.
154. Fuller, "Churches Walking," in *WAF*, 1:530–31.
155. Fuller, "Obedience of Churches," in *WAF*, 1:201.

hearer think that his carnal life was only to the injury of the pastor, Fuller went on to warn him that such conduct was also to his own peril.[156] In "The Reward of a Faithful Minister," Fuller instructed the congregation that all would be presented either as the minister's joy and crown or as rebellious children. It was, of course, the desire of Christian ministers that his people be saved and sanctified because they would be his hope, joy, and crown on the last day (1 Thess 2:19).[157]

CONCLUSION

The ordination service was an integral component of English Particular Baptist life in the long eighteenth century.[158] It was a significant moment in the life of the church, as was the case for the Baptist church in Bourton-on-the-Water when they called Thomas Coles after being without a pastor for six years. Fifty-eight years earlier, the same church had called Coles's predecessor, Benjamin Beddome, who was ordained to the pastorate of the Bourton church in 1743. The call to Bourton proved consequential for Beddome since he remained there until his death in 1795. These historical incidents demonstrate the significant role ordination services played in the ecclesial life of the Particular Baptists of this period.

A particular element of those services, the ordination sermon, has been the focus of this chapter. At the ordination of an English Particular pastor, it was customary for a visiting minister to give a charge to the ordinand and a different minister to preach a sermon to the church. Through these addresses, a visiting pastor urged the ordinand with respect to the significance, qualifications, duties, and motivations of the ministry.[159] Similarly, a visiting minister exhorted the church regarding their duties toward their newly appointed pastor and one another as members of the church.[160] These seasoned ministers drew their instructions from the Scriptures, their spiritual forebears, and their experience.[161] "The charge," says Wheeler, "which contained the pastoral advice of a more senior minister is central to understanding what was important to them concerning the ministry."[162] In addition to laying out the important role that ordination sermons played in

---

156. Fuller, "Obedience of Churches," in *WAF*, 1:200–201.
157. Fuller, "Reward," in *WAF*, 1:542–43.
158. Wheeler, "Eminent Spirituality," 117.
159. Wheeler, "Eminent Spirituality," 110.
160. Wheeler, "Eminent Spirituality," 111.
161. Wheeler, "Andrew Fuller's Ordination Sermons," 170.
162. Wheeler, "Eminent Spirituality," 117.

the life of the Particular Baptists, this chapter has also set Beddome in his denominational context. In chapter 4, Beddome's ordination sermons will be analyzed to construct his pastoral theology in the same manner as has been done for the Particular Baptists in this chapter. Before this, though, his letters will be analyzed in the next chapter.

CHAPTER 3

Pastoral Ministry According to Benjamin Beddome's Letters

SEVERAL OF BENJAMIN BEDDOME's letters are extant.[1] Many of these were published during the nineteenth century in *The Baptist Magazine*, *The Evangelical Magazine*, and the Bourton-on-the-Water Baptist Church history by Thomas Brooks, *Pictures of the Past*.[2] Recently, Beddome's letters have been republished for a contemporary audience, such as in *The Journal of Andrew Fuller Studies*, Roger Hayden's *Continuity and Change*, and Stephen Pickles's *The Life and Times of Benjamin Beddome*.[3]

Though they do not constitute a full biography, in their own way, Beddome's letters tell the story of his life. This chapter will begin with an overview of these published letters.[4] These will be categorized by type and theme and then organized in a loosely chronological fashion. After this, the collection of letters written to Beddome by his father, John Beddome, will be examined. John wrote most of these letters during the time his son was baptized and sensed a call to the ministry. In the last of these letters, John invited his son to come and minister with him in Bristol.

---

1. An adapted version of this chapter was presented as a paper at the annual meeting of the Evangelical Theological Society Ontario and Quebec, Toronto, October 12, 2024. That paper was published as Yuta Seki, "Pastoral Usefulness: Retrieving Wisdom from the Letters of Benjamin Beddome," *JAFS* 10 (Spring 2025). Used with permission.

2. Brooks, *POTP*. The letters published in the magazines will be individually cited below.

3. Hayden, *Continuity and Change*; Pickles, *Cotswolds Pastor*. The letters published in *JAFS* will be individually cited below.

4. While this chapter's focus will be on the letters that Beddome penned, there are several letters written to Beddome that are extant and will be included in this chapter.

The final section will form the core of this chapter. It will be a thorough analysis of a lengthy correspondence between the Bourton-on-the-Water Baptist Church and the Little Prescott Street Baptist Church in Goodman's Fields, London. Though these letters have been reproduced and briefly studied in several places, this book will be the first time they have been thoroughly analyzed.

To understand the purpose of this chapter in the overall argument of the book, the types of sources available to construct the pastoral theology of the eighteenth-century English Particular Baptists should be mentioned. First, there are systematic treatments of pastoral ministry, such as in John Gill's *Body of Practical Divinity*.[5] Catechisms and confessions of faith also fit into this category; though this book does not deal heavily with systematic treatments of *pastoralia*, Beddome's catechism is considered in chapter 4. Second, there are ordination sermons; this genre was explained and examined in chapter 2, and will also be the focus of chapter 4. Third, there are documents like letters and church minute books, which capture the correspondence of people in the past and the events in the life of a church, respectively. These sources provide a view of *pastoralia* in action; the minute books of the Bourton church are not considered in this book, but Beddome's letters are the focus of the current chapter. As noted, the life of the Cotswold divine will be considered from the vantage point of his correspondence, followed by analysis of the letters from his father, John, and those exchanged between the churches in Bourton and Goodman's Fields.

OVERVIEW OF BEDDOME'S LETTERS

There are several extant letters written by John Beddome to Benjamin in his earlier years (1739–1743). John wrote to his son: (1) on the occasion of his baptism;[6] (2) expressing hesitation about Benjamin being called to the min-

---

5. Gill, *Body of Practical and Doctrinal Divinity* (1810), 514–94.

6. John Beddome to Benjamin Beddome, n.d., in Brooks, *POTP*, 23; Anonymous, "Memoir," in Beddome, *SP*, xiii. For the letters from John Beddome to his son, Benjamin, the first names have been retained in the footnotes for the sake of clarity. Many of the letters were published in multiple locations; thus, sometimes, multiple works may be cited for a single letter. Also, if an original exists, then its current location will be indicated.

istry so hurriedly;[7] (3 and 4) urging his son to preach softer and shorter;[8] (5) regarding the younger Beddome's decision to go to Warwick or Bourton (July 1743 or later);[9] and (6) expressing regret to miss his son's ordination (the ordination was on September 23, 1743).[10] These letters from his father are instructive for a study of Beddome's pastoral theology, particularly because John wrote both as a father and an experienced pastor. During that same period, Beddome proposed to the Baptist hymnwriter Anne Steele (1717–1778) by letter.[11]

Once he was settled in Bourton-on-the-Water, there were two attempts to draw Beddome away from the Bourton church. The first came from his father in 1748, and the second came from the Goodman's Fields church in London during November 1750–February 1751. These letters will be discussed more thoroughly below.

Beddome was also involved in the Midland Association. He attended his first meeting in 1743 and made his final appearance in 1789.[12] According to Michael A. G. Haykin, these associations consisted of independent churches in a geographical area cooperating for the purposes of "evangelism and church planting, financial support of one another, and theological education. These associations [met] annually for two or three days of preaching and fellowship."[13] At his first associational meeting in Leominster, Beddome preached the annual sermon and did so on sixteen other occasions.[14] The Bourton church also hosted the annual meeting three times during

---

7. John Beddome and Rachel Beddome to Benjamin Beddome, May 21, 1740, in Brooks, POTP, 23; Anonymous, "Memoir," in Beddome, SP, xiii–xiv. This letter requires some explanation. Most of the father's portion of the letter was printed in Brooks, POTP; the full original is at Bristol Baptist College. Also, the date in Brooks, POTP, is May 21, 1740, but the date in the original is, apparently, May 26, 1740. For a discussion of the letter, including the mother's portion, see Brady, "Being Benjamin Beddome," 7–8.

8. John Beddome to Benjamin Beddome, May 17, 1742, in Brooks, POTP, 24; Anonymous, "Memoir," in Beddome, SP, xiv–xv; John Beddome to Benjamin Beddome, August 6, 1742, in Brooks POTP, 24–25; Anonymous, "Memoir," in Beddome, SP, xv.

9. John Beddome to Benjamin Beddome, n.d., in Brooks, POTP, 25–26; Anonymous, "Memoir," in Beddome, SP, xvi.

10. John Beddome to Benjamin Beddome, n.d., in Brooks, POTP, 26; Anonymous, "Memoir," in Beddome, SP, xvii.

11. Beddome to Steele, December 23, 1742, in Haykin and Haykin, Christian Lover, 34. A facsimile of the original is available as Beddome, "Letter of Proposal."

12. Rippon, "Rev. Benjamin Beddome," 325; Stokes, Midland Association, 88–90.

13. Haykin, Holy Spirit Now Descend, 89.

14. Oliver, English Calvinistic Baptists, 26. For a discussion regarding the number of times Beddome preached at the Midland Association's annual meetings, see Montgomery, "Benjamin Beddome," 146–47; and Rippon, "Rev. Benjamin Beddome," 325.

Beddome's lifetime.[15] He was the moderator for at least five meetings[16] and wrote the circular letter on a few occasions.[17]

The title and an excerpt of the 1765 circular letter give a sense of what was on the hearts of the ministers as they met in association. The title was *The Circular Letter from the Elders and Messengers of the Several Baptist Churches [. . .] Maintaining the Doctrines of Free Grace, in Opposition to Arminianism and Socinianism: and the Necessity of Good Works in Opposition to Libertinism and Real Antinomianism*. In that letter, Beddome exhorted the churches of the Midland Association thus:

> Look well, then, to the foundation upon which you are built, and seriously and frequently examine your state God-ward. See that you lay Christ at the bottom of your religion, as the support of it; that you place him at the top of it, as its glory; and that you make him the centre of it, to unite all its parts, and add beauty and vigour to the whole. Remember that growth in Christianity is growth in the knowledge of Christ. Seek that sorrow, that peace, that holiness, that establishment, which flow from Christ; let all your duties begin and end in Christ.[18]

Six letters were addressed to unknown relatives in 1759–60.[19] Though he was corresponding with family members, Beddome's spiritual concern for his recipients was also evident. For example, addressing his cousin who was facing trials related to poor health, Beddome wrote,

> Though the motions of the wheels of Providence are rough and intricate . . . I doubt not but all thing[s] are ordered by an infinitely wise God for your good and advantage. I hope you have found the school of affliction to be the school of Christ, and that you can say with David, in very faithfulness thou hast

---

15. Brady, "Red Letter Day," 65. Bourton hosted the annual meeting in 1753, 1765, and 1785.

16. This is the number given in Montgomery, "Benjamin Beddome," 147. However, in the statistics table given by Stokes, Beddome is listed as the moderator only four times, in 1746, 1749, 1753, and 1771; Stokes, *Midland Association*, 88–90.

17. Beddome, *Circular Letter* (1759); Beddome, *Circular Letter* (1765). The 1765 circular letter, excluding the "Breviates," also appears in Pickles, *Cotswolds Pastor*, 77–80. The circular letters of 1753 and 1758 were also penned by Beddome. The 1753 letter, according to Montgomery, was transcribed into the church books. Montgomery, "Benjamin Beddome," 143n69, 147. The 1758 letter was also transcribed into the church books and included in Pickles, *Cotswolds Pastor*, 255–57.

18. Beddome, *Circular Letter* (1765), 2.

19. These were recently published as Beddome, "Extracts from Six Letters," 59–65; these letters were originally published in *Evangelical Magazine* 8 (April–September 1800) 156, 197, 229–30, 272–73, 319, 370.

afflicted me [Ps 119:75]. . . . I shall be heartily glad to hear of the perfect restoration of your health and above all, of your spiritual welfare.[20]

Around that time, Beddome also wrote to a "Sister Reynolds" to confront her continual absence from the services of the church and the Lord's table. He warned her that the church would take further action if she did not appear before the membership to provide an explanation for her conduct.[21] Beddome clearly desired to preside over the house of God and ensure members were conducting themselves properly.

Several letters demonstrated the pastoral friendships Beddome had cultivated and enjoyed. First, there were three letters connected to John Collett Ryland, who was converted during a time of revival in early 1741 in Bourton; subsequently, Ryland was baptized by Beddome and brought into membership of the Bourton church.[22] These letters were: (1) a letter of dismission for Ryland from Bourton when he went to pastor at Warwick;[23] (2) a portion of a letter written by Ryland to Beddome;[24] and (3) a poetic epistle written by Beddome to Ryland.[25] Second, there was a letter from Daniel Turner (1710–1798) to Beddome to encourage the latter during a time of spiritual depression.[26]

Finally, there were three letters from the closing years of the Bourton pastor's life. The first letter was written in 1786 to the Midland Association and copied by Brooks into *Pictures of the Past*.[27] In the letter, which was representative of other associational letters from Beddome's later decades, the Bourton pastor lamented the church's decline in membership.[28] From 1766 until 1786, the membership had been reduced from 170 to about 100,

---

20. Beddome to His Cousin, October 18, 1759, in Brady, "Extracts from Six Letters," 61.

21. Beddome to Reynolds, March 8, 1761, in Brooks, *POTP*, 63.

22. Ivimey, *History*, 3:3; Rippon, "Rev. Benjamin Beddome," 323*.

23. Bourton Church to Warwick Church, July 8, 1750, in Newman, *Rylandiana*, 5–6.

24. Ryland to Beddome, May 11, 1766, in *Christian's Elegant Repository*, 62–63.

25. Beddome, "Original Poetic Epistle"; this letter was also included in Newman, *Rylandiana*, 137–39.

26. This was recently published as Turner, "Consolation in Spiritual Darkness," 59–70. Earlier, it was published as Turner, "Spiritual Darkness," 8–14; and Turner, *Consolation in Spiritual Darkness*.

27. Beddome to the Midland Association, 1786, in Brooks, *POTP*, 54–55. Another published associational letter is Bourton and Stow Churches to the Midland Association, July 19, 1772, in Stokes, *Midland Association*, 109–10.

28. Brooks, *POTP*, 54; Haykin, "Benjamin Beddome (1717–1795)," 4:265.

though the number of hearers, said Beddome, "keeps up surprisingly."[29] The second letter was also written to the association with the deacons in 1789.[30] The third letter was written to Andrew Fuller concerning the Baptist Missionary Society in 1792.[31] The Bourton pastor expressed hesitation concerning the Society, stating he once thought William Carey could have replaced him when the time came. Beddome's concern was broader than the Bourton church, however, and his fear was the lack of qualified ministers available in England.[32] During the final decade of his ministry, Beddome remained faithful in Bourton, but he had grown weary from a half-century of ministry and was deeply concerned about the state of the churches at home.[33]

This catalog of Beddome's letters is partial, just as the story they tell of the Cotswold divine's life.[34] Yet, they are instructive. The early letters from his father gave evidence of the kind of influence that was upon Beddome's life and ministry. The circular and associational letters provided a glimpse into the connection with other associational churches and their doctrinal commitments. The more personal letters to his relatives demonstrated his earnest concern for spiritual matters. The documents connected to Collett

---

29. Beddome to the Midland Association, 1786, in Brooks, *POTP*, 54–55. For a discussion of this letter, with insights from the Bourton church books, see Haykin, "Benjamin Beddome (1717–1795)," 4:265.

30. Beddome and Bourton Church Deacons to the Midland Association, May 31, 1789. The original is at the National Library of Wales, Aberystwyth. For information on this letter, see Mann, "Calendar of Letters" (Oct. 1932), 179–80. For a transcription of this letter, see Beddome, "Letter to the Association 1789."

31. Beddome to Fuller, October 2, 1793, in Pickles, *Cotswolds Pastor*, 388–89; the original is at the Angus Library. For a discussion of this letter, see Haykin, *Missionary Fellowship*, 59–62; Montgomery, "Benjamin Beddome," 151–57; and Pickles, *Cotswolds Pastor*, 387–90.

32. Beddome to Fuller, October 2, 1793, in Pickles, *Cotswolds Pastor*, 388.

33. Montgomery, "Benjamin Beddome," 155–56.

34. There are several letters not included above. There are some at the National Library of Wales: Benjamin Beddome to Henry Keene, September 14, 1772; Reynolds to Beddome, December 12, 1786. For information regarding these letters, see Mann, "Calendar of Letters" (Apr. 1932), 84; Mann, "Calendar of Letters" (Oct. 1932), 176–77. The letter from Beddome to Keene is also included in Pickles, *Cotswolds Pastor*, 221–23. There are some letters at the Angus Library also: Beddome to John Ryland, n.d.; Beddome to Hall, February 18, 1758 or 1764; information concerning these letters can be found through the Regent's Park Archive online catalog; see Seki, "Resurgence," 52n38.

There were also several letters transcribed into the Bourton church books, and these are largely not included here unless they have been published. For instance, Haykin remarks that Beddome wrote several letters on behalf of the church to the association lamenting the lack of growth in membership. These letters can be found, he says, "in the Bourton-on-the-Water Church Book 1719–1802, pages 232–317." Haykin, "Benjamin Beddome (1717–1795)," 4:265n26.

Ryland and Turner showed how the Bourton pastor prized pastoral friendships and endured spiritual discouragement in ministry. The proposal to Anne Steele portrayed Beddome's humanity.

While the above letters could be the basis of a study on various aspects of Beddome's life, the rest of this chapter will focus on two collections of letters that are fruitful in a study of his pastoral theology. First, there are several letters sent by Beddome's father, which were influential on the younger Beddome in his formative years as a minister of the gospel. Second, there are seven letters exchanged between the Baptist churches of Bourton-on-the-Water and Goodman's Fields concerning the request for Beddome's removal from Bourton to London.

LETTERS FROM JOHN BEDDOME TO BENJAMIN BEDDOME

Benjamin Beddome was spiritually awakened to his own sinfulness upon hearing a sermon on August 7, 1737, by a Mr. Ware of Chesham, at the Pithay church in Bristol.[35] Though he had grown up under the "winning affectionate ministry of his father," in the words of Rippon, it "had not effectually gained his attention before."[36] After his conversion, Beddome was concerned for the spiritual state of others and desired to enter the ministry. He enrolled at the Bristol Academy under the leadership of Bernard Foskett and then moved to London to attend the Independent Academy under John Eames (1686–1744). Until this time, Beddome had not joined a church, but in London, he became a member of the Little Prescott Street church in Goodman's Fields, having been baptized there, in September or early October 1739, by the pastor of the church, Samuel Wilson.[37]

His father, John, who was in Bristol, expressed his delight over this event: "I am pleased to hear that you have given yourself to a church of Christ."[38] Though John was elated about his son's baptism and membership in the church, he was hesitant when he heard Wilson had called him to ministry the following year.[39] Two years later, John heard reports about his son's preaching, specifically, that the sermon was delivered in a hurried manner,

---

35. Rippon, "Rev. Benjamin Beddome," 316.

36. Rippon, "Rev. Benjamin Beddome," 316.

37. For the details in this paragraph, I am indebted to Brooks, *POTP*, 22–23; Rippon, "Rev. Benjamin Beddome," 317.

38. John Beddome to Benjamin Beddome, n.d., in Brooks, *POTP*, 23.

39. John Beddome and Rachel Beddome to Benjamin Beddome, May 21, 1740, in Brooks, *POTP*, 23.

had too much content, and went on too long.⁴⁰ Thus, John wrote two letters to provide correction.⁴¹ Concerning the length, the father counseled his son, "Let two hours be the longest time you spend in the pulpit at any place."⁴² The goal of the letter was not to chastise but to develop Benjamin in his preaching. The words from his father surely encouraged Beddome to improve his preaching, such as when the former said, "I lately heard a great man say, that if you could deliver the matter you produce in the same manner as Mr. [Hugh] Evans, you would be more popular and useful than ever you are likely to be if you retain your harsh mode of speaking."⁴³ Beddome evidently heeded his father's advice⁴⁴ and eventually became a renowned preacher among Particular Baptists. Robert Hall Jr., writing over twenty years after the Bourton pastor's death, remarked, "As a preacher, [Beddome] was universally admired."⁴⁵

During this period from 1740 to 1743, Beddome regularly visited Bourton-on-the-Water and ministered both there and at Warwick. In July 1743, the Bourton church issued an invitation to Beddome to become their pastor, and on September 23, 1743, he was ordained to the office.⁴⁶ Though his father could not attend the ordination since he could not travel long on horseback, John sent a letter to encourage and strengthen his son.⁴⁷ Though John had initially expressed hesitation about the hurriedness with which Beddome was thrust into pastoral work, he was now satisfied with how Benjamin had given himself to the ministry.

John's approval of his son's ministry was demonstrated when he sought Beddome to be his co-pastor at the Pithay church in Bristol.⁴⁸ John pled with his son to remove to Bristol because the church greatly desired him to come, and they would provide him with a comfortable income. He went on to state his own reasons for desiring Beddome's removal to Bristol: many people would be prevented from spiritually "sinking," his children would be together, his wife would be comforted, and Benjamin would have a co-laborer

---

40. Brooks, *POTP*, 24; Anonymous, "Memoir," in Beddome, *SP*, xiv.

41. John Beddome to Benjamin Beddome, May 17, 1742, in Brooks, *POTP*, 24; John Beddome to Benjamin Beddome, August 6, 1742, in Brooks, *POTP*, 24–25.

42. John Beddome to Benjamin Beddome, August 6, 1742, in Brooks, *POTP*, 25.

43. John Beddome to Benjamin Beddome, August 6, 1742, in Brooks, *POTP*, 24–25.

44. Brooks said, "He held his voice with a tighter rein, and applied the scissors to his sermons." Brooks, *POTP*, 25.

45. Hall, "Recommendatory Preface," vi.

46. For the details of this paragraph, I am indebted to Brooks, *POTP*, 25–26.

47. John Beddome to Benjamin Beddome, n.d., in Brooks, *POTP*, 26.

48. Brooks, *POTP*, 29–30.

with whom he could have profitable conversations and an abundant harvest field as much as anywhere else.[49]

Though Beddome would have been closer to family and had ample opportunity for ministry in Bristol, he could not be easily swayed to leave Bourton. He was apparently fond of Bourton, which he had expressed in "The Wish," composed seven years prior:

> My dwelling place let Bourton be,
> There let me live, and live to thee!

In that same hymn, Beddome had prayed for a wife:

> Let the companion of my youth
> Be one of innocence and truth;
> Let modest charms adorn her face,
> And give her thy superior grace;
> By heavenly art first make her thine,
> Then make her willing to be mine![50]

Beddome may very well have had Anne Steele in mind as he prayed for a companion. Beddome proposed to the hymnwriter through a letter on December 23, 1742.[51] "The Wish," according to Rippon, was "composed about the year 1742."[52] However, Steele declined the proposal.

Beddome's wish for marriage was not granted until seven years later, when he was wed to Elizabeth Boswell on December 21, 1749.[53] Elizabeth was the daughter of Richard Boswell, one of the deacons of the Baptist church and "a most valuable man," according to Brooks.[54] Furthermore, Beddome initially took up residence in Lower Slaughter, a neighboring

---

49. John Beddome to Benjamin Beddome, October 28, 1748, in Brooks, *POTP*, 30. This letter also appeared in Anonymous, "Memoir," in Beddome, *SP*, xviii–xix; Dix, "Thy Will Be Done," n.p. The bulletin by Dix does not have pagination, but it is mostly devoted to Beddome and the two attempts to draw him away from the Bourton church.

50. Quoted in Rippon, "Rev. Benjamin Beddome," 318.

51. Beddome to Steele, December 23, 1742, in Haykin and Haykin, *Christian Lover*, 34.

52. Rippon, "Rev. Benjamin Beddome," 318.

53. Brooks, *POTP*, 30. In his memoir of Benjamin Beddome, Rippon extolled the piety and godly character of Elizabeth. Rippon, "Rev. Benjamin Beddome," 318–19n†.

54. Brooks, *POTP*, 31. Haykin says that Richard was "a wealthy jeweler." Haykin, "Benjamin Beddome (1717–1795)," 4:264. Richard's grandfather and father were both shopkeepers in Bourton, and it is likely that the younger Richard took over this business. That Richard was well-respected in the village was evident in how William Wilkins (d. 1812), the assistant minister of the church, referred to him as "the Father of the village, as well as of the Christian society to which he belonged." Rippon, "Rev. Benjamin Beddome," 318, 318*.

village, but moved to Bourton in September 1749 in preparation for marriage.[55] Thus, in marrying Boswell, his desires for a wife and remaining in Bourton were both granted.[56]

Brooks wondered whether Beddome's engagement to Boswell influenced his decision to stay in Bourton, though this could not be verified.[57] Either way, Beddome declined his father's invitation to remove to Bristol. Concerning the decision, Kenneth Dix said, "Benjamin was not to be moved by these entreaties. The allurements of a great city, and a city he had lived in for some 15 years, the seeming advantage of possibly being a well known and popular city minister, were not to move him from the people he loved, for whom he had given himself, and to whom the Lord had called him."[58] Thus, the Bourton church averted the first attempt to remove its pastor.[59] Two years later, there was another attempt to draw Beddome away from Bourton. The second appeal came from the Little Prescott Street church in Goodman's Fields, London, who desired Beddome to be their new pastor.

PRELIMINARY REMARKS CONCERNING BOURTON–LONDON CORRESPONDENCE

Seven letters were exchanged by the Baptist churches in Bourton-on-the-Water and Goodman's Fields in London. The main issue at hand was the Goodman's Fields church's request for Beddome to relocate to London and whether the Bourton church would comply with the request. These letters were numbered in *The Baptist Magazine*; the list below follows that numbering.[60] The letters were:

55. Anonymous, "Memoir," in Beddome, *SP*, xvii.

56. The connection between "The Wish" and Beddome's marriage to Boswell is made by Anonymous, "Memoir," in Beddome, *SP*, xix; Brooks, *POTP*, 30; Dix, "Thy Will Be Done," n.p.; Rippon, "Rev. Benjamin Beddome," 318. The connection between "The Wish" and Beddome's residence in Bourton is made in a few different ways. The connection between "The Wish" and Beddome's fruitful ministry in Bourton is made by Dix, "Thy Will Be Done," n.p. The connection between "The Wish" and his move from Lower Slaughter to Bourton is made by Anonymous, "Memoir," in Beddome, *SP*, xvii–xviii; and Rippon, "Rev. Benjamin Beddome," 317–18. The connection between "The Wish" and his remaining in Bourton (and not moving to Bristol) is made by Brooks, *POTP*, 30.

57. Brooks, *POTP*, 31.

58. Dix, "Thy Will Be Done," n.p.

59. Dix, "Thy Will Be Done," n.p.

60. Brooks, "Ministerial Changes" (July 1859), 425–29; Brooks, "Ministerial Changes" (Aug. 1859), 482–87.

1. Goodman's Fields Church, Letter to Benjamin Beddome, November 11, 1750
2. Goodman's Fields Church, Letter to Bourton Church, November 11, 1750
3. Benjamin Beddome, Letter to Goodman's Fields Church, [November 22, 1750]
4. Bourton Church, Letter to Goodman's Fields Church, December 16, 1750
5. Goodman's Fields Church, Letter to Bourton Church, February 3, 1751
6. Bourton Church, Letter to Goodman's Fields Church, February 24, 1751
7. Benjamin Beddome, Letter to Goodman's Fields Church, February 24, 1751

Furthermore, these seven letters can be grouped into four exchanges: (1) letters 1 and 2 comprise London's initial request; (2) letters 3 and 4 were Bourton's initial responses to London; (3) letter 5 was London's second appeal to Bourton; and (4) letters 6 and 7 comprise Bourton's second refusal. The analysis will be organized around these four exchanges.

These letters have been printed in several locations.[61] Since Brooks's *Pictures of the Past* has the most complete information, this will be the work that is primarily cited.[62] Also, the phrases Little Prescott Street church, Goodman's Fields church, and London church will be used interchangeably in this discussion. If another church in London is being referenced, this will be made clear.

The Death of Samuel Wilson

In a funeral sermon for his friend on October 14, 1750, John Gill preached:

> To you, the mournful widow of the deceased, give me leave to say, your loss is indeed great; you have lost a kind and indulgent husband; but remember, Christ your spiritual husband lives [Eph 5:31–32]; and from him, and his love, you can never be separated [Rom 8:39]; put your trust in him, he will never

---

61. In addition to *The Baptist Magazine* articles, they appeared in: Brooks, *POTP*, 32–47; Dix, "Thy Will Be Done," n.p.; Hayden, *Continuity and Change*, 82–86; Pickles, *Cotswolds Pastor*, 63–70.

62. Brooks, *POTP*, 32–47. Each letter will be individually cited below.

leave you nor forsake you [Heb 13:5]. To you his dear offspring, whom he most affectionately loved, you have lost one who has been, and still would have been, the guide of your youth, and constant monitor; follow his example, remember his instructions; shun the pleasures of sin [Heb 11:25], and the vanities of this world; flee youthful lusts [2 Tim 2:22]; seek the kingdom of God and his righteousness [Matt 6:33], and serve your father's God, and things will be well with you.[63]

Gill proclaimed these words to comfort his hearers. The words were couched in marital and familial terms, and yet, the intended audience was wider than the widow and children of the deceased. The funeral was for Samuel Wilson, the former pastor of the Little Prescott Street church in Goodman's Fields, and these words were aimed at the church mourning the loss of their shepherd.[64] Thus, Gill continued,

And to you, this church of Christ, among who, he has ministered many years, I would only say, abide by the truths he preached to you; imitate him in every thing praiseworthy, and of good report [Phil 4:8–9]; you have lost your shepherd, keep close to one another, and do not scatter and stray from the fold; preserve the order and discipline of God's house; seek peace and pursue it, unite in your counsels, be frequent and fervent in prayer; and I doubt not but in due time, God will send you a pastor to feed you with knowledge, and with understanding.[65]

In the wake of their pastor's death, the issue of Wilson's replacement weighed on the minds of the members and deacons of the Little Prescott Street church. Nineteenth-century Baptist historian Joseph Ivimey said that the first replacement the Goodman's Fields church considered was John Tommas (1724–1800). On the morning of Wilson's funeral, Tommas had preached at the Little Prescott Street church from Rev 1:18. Many were desirous to invite Tommas for a period of probation, but, according to Ivimey, "there were others who thought him not sufficiently gifted and accomplished to succeed their late pastor."[66] So, the London church turned

---

63. Gill, "Reverend Mr Samuel Wilson," in *S&T*, 1:498.

64. For sources on Wilson, see Anonymous, "Rev. Samuel Wilson," 141–45; Gill, "Reverend Mr Samuel Wilson," in *S&T*, 1:477–98; Stennett, "Funeral Sermon," 1–14; Wolever, "Samuel Wilson (1703–1750)," 4:183–209. For a history of the Little Prescott Street church from 1730 to 1768, see Ivimey, *History*, 3:542–61.

65. Gill, "Reverend Mr Samuel Wilson," in *S&T*, 1:498.

66. Ivimey, *History*, 3:554.

their attention to a former member who had enjoyed a decade of successful ministry in the rural Cotswolds of England: Benjamin Beddome.

EXCHANGE 1: GOODMAN'S FIELDS'S INITIAL REQUEST TO BOURTON

In this first exchange, letters 1 and 2 will be analyzed. These were written by the Goodman's Fields church deacons and addressed to Beddome and the Bourton church, respectively. The aim of the two letters was to request the removal of Beddome from Bourton to Goodman's Fields. The second was called a "Remonstrance" and indicated the reasons for their request.

Letter 1: Goodman's Fields to Beddome

The first letter was sent by five deacons and thirty members of the Goodman's Fields church to Beddome on November 11, 1750.[67] After the salutation, they wrote, "It is with great sorrow we mourn the loss of our beloved, laborious, and faithful pastor, and the present application is for your removal to London to succeed that excellent man."[68] The church's decision to call Beddome to London was unanimous, and they made the request with "the most strenuous importunity," which was evidenced in the remaining correspondence. The London church referred Beddome to the remonstrance, where they laid out their motivations for the request.[69]

If their prayers were answered that Beddome would become their pastor, they were ready to show "unfeigned affection and esteem, with all the assistance and respect in [their] power."[70] The duties of churches were set forth in the ordination sermons of English Particular Baptist pastors in the eighteenth century. At the ordination of George Braithwaite to the pastorate of Devonshire Square, London, on March 28, 1734, Wilson preached to the church regarding their duties.[71] He exhorted the church to have honorable thoughts of their pastor, converse with him respectfully, speak about him

---

67. Goodman's Fields Church to Beddome, November 11, 1750, in Brooks, *POTP*, 32–33.

68. Goodman's Fields Church to Beddome, November 11, 1750, in Brooks, *POTP*, 32.

69. Goodman's Fields Church to Beddome, November 11, 1750, in Brooks, *POTP*, 32.

70. Goodman's Fields Church to Beddome, November 11, 1750, in Brooks, *POTP*, 32.

71. Ivimey, *History*, 3:355.

with affection and esteem, pray for their pastor, not receive an accusing report against him, follow their minister as he followed Christ, and provide for him cheerfully and generously.[72] Thus, the London church echoed the instructions of their former pastor, saying that they would act properly toward Beddome if he would come and be their pastor.

The Goodman's Fields deacons tried to convince Beddome to remove to London on the grounds of usefulness. They envisioned that at the end of his life, Beddome could look back upon his labors in London and say, "Lord, thou deliverest unto me five talents; behold, I have gained besides them five talents more [Matt 25:20]."[73] By quoting the Matthean parable of the talents, the deacons were exhorting Beddome to be a good steward of his talents. In their minds, this entailed Beddome relocating to London. In the parable, three men were entrusted with a different number of talents: five, two, and one. Since the London deacons spoke of Beddome having five talents, it is clear they thought much of his gifting and abilities.

As will be demonstrated, usefulness was a prominent theme in the letters between Bourton and London. Beddome himself agreed that Christians should steward their talents according to their ability. In his sermon "Motives to Usefulness," Beddome preached that Christians "should not be remiss and negligent, but exert themselves to the utmost in the service, and for the honour of their blessed Redeemer."[74] He then gave several categories to help Christian people and ministers discern how they should serve Christ. The first category was natural and intellectual capacities. While God generally chose lowly persons to be part of his kingdom, he sometimes plucked those "whose intellectual powers fit him for a large sphere of usefulness. Now, where much is given, much is required: a greater improvement is expected from the man who has five talents, than from him who is possessed of two [Matt 25:14–30]."[75] Beddome here quoted the same passage as the London deacons did in their letter. He continued, describing the kind of talents he had in mind: "A clear understanding, penetrating judgment, lively imagination, strong memory, and the like, are given to men to profit withal; and

---

72. Gill and Wilson, *Mutual Duty*, 4–27.

73. Goodman's Fields Church to Beddome, November 11, 1750, in Brooks, *POTP*, 32.

74. Beddome, "Motives to Usefulness," in *TSD*, 1:88. This book will reference seven volumes of *Twenty Short Discourses* (*TSD*). These discourses were published in different years and multiple editions. To simplify the citations, the sermon title will be provided, followed by the volume and page range, e.g., Beddome, "Motives to Usefulness," in *TSD*, 1:88. Note, the eighth volume is titled *Short Discourses* (*SD*) and will be cited following a similar convention. The information for each volume is provided in the bibliography. The stand-alone work, *Sermons Printed*, will be cited as *SP*.

75. Beddome, "Motives to Usefulness," in *TSD*, 1:89.

the service they perform should certainly be proportioned to their superior abilities."[76] Thus, Beddome agreed with the London deacons that Christian people and ministers should strive for greater usefulness.

Letter 2: Goodman's Fields to Bourton

At that same church meeting on November 11, 1750, the deacons and members of the Goodman's Fields church wrote a letter to the Bourton church to request the removal of their pastor.[77] The London deacons expressed the great loss Wilson's death presented to the Goodman's Fields church and beyond. The Goodman's Fields deacons were also confident that the Bourton church would pray for God to provide a suitable replacement for Wilson, due to their concern for the honor of God and the prosperity of other Baptist churches.[78]

The deacons of the London church lamented the scarcity of qualified ministers in the city, especially when "compared with the other two denominations," a reference to the Congregationalists and Presbyterians.[79] The church desired a "learned and popular" pastor to replace Wilson. It is worth noting that both Wilson and Beddome were referred to as "learned" in this letter.[80] The state of the church in the city was poor, as evidenced by the decline of several churches and the spiritual carelessness of many professing Christians. Furthermore, the next generation was unpromising, and the existence and health of many country churches depended upon the "assistance, reputation, and influence of [the churches] in London."[81] Due to these reasons, the Goodman's Fields church felt compelled to urge

---

76. Beddome, "Motives to Usefulness," in *TSD*, 1:89.

77. Goodman's Fields Church to Bourton Church, November 11, 1750, in Brooks, *POTP*, 33–34.

78. Goodman's Fields Church to Bourton Church, November 11, 1750, in Brooks, *POTP*, 33.

79. Goodman's Fields Church to Bourton Church, November 11, 1750, in Brooks, *POTP*, 33.

80. Goodman's Fields Church to Bourton Church, November 11, 1750, in Brooks, *POTP*, 33–34. Some sixty years or so later, Beddome was remembered as having been learned, alongside Samuel Pearce and Benjamin Francis, in an address given by Andrew Fuller to the students of the Stepney Academical Institution. Fuller, "Young Minister Exhorted," in *WAF*, 1:520. There was no date for the address, but the Stepney Academical Institution was founded in 1810, and thus the figure of sixty years.

81. Goodman's Fields Church to Bourton Church, November 11, 1750, in Brooks, *POTP*, 33.

Beddome's removal, despite the Bourton church's love and affection for their pastor.[82]

They admitted that calling a pastor from the country to the city was not ideal, yet they also mentioned it had been done successfully by all three denominations in the city. The deacons conveyed that, had a suitable replacement other than Beddome been available, they would have been unjustified in requesting his removal. Their request was based solely on necessity.[83]

If the church waited for a suitable replacement, they were concerned that the people would disperse, and this might lead to the congregation's dissolution. A church recently under the care of Clendon Dawkes (d. 1758) was cited as an example of such a case.[84] The deacons were referring to the Joiners' Hall church meeting in Devonshire Square. Dawkes had been called there in 1735 and pastored the church for about sixteen years.[85] Though Joiners' Hall had once been "a church of the greatest popularity and reputation," it had evidently declined since. The Goodman's' Fields deacons were concerned that, without a suitable replacement, such fate might befall them also.[86] As it turned out, the deacons' prediction proved true: through deaths and removals, the Joiners' Hall church was greatly reduced and dissolved around 1761.[87]

Dawkes earlier pastored the Broad Street church, meeting on Old Gravel-Lane, Wapping, starting in 1719 or 1720. However, he was unpopular there and resigned on December 25, 1725.[88] Upon Dawkes's departure, the

82. Goodman's Fields Church to Bourton Church, November 11, 1750, in Brooks, *POTP*, 33–34.

83. Goodman's Fields Church to Bourton Church, November 11, 1750, in Brooks, *POTP*, 34.

84. Goodman's Fields Church to Bourton Church, November 11, 1750, in Brooks, *POTP*, 34.

85. Ivimey, *History*, 3:504.

86. Goodman's Fields Church to Bourton Church, November 11, 1750, in Brooks, *POTP*, 34.

87. Ivimey, *History*, 3:504.

88. Apparently, Dawkes had a habit of causing a decline in the churches under his care. Concerning the Broad Street church, Ivimey said, "This ancient church, which had enjoyed the rich labours of a Spilsbury, a Norcottt, and a Collins, and which had prospered under such culture, appears to have been gradually declining under the preaching of their successors (especially of Mr. Clendon Dawkes, who had contributed, it seems, to reduce several churches) until it experienced a temporary revival under Mr. Wilson." Ivimey, *History*, 3:310–11. Then, reflecting on the sermon preached at Dawkes's funeral by John Brine, Ivimey wrote,

> It would have been pleasant had Mr. Brine said something of the usefulness of Mr. Dawkes's labours, and shown that "his enlarged acquaintance with the evangelical scheme" had been the means of his building up and enlarging the church of God.

Broad Street church immediately invited Wilson, who had recently entered the ministry with much popularity. Under Wilson, the church revived from a low and declining state and eventually constructed a building in 1730 on Rosemary Branch, which later became Little Prescott Street. Though most of the church went with Wilson to the new building, there was a smaller group that remained at Broad Street; this group continued under the care of John Rhudd but eventually dissolved, at the latest by 1739.[89] It is not surprising then, some fourteen years later, when the Goodman's Fields church was seeking to replace Wilson, they insisted on securing a "learned and popular" minister.[90]

The Goodman's Fields deacons concluded with a closing appeal, entrusting the situation to the providence of God. They mentioned the presence of a suitable replacement for Beddome among the Bourton church's membership if Beddome were to leave Bourton. Also, the deacons described the potential relocation of Beddome to London as being "to more important services," which is connected to the concept of usefulness introduced in the previous letter.[91]

EXCHANGE 2: BOURTON'S FIRST RESPONSE TO GOODMAN'S FIELDS

Both Beddome and the Bourton church wrote a letter in response to the Goodman's Fields church. The pastor's reply came more quickly, within eleven days. However, the Bourton church, at their pastor's suggestion, took a month to pray and talk over the matter before providing their answer. Beddome, of course, signed his letter, and his father-in-law, Richard Boswell, along with two other deacons and thirty-seven members, signed the letter on behalf of the whole church. Their response, like London's request, was unanimous.

Instead of this, it should seem that the congregations he served in London declined under his hands, and soon became extinct. It is a very affecting circumstance, that "evangelical truth" should be preached without sinners being converted, and the church of God increased by it. (Ivimey, *History*, 3:505)

89. Ivimey, *History*, 3:306–7, 310. On Rhudd and the Broad Street church under his care, see Ivimey, *History*, 3:307–11.

90. Goodman's Fields Church to Bourton Church, November 11, 1750, in Brooks, *POTP*, 33.

91. Goodman's Fields Church to Bourton Church, November 11, 1750, in Brooks, *POTP*, 34.

Letter 3: Beddome to Goodman's Fields

The third letter was written by Beddome to the Goodman's Fields church.[92] Though it is technically undated, a later letter identifies the date as November 22, 1750.[93] The Bourton pastor began by expressing his condolences to the Goodman's Fields church concerning the recent loss of their pastor. While he rejoiced at the bliss that Wilson enjoyed, he looked with compassion upon the mournful church. Beddome was also a partaker of their loss since he had lost a friend and mentor in Wilson.[94] That Beddome called him "an instructor" could be traced back to the days when Beddome was baptized and called to the ministry under Wilson's care.[95] The Bourton pastor joined his friends in London in saying, "My father, my father, the chariot of Israel, and the horsemen thereof."[96] These words were uttered by the Old Testament prophet Elisha when the flaming chariots and horses separated him from his mentor, Elijah, who was taken up into heaven (2 Kgs 2:11–12).[97]

The Bourton pastor acknowledged the unanimous call they extended to him, saying that it was no small matter for either party. For the London church, it concerned their spiritual vitality, and for Beddome, he desired to have a clean conscience over the matter, whether he went to London or stayed in Bourton.[98]

He then responded concerning the necessity of their request: he agreed that they must have a minister, but he was not as certain that he was the most suitable option. For Beddome to be convinced that he was the man to replace Wilson, he would have needed to have a greater estimation of his abilities or a lesser one of his pastoral brethren.[99] It seems that Beddome may have had some hesitation in removing to London due to a modest assessment of his gifting and talents.

Beddome acknowledged the other strong motivations for his removal to Goodman's Fields. He contrasted his current situation in Bourton with the prospect of being in London. The church in Bourton was lowly and had much debt, whereas the London church was thriving and affluent. In the

---

92. Beddome to Goodman's Fields Church, n.d., in Brooks, *POTP*, 34–36.

93. Goodman's Fields Church to Bourton Church, February 3, 1751, in Brooks, *POTP*, 39.

94. Beddome to Goodman's Fields Church, n.d., in Brooks, *POTP*, 34–35.

95. Brooks, *POTP*, 23; Ivimey, *History*, 3:553.

96. Beddome to Goodman's Fields Church, n.d., in Brooks, *POTP*, 35.

97. The same words were spoken at the death of Elisha in 2 Kgs 13:14.

98. Beddome to Goodman's Fields Church, n.d., in Brooks, *POTP*, 35.

99. Beddome to Goodman's Fields Church, n.d., in Brooks, *POTP*, 35.

country, Beddome seldom enjoyed hearing and fellowshiping with other pastors, but London had "the best of preachers" and brother pastors who were united by a common cause and affection. Beddome was baptized and called to the ministry at Goodman's Fields, and the church sent Beddome to Bourton in the first place; thus, Beddome had a special regard for the London church. Bourton was clearly a place of less influence than London, and he acknowledged the Goodman's Fields perspective that Beddome would be of greater usefulness in the city.[100]

The Goodman's Fields church demanded respect since it was so "numerous and liberal," that is, generous.[101] Beddome again mentioned the unanimity of the call and said he would remember their invitation with gratitude.[102] However, even with such a favorable call, there were other factors to consider that gave Beddome reason to remain in Bourton. First, he was ordained over a people who had treated him with great affection, and many had been converted under his ministry. Second, the church was formerly divided but was now united. Moreover, Beddome had been fruitful in Bourton, as evidenced by the over one hundred people who were added to the church since his arrival. Fourth, the church's heart was engaged with its pastor. Fifth, they were committed to making Beddome comfortable. Last, Beddome had recently recovered from a life-threatening disease, and he attributed his recovery to the care and prayers of his people.[103]

The sickness took place shortly after his marriage to Elizabeth Boswell. Beddome contracted a serious disease that lasted for six weeks and brought him close to the grave. The Bourton pastor recovered, and the whole ordeal endeared the church to their pastor since he saw his restoration as an answer to his people's earnest prayers. Similarly, the fact they nearly lost their pastor strengthened the affection of the people for Beddome.[104]

There was tension in Beddome's mind as he placed the reasons for staying in Bourton and the motivations for his removal to London side by

---

100. Beddome to Goodman's Fields Church, n.d., in Brooks, *POTP*, 35.

101. Beddome to Goodman's Fields Church, n.d., in Brooks, *POTP*, 35. Brady says that the Little Prescott Street church was "London's largest Baptist church at the time." Brady, "Being Benjamin Beddome," 13.

102. Beddome to Goodman's Fields Church, n.d., in Brooks, *POTP*, 35.

103. Beddome to Goodman's Fields Church, n.d., in Brooks, *POTP*, 35–36.

104. For the information in this paragraph, I am indebted to Rippon, "Rev. Benjamin Beddome," 319. Rippon noted that, upon recovery, Beddome wrote a hymn of thanksgiving. Later, reflecting on his near-death experience, he wrote another hymn concerning the reality of death. The hymn of thanksgiving was likely Beddome, *Hymns*, #741. Pickles, *Cotswolds Pastor*, 60; see also Beddome, *Hymns*, #742. The later hymn was Beddome, *Hymns*, #778. There are two editions of the *Hymns* cited in this thesis; hereafter, unless otherwise noted, the individual hymns are cited from the 2020 edition.

side. He said, "I am in a great strait. I cry to God for direction, but what way I shall take, I know not."[105] Thus, Beddome entrusted himself into the hands of his church.[106]

The practice of a man entrusting a call to ministry to the church was commonplace among English Particular Baptists. When a man was called to be the pastor of a church (or to serve as what was called a probationer), it generally required a letter of dismission from the church where the candidate was a member. We see an example of this in the letter of the dismission of John Collett Ryland when he was called to the pastorate of the Baptist church at Warwick. In that letter, Beddome wrote of his joy that God had raised up Ryland from among the brethren in Bourton. Though he was threatened with illness, he had recovered and was now ready to settle as pastor of the people at Warwick. Beddome, on behalf of the church at Bourton, dismissed Ryland to Warwick with a hearty commendation. The Bourton pastor's desire was that his former member would be preserved in his character, and he and the friends at Warwick would "long be a mutual blessing one to another."[107]

---

105. Beddome to Goodman's Fields Church, n.d., in Brooks, *POTP*, 36. Benjamin Francis found himself in a similar situation twenty-two years later when he was requested to remove from his church in Horsley, Gloucestershire to the Carter Lane church in Southwark, London, to be John Gill's successor. In a letter to Caleb Evans, Francis expressed the perplexity he felt over the decision—whether to remove or to remain—in a manner akin to Beddome:

> My dear friend, I cannot express the astonishment, the shame, the concern, & perplexity, my mind has been overwhelmed with ever since. The thought of parting with my dear people, & of the unhappy consequences that may follow, dissolves my heart, & almost overpowers my spirits; while on the other hand a pleasing prospect of more extensive & general usefulness presents itself... I do not expect to be more happy in a people than I am at present: they love me exceedingly, as I also do them; nor have I but one material thing to complain of here, namely my being obliged to be so much from home, without which I cannot support my family... my poor wife is very lonesome & uncomfortable; I shall not be able so well to manage my children; I cannot visit my people so much as I would; & I have but little time for reading, study, etc.... *I am in a great strait*, & my mind is in a state of perpetual suspense. (Francis to Evans, February 22, 1772, in Nuttall, "Letters by Benjamin Francis," 7–8 [ellipses original, emphasis added])

For further information and sources on this episode in Francis's life, see n251.

106. Beddome to Goodman's Fields Church, n.d., in Brooks, *POTP*, 36.

107. Bourton Church to Warwick Church, July 8, 1750, in Newman, *Rylandiana*, 5–6. In his biography of Ryland, William Newman said that Ryland was called to the ministry on May 2, 1746, by the Baptist church in Bourton at a church meeting. Subsequently, he preached often at the Baptist church in Warwick and then, on September 21, 1746, was invited to preach for twelve months. He was eventually ordained to the pastorate of the Warwick church on July 26, 1750. In the case of Ryland, therefore, the probation period had already taken place when the letter of dismission was sent on

Though the situations were not exactly parallel—Ryland was entering his first pastorate while Beddome was being requested to remove to another place—this letter demonstrates the crucial role of the local church in the sending and receiving of pastors among Particular Baptist churches in the eighteenth century. To put it in modern parlance, Beddome did not view himself as a free agent, able to remove to the church of his choosing. Rather, he placed himself at the disposal of the Bourton church in this decision of whether he would remove to London or not.

So, Beddome placed the London church's arguments before his own church with sincerity. As their pastor, he desired that the membership pray both privately and corporately concerning the matter, "[entreating] guidance from him who hath power over all spirits, and can turn them as the rivers of water are turned [Num 16:22; Prov 21:1]."[108] To discourage a hasty decision, Beddome instructed the church to take a month to pray and talk about the matter, at which point, a response could be sent to London. This answer, Beddome trusted, would "appear most equitable and consistent with their duty."[109]

Beddome closed his letter with some reflections. When he looked back at his time in Bourton and how he had "been amongst them, in weakness and fear, and much trembling [1 Cor 2:1]," he wondered at how much he had been accepted by the people.[110] He also thought about the prospect of a new minister coming to Bourton and pondered if such a change might be warmly welcomed by the people.[111] In this, Beddome spoke modestly, but as it turned out, the Bourton church opposed the idea of a new pastor. Yet, he was reticent to succeed such an eminent minister in the most prominent city in England. To do so would require much wisdom, courage, and "superior abilities of every kind."[112] Ultimately, though, Beddome said that he had no will of his own and cast himself on the providence of God, asking also for the prayers of the Goodman's Fields church.

July 8, 1750. Newman, *Rylandiana*, 4–6. There were other dismissal letters that were recorded in the Bourton church books; some of these have been reproduced in Pickles, *Cotswolds Pastor*—on the occasion of Haines's dismissal: Bourton Church to Bradford on Avon Church, March 1750, in Pickles, *Cotswolds Pastor*, 194; on Rawlings's dismissal: Bourton Church to Trowbridge Church, October 5, 1766, in Pickles, *Cotswolds Pastor*, 198–99; on Reynolds's dismissal: Bourton Church to Cripplegate Church, September 14, 1766, in Pickles, *Cotswolds Pastor*, 202–3.

108. Beddome to Goodman's Fields Church, n.d., in Brooks, *POTP*, 36.
109. Beddome to Goodman's Fields Church, n.d., in Brooks, *POTP*, 36.
110. Beddome to Goodman's Fields Church, n.d., in Brooks, *POTP*, 36.
111. Beddome to Goodman's Fields Church, n.d., in Brooks, *POTP*, 36.
112. Beddome to Goodman's Fields Church, n.d., in Brooks, *POTP*, 36.

Letter 4: Bourton to Goodman's Fields

The Bourton church had met on December 16, 1750, to decide concerning the request from Goodman's Fields for the removal of their pastor.[113] Brooks said that the letter was drawn up by John Reynolds, John Reynolds Jr., and Beddome's father-in-law, Richard Boswell, and then approved and signed by the church.[114]

The deacons of the Bourton church expressed sympathy for their brothers and sisters in Goodman's Fields over the tragedy that had befallen them. Echoing the words in the letter sent to them, they assured the London church that they too were concerned "for God's honour, his worship" and would join them in praying to "the great Shepherd of Israel [Heb 13:20]" to provide them with a minister.[115] Regarding the spiritual state of the city, they condoled with the church in London but observed the same to be true in the country as well.[116]

The Bourton deacons agreed with the Goodman's Fields church that there should be "more learned and popular ministers" in London since the churches in the country benefited from those in the city. The Baptist church at Bourton, however, had not required such assistance, though they acknowledged the generosity of the Christians in London who provided help to other country churches. They again expressed a hope that, even as God raised up Wilson in the past, he would now provide another pastor for the brethren in Goodman's Fields, and they added, "without your being driven to such extremes as to deprive another church of its pastor."[117]

From this point in the letter, the Bourton deacons presented the alternative perspective to the request of Goodman's Fields, namely, that Beddome should not remove to London. They began by turning around the London church's arguments. If they were arguing from the perspective of "the church's necessity" and its potential dispersion or dissolution, the stronger case would be for Beddome to remain in Bourton and not relocate

---

113. Bourton Church to Goodman's Fields Church, December 16, 1750, in Brooks, *POTP*, 37–39.

114. Brooks, *POTP*, 37.

115. Bourton Church to Goodman's Fields Church, December 16, 1750, in Brooks, *POTP*, 37.

116. Bourton Church to Goodman's Fields Church, December 16, 1750, in Brooks, *POTP*, 37.

117. Bourton Church to Goodman's Fields Church, December 16, 1750, in Brooks, *POTP*, 37.

to London. For Goodman's Fields to see this, though, it would require them to have an impartial view of the matter.[118]

Additional considerations were given to demonstrate the case of the Bourton church to retain its minister. First, the Bourton church expressed "love and esteem for this our learned and faithful pastor."[119] Parting ways with Beddome would be extremely difficult to experience, and so this alone was sufficient to deny London's request. There were further reasons, though, such as a consideration of the history of the church in that parish. Recounting that history, the deacons claimed that there had been a professing people in that region for 150 years—initially called Puritans, then Baptists and Independents. During that period, they had lost many ministers, and there were also two or three who were "very eminent and valuable."[120]

Third, the Bourton church had been in a destitute state and prayed to God concerning their situation. He withheld an answer to their pleas, that is, until he raised up, qualified, and sent Beddome to be their pastor. Moreover, Beddome had been fruitful during his time in Bourton: decayed religion had been restored, the church's membership increased, and men had been raised up for ministry, some of whom were already called as pastors of other churches.[121] Last, the deacons relayed the episode of their pastor's sickness

---

118. Bourton Church to Goodman's Fields Church, December 16, 1750, in Brooks, *POTP*, 37–38.

119. Bourton Church to Goodman's Fields Church, December 16, 1750, in Brooks, *POTP*, 38.

120. Bourton Church to Goodman's Fields Church, December 16, 1750, in Brooks, *POTP*, 38.

121. Bourton Church to Goodman's Fields Church, December 16, 1750, in Brooks, *POTP*, 38. According to Rippon, the men raised up for ministry under Beddome were John Collett Ryland, Richard Haynes, John Reynolds Jr., Nathaniel Rawlins, and Alexander Payne. Collett Ryland and Haynes were already fixed as pastors. Collett Ryland had been called to the pastorate of the Castle Hill Baptist church in Warwick on July 22, 1750, and Haynes to the pastorate of the church at Bradford in Wilts in March of 1750. Reynolds had trained at the Bristol Baptist Academy and been engaged in ministry, though not called as a pastor of a church yet; for more on Reynolds, see n228; Rawlins was dismissed to Trowbridge on January 14, 1766; Payne was dismissed to Bengworth on his own initiative on October 26, 1780; the call of Payne to the ministry was not unanimous by the Bourton church; this is likely the reason for Rippon saying, "*four or five* persons in his time were called to the work of the ministry by [Beddome's] church," in his obituary of Beddome (emphasis added). For the details in this paragraph, see Holmes, "Early Years (1655–1740)," 42–52, appendix 12; Rippon, "Rev. Benjamin Beddome," 323, 323*.

Brooks listed another man who was called to the ministry under Beddome, Richard Strange, who settled "at or near Stratton, Wilts," in 1752. Holmes also listed another man, Thomas Coles. Though Coles was quite young, being only sixteen when Beddome passed, the Bourton pastor had an impact on him. For example, he took extended notes of Beddome's sermons when he was eleven and, at the age of thirteen, read his notes

that brought him close to death. In response to their prayers, God restored Beddome to health and, they hoped, to usefulness as before. This usefulness was evidenced recently in that some had been converted under Beddome's ministry and now wanted to join the church.[122]

The Bourton church saw their pastor as a merciful answer to their prayers from God—both when he was first given to them and when he was restored to health after a period of sickness. To consent to his removal would have been a rejection of God's mercy and answer to their prayers. Therefore, it would have displayed an ingratitude and been harmful to the church, their families, and those around them. In their minds, to let Beddome go from Bourton would have been provoking to God. So, the Bourton deacons wrote, "On these accounts we cannot consent to his removal, but must, till we see occasion to alter our minds, absolutely refuse it."[123]

They concluded the letter by stating they had and would continue to plead with "God, the great Shepherd of Israel, and bishop of souls, would qualify and send you a minister and pastor after his own heart, to your abundant joy and satisfaction [1 Sam 13:14; Heb 13:20; 1 Pet 5:4]."[124] Thus, they finished in the same way they began—with intercession to "the Shepherd of Israel" to supply a pastor to the Goodman's Fields church. The Bourton deacons were convinced that it was ultimately God and not other churches that would provide the Little Prescott Street church with a pastor.

---

at the weekly prayer meeting. He was baptized at age fifteen on August 9, 1795, and joined the church two weeks later, on August 16, 1795. This was evidently a busy month for Coles. After he was received into the church, he left to train at the Bristol Baptist Academy on August 24. On August 31, he turned sixteen, and on September 3, 1795, his pastor passed away. Coles eventually succeeded Beddome in 1801. For the details of this paragraph, see Brooks, *POTP*, 60, 82; Holmes, "Early Years (1655–1740)," 52; Rippon, "Rev. Benjamin Beddome," 326. For other works that address the men who were called to ministry under Beddome, see Brady, "Benjamin Beddome 1717-1795," 158–59; Oliver, *English Calvinistic Baptists*, 27–29; Pickles, *Cotswolds Pastor*, 185–208.

122. Bourton Church to Goodman's Fields Church, December 16, 1750, in Brooks, *POTP*, 38.

123. Bourton Church to Goodman's Fields Church, December 16, 1750, in Brooks, *POTP*, 38.

124. Bourton Church to Goodman's Fields Church, December 16, 1750, in Brooks, *POTP*, 38–39.

EXCHANGE 3: GOODMAN'S FIELDS'S SECOND APPEAL TO BOURTON

In reading the previous four letters, one would expect the correspondence to have stopped. The church in the city put forward a strong case for Beddome's removal to London, but the country church denied the request with equal force.[125] However, like the importunate widow in the Gospel of Luke, the London church persisted in their request (Luke 18:1-8).[126] After a month and a half, the Goodman's Fields deacons composed another letter to appeal for Beddome to come and pastor the Little Prescott Street church. While this decision caused consternation for Beddome and the Bourton church, it yielded three further letters for posterity.[127]

Letter 5: Goodman's Fields to Bourton

The second appeal made by the Little Prescott Street church was signed by the five deacons and sent on behalf of the whole church. It was dated February 3, 1751.[128] The deacons acknowledged their receipt of both letters from Bourton. In Beddome's letter, they particularly noted the reasons he gave for and against his removal to London, his consternation over what direction to take, and his deference to the church's decision on the matter. In the church's letter, they acknowledged the Bourton church's reasons for objecting to Beddome's removal and their absolute refusal to comply with London's request.[129]

The Little Prescott church deacons then brought up a "maxim" they said applied in all areas of life, whether civil or religious: "The service of all is to be preferred to that of the part." They continued, "No man ever said that the interest of one member is of equal importance with that of society in general."[130] This premise served as the basis for the thrust of their appeal

---

125. Holmes, "Early Years (1655–1740)," 55.

126. Dix, "Thy Will Be Done," n.p.

127. Rippon said, "He had not, however, been long restored to his people and his pulpit [a reference to his recovery from sickness], before another unexpected providence excited their fears [a reference to the Goodman's Fields church's first attempt to remove Beddome to London]." Rippon, "Rev. Benjamin Beddome," 319.

128. Goodman's Fields Church to Bourton Church, February 3, 1751, in Brooks, *POTP*, 39-42.

129. Goodman's Fields Church to Bourton Church, February 3, 1751, in Brooks, *POTP*, 39.

130. Goodman's Fields Church to Bourton Church, February 3, 1751, in Brooks, *POTP*, 39.

in the letter. From their perspective, the question at hand was whether "the prosperity of the churches in general of our faith and order, or that of the church at Bourton singly, [was] to be preferred."[131]

The Goodman's Fields church stated that their desire for Beddome's removal to London was not merely for their personal benefit. If Beddome moved to London, in their minds, he would be much more useful in the cause of Christ than if he were to remain in his "retired situation" in the rural region of the Cotswolds. Their ambition for Beddome was that he would become a celebrated preacher in the city and lend credibility to the Baptist cause, which was so often criticized by Dissenters and those of the national church.[132] The argument of the Goodman's Fields church was that Beddome would have been more useful in London and had a more influential and fruitful ministry there. Considering their comments, though, causes one to wonder whether a desire for prestige and respectability had tinged the motives of the London church.

The deacons at Goodman's Fields asserted that "an able and learned ministry" needed to be preserved at Little Prescott Street. They also urged the Bourton church to change their minds on the issue and reproved them for taking only the interest of Bourton and its surrounding areas into consideration.[133] The London deacons declared the necessity of their case and said there was not a suitable minister besides Beddome who could have replaced Wilson adequately.[134] This was already articulated in their first letter to the Bourton church. There, they said that they only felt warranted in their request because there was not a minister "fit and proper in all respects to succeed that eloquent preacher," a reference to Wilson.[135]

The Goodman's Fields deacons made clear that their concern was not merely for their church but for the interest of the churches in general. The reason why they saw themselves as more pivotal to the general cause than the Bourton church was because city churches had a proportionately greater impact upon the general interest of the Baptist churches. Additionally, the positive impact the city churches would have on the general interest was

---

131. Goodman's Fields Church to Bourton Church, February 3, 1751, in Brooks, *POTP*, 39.

132. Goodman's Fields Church to Bourton Church, February 3, 1751, in Brooks, *POTP*, 40.

133. Goodman's Fields Church to Bourton Church, February 3, 1751, in Brooks, *POTP*, 40.

134. Goodman's Fields Church to Bourton Church, February 3, 1751, in Brooks, *POTP*, 40.

135. Goodman's Fields Church to Bourton Church, November 11, 1750, in Brooks, *POTP*, 34.

proportionate to the quality of its ministers. If the Bourton church were to argue to retain Beddome from the standpoint of necessity, they were only concerned about the village of Bourton and the surrounding area. So, the need of London should have been preferred over that of Bourton, in the mind of the Goodman's Fields church.[136]

In a surprising aside, the deacons of the Little Prescott Street church proposed a hypothetical situation to argue for their case. They said that even if the situation was between the Bourton church and a single church in London, without any consideration of the general interest, Beddome would have been more useful in London than in the obscure village of Bourton.[137] Even in this hypothetical situation, the metropolis was to be preferred over the country village.[138]

The Goodman's Fields church proceeded to speak of the hazard that awaited them as a church if they could not secure Beddome as their pastor. Since there were forty congregations in the vicinity, the London deacons were concerned that the people would disperse to them. In their letter, the Bourton deacons mentioned how their church had been in a destitute state in the past. The Goodman's Fields deacons responded by asking how a church in London could survive similar challenges. Simply put, the situations in London and Bourton were not the same, and this too was an argument for Beddome's removal to the city.[139]

According to London, Bourton's fears of dispersion or dissolution were unfounded: first, because the people at Bourton did not have forty congregations close by to disperse to, and second, because they had a

---

136. Goodman's Fields Church to Bourton Church, February 3, 1751, in Brooks, POTP, 40.

137. Goodman's Fields Church to Bourton Church, February 3, 1751, in Brooks, POTP, 40. In the recommendatory preface to Beddome's hymns, Hall acknowledged the obscurity of Bourton, which accorded with the perspective of the Goodman's Fields church. However, with the advantage of hindsight (he wrote nearly seventy years after the correspondence and over twenty years after Beddome's death), Hall also saw the suitability of a gifted and learned man such as Beddome to have spent his days in a country village in the Cotswolds. Hall, "Recommendatory Preface," vi.

138. Goodman's Fields Church to Bourton Church, February 3, 1751, in Brooks, POTP, 40. We have the total membership of the Bourton and Goodman's Fields churches from around that time. Brooks said that the Bourton membership was 180 in 1751, and Ivimey estimated that the Goodman's Fields church had 150 members in 1753. Brooks, POTP, 50; Ivimey, History, 3:278. The Bourton church had a larger membership than the Goodman's Fields church. Considering this, the argument made by London here—that even if the situation involved the Bourton church and a single church in London, without regard for the general interest—held less weight.

139. Goodman's Fields Church to Bourton Church, February 3, 1751, in Brooks, POTP, 40–41.

suitable replacement in John Reynolds Jr.[140] The London church's first letter to the Bourton church had already alluded to Reynolds, though he was not named.[141] In the estimation of the Goodman's Fields church, Reynolds was the right replacement for Beddome, and Beddome for Wilson. The latter judgment arose from the London church's plight that there were no suitable candidates to take Wilson's place. In their minds, since Beddome was "learned and popular," he belonged in the city and not in the country.[142]

The Goodman's Fields church prepared arguments for their case and rebutted Bourton's reasons against Beddome's removal. In their letter, the Bourton church stated that their love and esteem for their pastor was sufficient to have caused them to refuse London's request. They wrote, "Our great love and esteem for this our learned and faithful pastor would make the parting stroke very severe and unsupportable, so that, if there were no other reason than this—this would restrain us from giving our assent to his removal."[143] Even this objection was quickly dismissed by the Goodman's Fields church since, according to them, the Bourton church was not considering the general interest and, by their refusal, constraining Beddome's usefulness in the city.[144]

The London deacons continued by quoting Prov 16:33, "The lot is in the lap, but the disposal is of God," and then admitting that their sight was "as through a glass, darkly," a reference to 1 Cor 13:12.[145] By saying that their sight was dim, the deacons were admitting that their design for Beddome's removal may not play out exactly as they had planned. Since it was probable, though, that was sufficient for them.[146] To support their case that

---

140. Goodman's Fields Church to Bourton Church, February 3, 1751, in Brooks, *POTP*, 40–41.

141. Goodman's Fields Church to Bourton Church, November 11, 1750, in Brooks, *POTP*, 34.

142. Goodman's Fields Church to Bourton Church, February 3, 1751, in Brooks, *POTP*, 41. In 1796, Fuller noted that the greater part of the Baptist ministers in the Northamptonshire Association did not have an "academical education." Fuller, "Discipline," in *WAF*, 3:481. Nearly a half-century earlier, when the Goodman's Fields church was looking for a learned minister, an even smaller percentage of ministers would have been educated.

143. Bourton Church to Goodman's Fields Church, December 16, 1750, in Brooks, *POTP*, 38.

144. Goodman's Fields Church to Bourton Church, February 3, 1751, in Brooks, *POTP*, 41.

145. Goodman's Fields Church to Bourton Church, February 3, 1751, in Brooks, *POTP*, 41.

146. Goodman's Fields Church to Bourton Church, February 3, 1751, in Brooks, *POTP*, 41.

Beddome would be useful in London, they referred to the evidence that the Bourton deacons had brought forth to demonstrate Beddome's usefulness in Bourton—"the restoration of decayed religion," the increase in membership at Bourton, and the calling of men to the ministry under Beddome's leadership.[147]

The Little Prescott Street deacons acknowledged that Beddome's call to Bourton and recovery from a life-threatening illness were answers to the prayers of the Bourton church. Yet, such a man with his gifting and graces was "qualified for extensive service," said the London deacons, and thus "was not one of those mercies that you can keep or we can take."[148] In a corrective manner, the London church said that if Beddome, after prayer and deliberation and with an unbiased approach to the situation, discerned that he should remove to London, then he would accept the call and the Bourton church's reluctance could not stop him.[149] Perhaps there was speculation on the part of the Goodman's Fields church that the Bourton church was seeking to retain Beddome even though he had an inclination to relocate to London. Either way, it should be observed that this was the exact opposite of what Beddome claimed he would do, namely, to entrust his decision to the will of the church.[150]

The letter concluded with some general pleasantries. The London deacons acknowledged their assertiveness in the letter. They were in regular prayer for the prosperity of the Bourton church, the Goodman's Fields church, and all the churches. There was a request that the Bourton church and its pastor pray for their friends in London. The deacons also expressed thanksgiving for the Bourton church's kind words and concern. They closed with a plea for a favorable response to their request.[151]

Usefulness and London

The main assertion of Goodman's Fields was that Beddome would be more useful in London than in Bourton. This thinking was built on the maxim

---

147. Bourton Church to Goodman's Fields Church, December 16, 1750, in Brooks, *POTP*, 38; Goodman's Fields Church to Bourton Church, February 3, 1751, in Brooks, *POTP*, 41.

148. Goodman's Fields Church to Bourton Church, February 3, 1751, in Brooks, *POTP*, 41.

149. Goodman's Fields Church to Bourton Church, February 3, 1751, in Brooks, *POTP*, 41.

150. Beddome to Goodman's Fields Church, n.d., in Brooks, *POTP*, 36.

151. Goodman's Fields Church to Bourton Church, February 3, 1751, in Brooks, *POTP*, 41–42.

quoted above and was a prevalent notion in eighteenth-century British society. Christopher W. Crocker indicated that the term "usefulness" came from the Enlightenment. Particularly influential was "the philosopher, jurist, and social reformer Jeremy Bentham (1748–1832) [who] is widely credited as being the father of the modern philosophy known as utilitarianism." Crocker continued, "Bentham argued that the greatest good is that which brings the greatest happiness [for society]."[152] John Stuart Mill (1806–1873) built on Bentham and argued, in the words of Crocker, "The morally right action is that which maximizes human welfare." This popular ethic asserted "that an action is right if it results in the greatest good for the greatest number of people."[153]

In his 2018 dissertation, Crocker demonstrated the "considerable usefulness" of John Ryland Jr.[154] The phrase came from a letter penned to Ryland by his mentor, John Newton, in which he wrote,

> But I correct myself, I had better not praise you at all, but rather praise the Lord on your behalf, who has given you, together with the knowledge of his truth, and a zeal for his service, a competent measure of abilities which when farther ripened by experience and study, and sanctified by his special blessing, will qualify you for considerable usefulness.[155]

Newton's sense of the term, according to Crocker, was not the utilitarian usefulness of Bentham but rather an understanding of the word rooted in the Puritan tradition, namely, a usefulness that was grounded in one's faithfulness to God. Crocker captured the idea in this way: "The greater the faithfulness the greater the usefulness and in turn the greater glory given to the one to which they sought to be faithful."[156] He added,

> Usefulness then, in the sense described above, may be defined as someone having the ability or qualities to advance the cause of the Gospel of Jesus Christ to the benefit of humanity and for the end of glorifying God. It is a dutiful outworking of faithfulness to God's grace. This is what was meant when Newton referred to Ryland as a man of *considerable usefulness*.[157]

152. For the sake of clarity, Crocker is summarizing Bentham's argument and not directly quoting him; the phrase in square brackets is original to Crocker.

153. Crocker, "John Ryland Jr.," 3–4.

154. Crocker, "John Ryland Jr.," 2–3.

155. Newton to Ryland, October 17, 1771, in Newton, *Wise Counsel*, 12.

156. Crocker, "John Ryland Jr.," 3–4.

157. Crocker, "John Ryland Jr.," 8 (emphasis original). This understanding of usefulness accords with that of Fuller who said—at the ordination of Robert Fawkner to the church in Thorn, Bedfordshire, on October 31, 1787—

With that operative understanding of usefulness, one could wonder how Newton would have advised Beddome on whether he should remove to the more influential London or remain in Bourton with a beloved people and in a field where he had enjoyed success. Though Newton did not counsel Beddome on the matter, he advised Ryland Jr. when the latter found himself in a comparable situation over forty years later.

Ryland had served at the College Lane church in Northampton since 1781, initially as a co-pastor with his father, then as the sole pastor from 1782 onward. Ten years later, in 1792, Ryland was invited to supply the pulpit at the Broadmead Baptist Church in Bristol. The reason the Broadmead church invited Ryland to fill the pulpit was because their pastor, Caleb Evans, had passed the previous year on August 9, 1791. Evans had served as the pastor of the Broadmead church and as the principal of the Baptist Academy. Thus, the church had sought a replacement. First, a Mr. Jenkins was considered, but he was passed over; then, John Fawcett (1740–1817) was invited, but he declined the offer.[158] Ryland was then asked by the Broadmead church to preach for one month. Newton, who was advising Ryland through correspondence, supposed that Ryland would soon be invited as Evans's successor.[159] It was in that context Newton wrote,

> I think it may be laid down as a rule, which both Scripture and experience will confirm, that *eminent spirituality in a minister is usually attended with eminent usefulness*. I do not mean to say our usefulness depends upon our spirituality, as an effect depends upon its cause; nor yet that it is always in proportion to it. God is a Sovereign; and frequently sees proper to convince us of it, in variously bestowing his blessing on the means of grace. But yet he is not wanting in giving encouragement to what he approves, wherever it is found. Our want of usefulness is often ascribed to our want of spirituality, much oftener than to our want of talents. God has frequently been known to succeed men of inferior abilities, when they have been eminent for holiness, while he has blasted others of much superior talents, when that quality has been wanting. Hundreds of ministers, who, on account of their gifts, have promised to be shining characters, have proved the reverse; and all owing to such things as pride, unwatchfulness, carnality, and levity. (Fuller, "Qualifications and Encouragement," in *WAF*, 1:143 [emphasis original])

For Fuller, usefulness was integrally tied to a minister's godliness or spirituality, and God was the one who granted usefulness. Thus, a pastor's usefulness was dependent more upon his spirituality and whether God willed him to be fruitful than the station in which he ministered.

158. For further information and sources on this episode in Fawcett's life, see n251.

159. For the details in this paragraph and further information, see Crocker, "John Ryland Jr.," 142–52; Culross, *Three Rylands*, 82–83; Gordon, "Call," 214–27; Gordon, "John Ryland, Jr. (1753–1825)," 2:80–82, 84–85; see editor's notes by Grant Gordon, in Newton, *Wise Counsel*, 259–60. There was a long-standing letter correspondence between Ryland and John Newton (1725–1807), with the letters from Newton having been preserved. For the letters from Newton to Ryland during this period, as well as background information, see Newton, *Wise Counsel*, 259–302.

I am always afraid of the transplanting of ministers from places where they are useful and acceptable. It seems like the transplanting of a full grown tree, which perhaps may strike its root into new soil, and thrive, but it is often otherwise. The inconveniencies of a present situation are known and felt, and may be escaped by a removal, but others will be found elsewhere, which will likewise be felt when they are known. Considering that our Lord's kingdom is not of this world [John 18:36], I have thought it a little strange, that when his ministers think He calls them to leave one charge for another, it should almost universally be from less to more; to a better income, a larger town or a more genteel congregation. We seldom have an instance of a retrograde [editor: that is, a move backwards or downwards] call. Ministers frequently remove from the country to London, but for one to leave London, for a charge in the country is rare indeed. I make no apology for this hint; you will probably hear enough on the other side.[160]

Ryland eventually removed to Bristol and thus differed in his actions from Beddome. This notwithstanding, Newton's counsel represented a view of usefulness different than the utilitarian usefulness of Bentham. It seems that Goodman's Fields—though not entirely illegitimate in their claims for Beddome's removal to London—adopted and employed an understanding of usefulness that was more aligned with Bentham than Newton.

Another element that factored in this correspondence between Bourton-on-the-Water and London was the latter's prominence in eighteenth-century society. London's population had grown from 200,000 in 1600 to 575,000 toward the end of the century, to 675,000 in 1750, and to 900,000 in 1800. The population of Paris—which was the second largest city in Europe at the time—grew from 400,000 at the beginning of the seventeenth century to just less than 550,000 in 1801. Another metric that demonstrates London's supremacy is the proportion of England that lived in the capital. In 1650, Londoners comprised 7 percent of England's population, but by 1750, that figure had risen to 11 percent. By way of contrast, from 1650 to 1750, the percentage of France that resided in Paris remained at a steady 2.5 percent.[161] By 1680, London's population exceeded that of the sixty largest provincial towns in England; Norwich, the next largest city, had a population of only 30,000. In 1750, when the letter exchange between Bourton

---

160. Newton to Ryland, April 10, 1792, in Newton, *Wise Counsel*, 262.
161. For the statistics until here, I am indebted to Wrigley, "Simple Model," 44–45.

and London took place, Bristol had eclipsed Norwich as the second largest city in England, and its population was 50,000, compared to London's 675,000.[162]

The growth in London was particularly remarkable when one considers the increasing mortality rates after 1670 and into the early eighteenth century. The expansion was fueled not by births but by migration to the city. The sentiment of London at this time was well captured by a customs commissioner, Corbyn Morris, in 1751, who said, "London will not feel any want of recruits till there are no people in the country."[163] Among those who flocked to the city were young people seeking employment and wealth; by about 1700, eight thousand men and women were arriving in London each year.[164]

The commerce and politics of the nation were centered in the capital, and this increased London's supremacy.[165] Porter writes, "People were sucked into London. And those who remained in the country increasingly had their lives shaped by the demands of the metropolis."[166] He went on to quote Daniel Defoe, who said, "This whole kingdom are employed to furnish something, and I may add, the best of everything, to supply the city of London with provisions."[167] The volume of these provisions was enormous. "Georgian London," said Porter, consumed "each year 2,975,000 bushels of flour, 100,000 oxen, 700,000 sheep and lambs, 238,000 pigs, 115,000 bushels of oysters, 14,000,000 mackerel, 160,000 pounds of butter and 21,000 pounds of cheese."[168]

Additionally, London was "the nation's only dynamo of fashion, [and so] attracted provincials to come and spend on clothes, and finery, pictures, *objets d'art*, books and the theatre."[169] Landowners and provincials could enjoy such pleasures and utilize the professional services available in the metropolis, such as "doctors, architects, face-painters, barristers, attorneys and scriveners, bankers, [and] brokers."[170] By this time, London played a larger role in Britain's legal proceedings, and it had become the financial

---

162. For these statistics, I am indebted to Research Centre, "Demography"; Porter, *London*, 131.
163. Quoted in Porter, *London*, 132.
164. Porter, *London*, 132–33.
165. Porter, *London*, 131–32.
166. Porter, *London*, 133.
167. Quoted in Porter, *London*, 133.
168. Porter, *London*, 134.
169. Porter, *London*, 134.
170. Porter, *London*, 134.

capital of the nation. Those in the ruling classes were drawn to the city more frequently, so their accommodations and services were improved. Communication and travel were also bettered, increasing the nation's connection to the capital. Porter said, "All such developments enhanced London's dominance."[171]

However, there were mixed perspectives on the dominance of the capital. Defoe said there are some "who pretend the growing greatness of [London] is too much for the whole country; alleging ... that the city draws away the nourishment from the country; like a dropsy, which swells the body, but draws the nourishment away from the extreme parts."[172] Though Defoe's words captured the thinking of some in the nation who objected to the ascendance of the great metropolis, he held the opposite view. According to Defoe, those who objected to the dominance of the capital were "greatly mistaken." In support of London's supremacy, he continued,

> As every part of the kingdom sends up hither the best of their produce, so they carry back a return of wealth; the money flows from the city into the remotest parts, and furnishes them again to increase that produce, to improve the lands, pay rent to their landlords, taxes to their governors, and supply their families with necessaries; and this is trade.[173]

According to Defoe, everything in England necessarily revolved around London. Porter remarked that "London's position peaked around 1750."[174]

It was exactly at this time, at the height of London's preeminence in English society, that the exchange between the Goodman's Fields and Bourton took place. Therefore, it seems a safe conclusion that the notion of London's supremacy had influenced the thinking of the Goodman's Fields deacons in their request for Beddome's removal. This helps to explain why the Little Prescott deacons called pastoring in London a "more important service,"[175] faulted the Bourton church for not being concerned for the Baptist cause generally in retaining Beddome,[176] tied the general interest

---

171. Porter, *London*, 136. For the information in this paragraph, I am indebted to Porter, *London*, 134–36.

172. Porter, *London*, 136, quoting Daniel Defoe, *Complete English Tradesmen*, London, 1726.

173. Porter, *London*, 136, quoting Daniel Defoe, *Complete English Tradesmen*, London, 1726.

174. Porter, *London*, 136.

175. Goodman's Fields Church to Bourton Church, November 11, 1750, in Brooks, *POTP*, 34.

176. Goodman's Fields Church to Bourton Church, February 3, 1751, in Brooks, *POTP*, 40.

of Baptist churches integrally with the state of the churches in London,[177] and asserted that there was hardly a place for learned ministers in country churches.[178]

EXCHANGE 4: BOURTON'S SECOND RESPONSE TO GOODMAN'S FIELDS

The Little Prescott Street church considered themselves to be in dire need due to the recent death of their pastor. If Bourton did not grant their request, the church could disperse and, in a worst-case scenario, dissolve. Beddome—who was the only suitable replacement for Wilson according to Goodman's Fields—needed to relocate to London. This was in the best interest, not only for the church at Little Prescott Street but for the general interest of the Baptist cause in England. Since "the service of all is to be preferred to that of the part,"[179] any reason Bourton cited as grounds to retain Beddome—such as their love for their pastor and their understanding that he had been given as a gift to the Bourton church—was easily dismissed by London. Additionally, the deacons at Goodman's Fields pointed out that Bourton had a suitable replacement for Beddome. With such strong solicitation, it would have been no surprise if the Bourton church gave up their beloved pastor "to more important services," to borrow the words of the Goodman's Fields deacons from an earlier letter.[180] This, however, was not how the situation unfolded. In this section, we will analyze Bourton's second response to Goodman's Fields.

There are two letters, one from the church and one from the pastor. Brooks noted that the letter from the church was written by the same men as before—Reynolds Sr., Reynolds Jr., and Boswell. It was then "read, approved, and signed" at a church meeting on February 24, 1751.[181] Brooks listed the following men as the signatories: the drafters of the letter, Joseph Strange (who also signed the previous letter), John Wood, Jeremiah Cresser,

---

177. Goodman's Fields Church to Bourton Church, February 3, 1751, in Brooks, *POTP*, 40.

178. Goodman's Fields Church to Bourton Church, February 3, 1751, in Brooks, *POTP*, 41.

179. Goodman's Fields Church to Bourton Church, February 3, 1751, in Brooks, *POTP*, 39.

180. Goodman's Fields Church to Bourton Church, November 11, 1750, in Brooks, *POTP*, 34.

181. Brooks, *POTP*, 42.

Henry Collett, and others.[182] At the same church meeting, which took place on a Sunday, Beddome read his letter to the congregation.[183]

Letter 6: Bourton to Goodman's Fields

The Bourton church acknowledged their receipt of the letter from Goodman's Fields, dated February 3. In that letter, the London church had made a second appeal for Bourton to release their pastor to the city and sought to strengthen their case with further reasons and arguments. Such solicitation was not warmly received by Bourton. Their sympathies were with their brethren at Little Prescott Street, but they seemed bothered at London's forwardness in the matter. Bourton wrote, "We are sorry you should desire, much more endeavour, to deprive another church of its fixed pastor, in order to repair the distressing loss of your worthy minister deceased."[184] The distress of the Goodman's Fields church at not being settled from a lack of a pastor should not have caused them to earnestly seek the removal of a pastor from another church, for that would leave the latter in the same distress. The Bourton deacons asked a hypothetical question to make their point. Suppose a church that was larger than Little Prescott Street had lost its pastor through death. If this happened while Wilson was alive and that larger church came and sought Wilson's removal, how kindly would the Goodman's Fields church have looked upon such a request?[185]

Bourton then responded to the major premise underlying Goodman's Fields argument in their letter. The Bourton deacons quoted their counterparts in London: "It is a maxim in the religious, as well as civic life, that the service of all is to be preferred before that of a part."[186] Goodman's Fields had applied this maxim to the situation and contended that Beddome would have been "more extensively useful in London than in the country."[187] Bourton's response here was significant since usefulness was an argument that Goodman's Fields had employed from the beginning.

---

182. Bourton Church to Goodman's Fields Church, February 24, 1751, in Brooks, *POTP*, 44.

183. Brooks, *POTP*, 42.

184. Bourton Church to Goodman's Fields Church, February 24, 1751, in Brooks, *POTP*, 42.

185. Bourton Church to Goodman's Fields Church, February 24, 1751, in Brooks, *POTP*, 42.

186. Bourton Church to Goodman's Fields Church, February 24, 1751, in Brooks, *POTP*, 42.

187. Bourton Church to Goodman's Fields Church, February 24, 1751, in Brooks, *POTP*, 42.

In the minds of the Goodman's Field church, London was to be prioritized over any country church because of the influence and impact that the churches in the city could have. Furthermore, the impact of those churches was proportionate to the quality of its pastors. Therefore, the best pastors should be in the cities.[188] In the previous letter, Goodman's Fields argued for the propriety of eminent ministers relocating from the country to the city. In this letter, Bourton articulated the alternate perspective: there was a reasonableness for an eminent minister such as Beddome to remain in an obscure station such as Bourton-on-the-Water. In fact, in some places in the letter, the Bourton deacons argued that eminent ministers are more needed in the country than in the city, the very opposite of London's position.

By asking a series of rhetorical questions, the Bourton church made the point that the source of a minister's gifting, fruit, and usefulness was God. Drawing on the imagery in the letter of Revelation, the deacons referred to pastors as stars in Jesus's right hand, and thus it was from him that ministers received their brightness and splendor (Rev 1:16, 20; 2:1; 3:1). Continuing the metaphor, if Jesus had placed stars to shine in darker parts of the world, their light was more necessary in those places than in other regions where he had set up a constellation of ministers.[189] Thus, the Bourton deacons began with scriptural and theological arguments.

Bourton then appealed to experience and observation. In their letter, the Goodman's Fields church admitted that the success of their plan for Beddome's removal to the city and accompanying usefulness was only probable and not certain, yet this was sufficient grounds to appeal for Beddome's removal. Bourton questioned how Goodman's Fields knew that probability was on their side. The Bourton deacons observed that, in many cases, when a minister had been removed from a station where God had placed him, it was not accompanied by great success, though they admitted there were situations where this had been the case. The Goodman's Fields church had left out this detail, though they hinted at it in their earlier letter.[190]

Beddome had enjoyed success in Bourton as a pastor; this success led to Goodman's Fields's thinking that it was probable the Bourton pastor would have a similarly successful ministry in London. A look at the parallel situations in which ministers had been removed to another station did not consistently show this, however. Also, if ministers had been appointed to a

---

188. Goodman's Fields Church to Bourton Church, February 3, 1751, in Brooks, *POTP*, 40.

189. Bourton Church to Goodman's Fields Church, February 24, 1751, in Brooks, *POTP*, 43.

190. Bourton Church to Goodman's Fields Church, February 24, 1751, in Brooks, *POTP*, 43.

place by God and then were made to leave that station, it could not be assumed that they would have continued to be useful. From the vantage point of Bourton, "Usefulness consists not barely in preaching to a very great auditory, but in honouring religion by serving God and our generation in that post in which he sets us."[191]

This was a different perspective to that of the Goodman's Fields church. To the Londoners, removal to the city was the only plausible outcome since there was more opportunity for influence and impact upon not just a single church but other churches, particularly of the Baptist cause. There was not a category in the Londoners' minds in which a faithful, and particularly learned, minister could remain in an obscure village in the Cotswolds, whereas the Bourton deacons operated on the principle that God could call men to minister in less prominent places. Therefore, it was not a foregone conclusion, based on Beddome's education, gifting, and success, that he should remove to London. To the contrary, if he was called to Bourton—and more factors than simply opportunities for impact and influence needed to be considered to discern this—then in Bourton he should remain.

That the Bourton church was open to God's leading over the matter was made clear in the next section of the letter. They were open to the leadings of Providence but, in this case, did not see that God was leading them to give up their pastor in compliance with London's request. Beddome was God's gracious gift in answer to their prayers and a minister who had been exceedingly useful in their midst. It was their hope that God would cause such usefulness to continue.[192]

The Bourton deacons then proceeded to address the matter of how the general interest was so strongly connected with the London churches. It was true, Bourton admitted, that the London churches consistently helped country churches. However, if this was the rationale supporting why city churches could always draw ministers from the country churches, the London churches would have been simultaneously helping and harming the churches in the rural areas. Such action on the part of the city churches would lead to friction and division between them and the country churches.[193] This would be the inevitable result since the country churches would have been regularly losing their ministers "whom God [had] fixed over

---

191. Bourton Church to Goodman's Fields Church, February 24, 1751, in Brooks, *POTP*, 43.

192. Bourton Church to Goodman's Fields Church, February 24, 1751, in Brooks, *POTP*, 43.

193. Bourton Church to Goodman's Fields Church, February 24, 1751, in Brooks, *POTP*, 43–44.

them, and whom they dearly [loved]."[194] There was also the danger of such removals resulting in dispersion or the country churches becoming dependent on the city churches even though, at that time, they had been independent.[195]

In their previous letter, the Goodman's Fields church had inquired of the Bourton church as to why they had fears for dispersion or dissolution if Beddome were to be removed, particularly because they had a suitable replacement in Reynolds.[196] The Bourton church's response turned the question around, asking the source of the London church's fears if Beddome were not to come. Bourton contended that the London deacons could not point to a lack of ministers, as they had done in their letters,[197] since there were many adequate candidates. Also, Bourton had been informed by credible sources that dispersion in London churches was more due "to a bad settlement," that is, the wrong pastor having been appointed, than the lack of a pastor.[198]

In concluding the letter, the Bourton church resolutely refused London's request for Beddome's removal. They pointed out that, in their view, such a refusal was not inconsistent with a concern for the general interest of religion or the welfare of the Little Prescott Street church. The deacons requested the continued prayers of the London church, and they expressed their desire to pray for the general cause of Christ and a pastor to be placed over the Little Prescott Street Baptist Church once again.[199]

Much had taken place since November 22, 1750, when Beddome wrote his first letter to the church at Goodman's Fields. There had, of course, been the initial response from the Bourton church to London, as well as their second response, which was just analyzed. There was also the second appeal, sent by the deacons at Little Prescott Street, which was an even stronger petition than the first. Two months had elapsed, and while Beddome had heard from London, London had not heard from Beddome. Also, there was

194. Bourton Church to Goodman's Fields Church, February 24, 1751, in Brooks, *POTP*, 44.

195. Bourton Church to Goodman's Fields Church, February 24, 1751, in Brooks, *POTP*, 44.

196. Goodman's Fields Church to Bourton Church, February 3, 1751, in Brooks, *POTP*, 41.

197. Goodman's Fields Church to Bourton Church, November 11, 1750, in Brooks, *POTP*, 34; Goodman's Fields Church to Bourton Church, February 3, 1751, in Brooks, *POTP*, 40.

198. Bourton Church to Goodman's Fields Church, February 24, 1751, in Brooks, *POTP*, 44.

199. Bourton Church to Goodman's Fields Church, February 24, 1751, in Brooks, *POTP*, 44.

some indication that the London church suspected the Bourton church of unduly retaining Beddome when he had the inclination to remove to the city.[200] We now turn to the final letter of this correspondence.

Letter 7: Beddome to Goodman's Fields

Beddome's letter accompanied the Bourton church's response to the Goodman's Fields church.[201] He reassured the church at Goodman's Fields that he had not influenced the church's decision or taken any part in drafting their letter. On the contrary, Beddome spoke on behalf of the London church, putting forth their arguments in ways he thought would bear the most weight.[202] However, the church had refused London's request for a second time after much deliberation and prayer, and thus, Beddome could do no other than submit to the will of the church. He provided several reasons for his decision. First, Beddome thought that if a pastor was settled and had been useful among a people, it was not lawful to leave them "without their consent."[203] The only exception was if there was a deficiency on the part of the church, such as a lack of love for the pastor, stinginess in giving, divisions, and opposition.[204]

Beddome was outlining the basic duties of a church toward one another and their pastor. These duties were captured in the sermons to the church at ordination services of English Particular Baptist pastors in the eighteenth century.[205] Beddome had just written that he would not remove to London. Thus, when he claimed that a church's failure in these duties legitimized a pastor's removal, the Bourton pastor was indirectly stating that his people had been adequately fulfilling their duties toward him and one another. This whole episode, in fact, had led the church toward deeper unity and paying off a large, long-standing debt.[206]

---

200. This was intimated in Goodman's Fields Church to Bourton Church, February 3, 1751, in Brooks, *POTP*, 41.

201. Beddome to Goodman's Fields Church, February 24, 1751, in Brooks, *POTP*, 45–47.

202. Beddome to Goodman's Fields Church, February 24, 1751, in Brooks, *POTP*, 45.

203. Beddome to Goodman's Fields Church, February 24, 1751, in Brooks, *POTP*, 45.

204. Beddome to Goodman's Fields Church, February 24, 1751, in Brooks, *POTP*, 45.

205. On the duties of a church according to the ordination sermons of the English Particular Baptists in the long eighteenth century, see chapter 2 of this book.

206. Beddome to Goodman's Fields Church, February 24, 1751, in Brooks, *POTP*, 47.

Second, Beddome's decision to remain in Bourton was buttressed by the witness of church history. He wrote, "And herein I have the greatest writers on church government on my side."[207] First, while some pastors had left their churches in the past in an unwarranted manner, virtually none had sought to defend such actions. Then, Beddome leaned on the Congregationalist minister John Owen (1616–1683).[208] The seventeenth-century English divine taught that the removal of a pastor was only lawful if all the churches involved gave their consent, and there was the affirming counsel of other churches or their elders "with whom they [walked] in communion."[209] During the early centuries of the church, it became common practice for bishops to plot their own removal from a lesser to a greater ecclesial office because some churches "increased in numbers, reputation, privileges and wealth above others."[210] Continuing his dependence on Owen, Beddome said this practice was forbidden by the canons of the council of Nicaea, which stated that a man may become a bishop or presbyter in only one place, namely, the church in which he was initially ordained.[211] If a man chose to remove himself to another office, he should be sent home and remain there or cease to be a church officer.[212]

In *The True Nature of the Gospel Church and Its Government*, Owen cited the ancient church's prohibition of the removal of a pastor. In response to the question "May a pastor remove from one congregation unto another?" he said, "This is a thing also which the ancient church made great provision against."[213] After summarizing the practice of the ancient church and the rel-

---

207. Beddome to Goodman's Fields Church, February 24, 1751, in Brooks, *POTP*, 45.

208. Owen, *True Nature*. Beddome was specifically drawing from a section answering the question "May a pastor remove from one congregation to another?" Owen, *True Nature*, 113.

209. Beddome to Goodman's Fields Church, February 24, 1751, in Brooks, *POTP*, 45.

210. Beddome to Goodman's Fields Church, February 24, 1751, in Brooks, *POTP*, 45.

211. Beddome to Goodman's Fields Church, February 24, 1751, in Brooks, *POTP*, 45. This practice was denounced at the Council of Nicaea in 325 and the Council of Chalcedon in 451. These councils—which are often associated with the respective creedal statements on Trinitarian theology and Christology—issued canons, or laws, that governed ecclesial practice. Owen referred to Canons 15 and 16 from Nicaea and Canons 5 and 20 from Chalcedon. Owen, *True Nature*, 113; also, see Owen, *True Nature*, 112. For the canons from Nicaea, see Percival, "Excursus," in *NPNF2* 14:32, 35. For the canons from Chalcedon, see Percival, "XXX Canons," in *NPNF2* 14:271, 282.

212. Beddome to Goodman's Fields Church, February 24, 1751, in Brooks, *POTP*, 45.

213. Owen, *True Nature*, 113.

evant canons, the Puritan pastor went on, "Yet it cannot be denied, but that there may be just causes of the removal of a pastor from one congregation unto another."[214] Though the goal of every local church was to promote the welfare of the universal church, in special cases, removal would be particularly useful to the cause of the church at large and so should be permitted.[215] The Puritan pastor wrote that in such situations, a multiplicity of factors needed to be considered, and the decision was not merely contingent upon prospective usefulness.[216] The potential for extensive usefulness occasioned the consideration of a pastor's removal from one station to another, but it was not the grounds for an immediate and certain removal. To avoid offense in such removals, Owen laid out two requirements: first, the consent of the churches involved, and second, the affirming counsel of other churches and their elders of the same denomination. Owen indicated there were good examples of this kind of removal in the early church. He noted the removal of Gregory of Nazianzus (ca. 329/330–391) from Sasima to Constantinople, though, admittedly, it had failed.[217] Thus, in responding to a contemporary ministerial crisis, Beddome leaned on the wisdom of Owen from the seventeenth century, who, in turn, was leaning on the rulings of Nicaea and Chalcedon from the fourth and fifth centuries.

A third reason that Beddome chose to acquiesce to the church's decision to refuse London's request was the counsel he had received from his friends. Over the past two months, he had evidently consulted with others regarding the situation. This took place through personal conversations with those who lived closer to him and by letter with others who lived farther away. He spoke with fellow pastors and others, and among his counselors were, in Beddome's words, "those persons of great judgment and distinguished piety."[218] With a near unanimous voice, they advised Beddome to stay with his people in Bourton unless they gave consent to his removal.[219]

The fourth reason why Beddome chose to remain in Bourton was because it was rare for great success to result from the removal of a pastor. On this point, Beddome brought up the example of Matthew Henry

214. Owen, *True Nature*, 113–14.
215. Owen, *True Nature*, 114.
216. Owen, *True Nature*, 114.
217. Owen, *True Nature*, 114. On Nazianzen, see Beeley, *Gregory of Nazianzus*; Daley, *Gregory of Nazianzus*; McGuckin, *St. Gregory of Nazianzus*; Norris, "Introduction," 1–82.
218. Beddome to Goodman's Fields Church, February 24, 1751, in Brooks, *POTP*, 45.
219. Beddome to Goodman's Fields Church, February 24, 1751, in Brooks, *POTP*, 45.

(1662–1714), who had left Chester for Hackney in London. Rather than resulting in greater usefulness, Henry was not overly successful at Hackney, though he labored diligently to the end of his life. As for Chester, Beddome had heard reports that the communicants under Henry were greater than the hearers under his successor, a Mr. Gardiner.[220]

Beddome discussed the issue of usefulness by pointing out a hole in the argument of the London church. If their premise was true—that greater usefulness was a sufficient reason to warrant the removal of a pastor—then it would be impossible for smaller and less significant churches to retain their pastors. This would also have justified the removal of a pastor in every situation since greater usefulness was nearly always cited as a cause for removal.[221] For Beddome, usefulness in another station was one factor among many to be considered at the prospect of removal and not the deciding element in every case.

As mentioned earlier, Gill preached the funeral sermon for Wilson.[222] Beddome had access to that sermon, and he referred to it in his letter, saying Gill "entirely left out the prospect of greater usefulness, among the motives which he looks upon as sufficient to authorize the removal of a pastor from one place to another."[223] In the respective section, Gill talked about the affliction that befalls a church when it could no longer see their pastor's face. He was contrasting situations in which a pastor might be temporarily separated from a people with the permanent separation that occurred through death. Without question, the latter was more grievous, because the people would never see their pastor again in this life. The examples of temporary separation included a pastor's absence from his church for a season, persecution and imprisonment, being laid low by sickness, or removal "from one church to another."[224]

Beddome referred to the section on the pastor's removal from one place to another in his letter. Earlier, Beddome articulated that a pastor should not leave his people without their consent except in situations where there was a lack on the church's end.[225] Gill expounded on the same concept

---

220. Beddome to Goodman's Fields Church, February 24, 1751, in Brooks, *POTP*, 45–46. For Henry's move from Chester to Hackney, see Harman, "Matthew Henry's Move," 155–73.

221. Beddome to Goodman's Fields Church, February 24, 1751, in Brooks, *POTP*, 46.

222. Gill, "Reverend Mr Samuel Wilson," in *S&T*, 1:477–98.

223. Beddome to Goodman's Fields Church, February 24, 1751, in Brooks, *POTP*, 46.

224. Gill, "Reverend Mr Samuel Wilson," in *S&T*, 1:483–85.

225. Beddome to Goodman's Fields Church, February 24, 1751, in Brooks, *POTP*, 45.

in his funeral sermon and provided a more expansive list of what could have constituted a lack on the part of the church. According to Gill, a pastor may lawfully remove from one church to another if heresies in the church could not be rooted out, immorality was prevalent, discipline was neglected, people refused to submit to Christ's laws, the church could not and would not adequately provide for the pastor and thereby invited the reproach of the world, or "disaffection between him and the people rises so high, on one account or another, that peace and fellowship cannot be maintained, nor the ends of the ministration of the word, and administration of ordinances be answered."[226] There was, as Beddome pointed out, no mention of the prospect of greater usefulness being grounds for the removal of a pastor.[227]

The way Gill phrased his last reason for the lawful removal of a pastor was instructive. If there was a lack of love between a pastor and his people, it undermined the effectiveness of the ministry of the Word and ordinances. To state it positively, when there was a strong bond of love between a pastor and his people, it caused the preaching and the administration of the ordinances to be more effective. One could deduce from Gill's words that a strong bond of love between a pastor and the people was an argument for him to remain in his current station. That accords with what Bourton and Beddome argued in their letters.

Goodman's Fields had suggested that Reynolds could have been a suitable replacement for Beddome. Beddome agreed with the Goodman's Fields church regarding the quality of said church member and his suitability for ministry. If Beddome were to leave Bourton, Reynolds would have been the best person to replace him as minister. However, Reynolds had already received calls from two churches and would have preferred to serve in one of those places over Bourton.[228]

226. Gill, "Reverend Mr Samuel Wilson," in S&T, 1:484.

227. Beddome to Goodman's Fields Church, February 24, 1751, in Brooks, POTP, 46.

228. Around age eighteen, Reynolds attended the Bristol Baptist Academy under Bernard Foskett for nearly two years. Then, he was permitted to exercise his gift until the church saw fit to call him more fully to the ministry in 1751. In his obituary, Rippon remarked that he "preached occasionally at 20, chiefly at Bromsgrove, Bratton, Cirencester, and Cheltenham, and more constantly at Oxford about three years and a half." Rippon, "Rev. John Reynolds," 41. Holmes observed, "It appears that for the next fourteen years he occasionally deputized for Mr. Beddome and there are several entries recording his services to the church." Holmes, "Early Years (1655–1740)," 46. On September 14, 1766, Reynolds was called to the pastorate of the Cripplegate church, London. For the information in this paragraph and the life of Reynolds, see Brooks, POTP, 31; Holmes, "Early Years (1655–1740)," 45–47; Rippon, "Rev. John Reynolds," 41–44; Rippon, "Rev. Benjamin Beddome," 323*. Reynolds was baptized at age fourteen on June 10, 1743, by Beddome. There is no information regarding the two churches that Reynolds had received calls from that Beddome mentioned.

If Beddome left, the church would have likely been destitute for a long time.[229]

At this point, Beddome's decision was made: he needed to remain in Bourton. Had he complied with a call to the city, he supposed it would have been miserable both for the London church and himself since he would have been acting contrary to his conscience. The Bourton pastor expressed his hope that he had conducted himself uprightly and with sincerity throughout the situation. He also made it clear that had his church consented to his removal, he would have accepted London's call with no reluctance, though such a removal would have required sacrifice on his part since he deeply loved his people. Since the membership refused his removal, though, Beddome concluded, "The will of the Lord be done [Acts 21:14]."[230] The beloved pastor of the Baptist church at Bourton was resolved that he would not violently tear himself away from his people. Beddome said that he would rather serve God in a lower and less significant station where God had placed him (that is, Bourton) than "intrude" in a higher and more significant station where God had not directed him (that is, London).[231]

The way the Bourton church sought to discern God's guidance over the matter was different from the approach of Goodman's Fields. Beddome began by asking, "To what station has God called me?" Having determined that (through several factors, not excluding the question of usefulness), the Bourton pastor resolved to be faithful in that place. Goodman's Fields, however, began by asking, "Where will this man be most useful?" with useful being defined as ministering in the most prominent church and having the largest influence on the greatest number of people from that station. Thus, usefulness, understood in this way, was the supreme consideration above all others. Beddome should have removed to London, according to Goodman's Fields, because he would have been most useful there as a pastor. For Goodman's Fields, the other factors that Bourton cited to argue for the retention of their pastor—the love of the church for their pastor, the reading of Providence that Beddome was God's gift to the Bourton church, the necessity of country churches to have continuing pastors, the danger that Beddome's removal would pose to the country church, and the unanimous decision of the Bourton church to refuse London's request—were all subordinate to the

---

229. Beddome to Goodman's Fields Church, February 24, 1751, in Brooks, *POTP*, 46.

230. Beddome to Goodman's Fields Church, February 24, 1751, in Brooks, *POTP*, 46.

231. Beddome to Goodman's Fields Church, February 24, 1751, in Brooks, *POTP*, 46–47.

sole consideration of usefulness. To Beddome, this seemed too simplistic an approach.

The pastor of the Bourton church mentioned that though the invitation had come to nothing as far as the London church was concerned, it had proved beneficial for Bourton. Beddome reported that his people were more united and motivated to pay off a large and long-standing debt of nearly one hundred pounds.[232] These events were recorded in *Pictures of the Past*. Brooks commended Beddome for his conduct throughout the ordeal and captured the church's affectionate response toward him. With a renewed zeal, the Bourton church sought to make their pastor's situation more comfortable, and they, as an initial action, determined to rid their debt. The debt had been incurred through three building projects—the construction of the parsonage in 1741, the expansion of the chapel in 1748, and the strengthening of it in 1750. London's request for the removal of Pastor Beddome and the ensuing deliberations in the church stirred them to pay off these debts.[233]

The Bourton pastor then endeavored to comfort and strengthen his friends at Goodman's Fields. He began by reminding them of the words of Isaiah, "the evangelical prophet," who said, "He that believeth will not make haste [Isa 28:16]."[234] Their task was to wait upon God and continue in their prayers and, in due time, "the great Head of the church [Eph 1:22–23; Col 1:18]"[235] would provide for the Little Prescott Street church in ways far better than they could have designed themselves. Even if there was a short delay in securing a pastor, this was not as dangerous as they imagined it to be particularly since there were suitable men in London and people were generally interested in new things. Even if the worst should happen and the hearers at Little Prescott Street were to disperse and the membership of the church significantly decline, God was able to raise them up as he had done previously.[236] The reference here was to the renewal of the church that had taken place under Wilson's ministry. When he came to the church, it

---

232. Beddome to Goodman's Fields Church, February 24, 1751, in Brooks, *POTP*, 47.

233. Brooks, *POTP*, 47–48; Beddome to Goodman's Fields Church, February 24, 1751, in Brooks, *POTP*, 47.

234. Beddome to Goodman's Fields Church, February 24, 1751, in Brooks, *POTP*, 47.

235. Beddome to Goodman's Fields Church, February 24, 1751, in Brooks, *POTP*, 47.

236. Beddome to Goodman's Fields Church, February 24, 1751, in Brooks, *POTP*, 47.

was "in a low and declining state," according to Ivimey.[237] Over the next twenty-five or twenty-six years, the church revived under Wilson's ministry with many people being converted and edified.[238] In his funeral sermon for Wilson, Gill reflected, "The low estate in which you were, when he came to this place, and the numbers of which you now consist, and the flourishing condition in which you now are, abundantly show the success of his ministration among you."[239] In their heartache at the loss of their pastor and the anxiety with which they sought his replacement, the Goodman's Fields church had forgotten their own history. If God raised them up under Wilson, he was able to do it again through another.[240] Either way, he exhorted his friends in London to trust the Lord by quoting Ps 37:5, "Commit, then, your way unto the Lord; trust also in him, and he will bring it to pass."[241]

He expressed his hope that the London church would receive his letter with their "usual candour" and requested that they remember him in their prayers, even as he would remember them at the throne of grace. He signed the letter, "Your affectionate friend and brother in gospel bonds, B. Beddome."[242] In his own mind, Beddome belonged to God as his servant, and he was gifted and called by Christ to serve in whatever station his master placed him.

Brief Evaluation and Aftermath

Therein concludes the analysis of the correspondence between the Bourton-on-the-Water Baptist Church and the Little Prescott Street Baptist Church concerning the request for Beddome's removal to London. In the end, the Bourton pastor chose to remain with his people in compliance with their wishes, which he understood to be the divine will for his life. Those two months must have been quite trying—both for the pastor and the church—since the request from London was no small ask. If Beddome obliged, this would have been a significant move for him and Elizabeth, who had married just a year prior. It also would have torn Elizabeth away from her

---

237. Ivimey, *History*, 3:307.

238. Gill, "Reverend Mr Samuel Wilson," in *S&T*, 1:496.

239. Gill, "Reverend Mr Samuel Wilson," in *S&T*, 1:496.

240. Beddome to Goodman's Fields Church, February 24, 1751, in Brooks, *POTP*, 47.

241. Beddome to Goodman's Fields Church, February 24, 1751, in Brooks, *POTP*, 47.

242. Beddome to Goodman's Fields Church, February 24, 1751, in Brooks, *POTP*, 47.

father, Richard, and their whole family, and Beddome would have had to leave Bourton, the place where he wished to dwell and serve his God.[243] Perhaps, there was also the additional awkwardness of needing to explain to his father that he was willing to remove to London but not Bristol. Most of all, though, Beddome must have been consternated because it was a situation in which he needed to proceed carefully so that he could have a clear conscience.[244]

It would have been distressing for the church since this was now the third time that their pastor could have been taken from them: the first being the attempt by his father to have his son removed to Bristol, and the second being the six-week-long illness that nearly took the Bourton pastor's life. The Bourton church had prayed for a minister, and God had answered their prayers twice in this regard—in Beddome's arrival and in his recovery from sickness—and now there was the potential that they might lose him to a more prominent and popular church in the city. How relieved must have the Bourton membership been when their pastor read his letter of refusal to London's request at the church meeting on the Lord's Day, February 24, 1751.[245]

This whole correspondence, which was captured in the minute books of the Bourton church, greatly impressed Beddome's later successor, Thomas Brooks, who became the pastor of the church in August 1855. He commended Beddome in his church history with these words:

> Comparatively few ministers are ever called to pass through an ordeal as trying as the one disclosed in the above correspondence, and it may be safely affirmed, that none ever came out with more credit to themselves. By this circumstance, Mr. Beddome's uprightness, disinterestedness, and simplicity, are placed above suspicion. We are not surprised to hear that his people were provoked to love and good works. "Shame and confusion" would have belonged to them, had they failed to love him heartily.[246]

This perspective was shared by Holmes, who said, "Throughout the correspondence there are glimpses of the stature of Mr. Beddome's character and

---

243. Rippon, "Rev. Benjamin Beddome," 318.

244. Beddome to Goodman's Fields Church, February 24, 1751, in Brooks, *POTP*, 46.

245. Brooks wrote, "At the same time the pastor read his answer to the said letter, for which being also in the negative, the church expressed their thankfulness." Brooks, *POTP*, 42.

246. Brooks, *POTP*, 47.

by his replies it can be seen that he acted with the care, integrity and dignity that the office of 'Teaching Elder' demands."[247] Dix, who was writing in the twentieth century along with Holmes, concurred,

> It reveals a Pastor who loved his people, and a people who in turn held him in lasting and true affection. There was a bond of union between them, which was not to be easily broken. It was like a marriage in which all the wooing of a third party proves ineffectual. That Beddome was able to defer the decision into the hands of the church shows the depth of love and trust between them, something which is often sadly lacking in our day. But the story also shows us a man who was not concerned for himself. It was not merely that he refused to seek great things for himself, he also refused a way which might seemingly have brought him to great things, because he was not able to see the providential leading of the God whom he served. In what must have been one of the supreme crises of his life, he comes to us as a practical demonstration of what it means when we say, "Thy will be done [Matt 6:10; 26:42]."[248]

As to the discovery of the letters, Brooks said that he had come across them as he was perusing the Bourton church's minute books. He rightly deemed the letters to be of value and interest to the Baptist denomination and submitted them to the editor of *The Baptist Magazine*. The letters gave insight into how pastoral removals took place a century prior and "how two churches could contend for the prize of a pastor." Notably, it would also give the readers of the magazine a sense of the relationship between a pastor and his people.[249]

Brooks closed the chapter in the church history book by relating one further incident related to this period in Beddome's life. Given that both Beddome and the Bourton church issued such strong refusals to London's request, it is somewhat surprising that the Goodman's Fields church sent another request for Beddome's removal later that year. The details were recorded in the church minute books on December 15, 1751, which Brooks transcribed into the church history. Beddome had received a letter from members of the Goodman's Fields church requesting that he leave Bourton and relocate to London. The reason for their urgent request was because the church was divided over two potential candidates—Reynolds and Thomas— and the church would be distressed and even "broken in pieces" if Beddome

---

247. Holmes, "Early Years (1655–1740)," 53.
248. Dix, "Thy Will Be Done," n.p.
249. Brooks, "Ministerial Changes" (July 1859), 425.

did not come. There were also renewed solicitations from two individuals in the church, who employed the former arguments in the letters as well as their current situation, which, in their view, was urgent. Beddome requested that his people pray over the matter for two weeks, at which time he would call a church meeting and receive their answer. The Bourton pastor was intending, as before, to allow the church's response to guide his. Bourton refused London's request for a third time, stating that they could not envision the state of the church in London to be as bad as they had claimed, and if it was, they continued, "We could not consent to cast ourselves into the same or greater distress in order to help them."[250]

COMPARATIVE STUDIES: THE REMOVAL OF A PASTOR

The topic under consideration in this chapter has been a pastor's removal from one church to another. A more influential and affluent church in the nation's capital had requested for a church in the country to release their pastor to a ministry of greater usefulness in London. In the correspondence, in which seven letters were exchanged between Bourton and London, both parties ardently argued their case—London for Beddome's removal and Bourton for his remaining. In the end, the London church was left wanting and needed to look elsewhere for a replacement for Wilson, their late, popular, and learned pastor. As for Beddome, he remained in Bourton for the rest of his days until his death in 1795.

Among Beddome's contemporaries, there were other requests for the removal of a pastor. These requests were necessary since pastors needed to be replaced for various reasons, such as illness or death. Sometimes, a pastor chose to remain in his previous station, as Beddome had done. Two further examples were John Fawcett and Benjamin Francis, who decided not to relocate to a different church, though both were called to places of potentially greater usefulness.[251] In other scenarios, however, a pastor complied with

---

250. Brooks, *POTP*, 48–49.

251. Fawcett had pastored the Baptist church in Wainsgate since 1764. When John Gill passed on October 14, 1771, Fawcett was soon asked to be his successor. This would have been a sensible move for Fawcett since the Wainsgate church could not adequately support him financially—his salary was only twenty-five pounds a year, and his house was too small for a growing family. Fawcett made the decision to remove to the Carter Lane church in Southwark, but when the time came to move to London, he was overcome with a love for his people and chose to remain. For the details in this paragraph and further information, see Fawcett, *Rev. John Fawcett*, 171–75; Haykin, *Remembering John Fawcett*, 16, 23–25; Haykin, "John Fawcett (1740–1817)," 5:193–217.

Francis had served as the pastor of the Baptist church in Horsley, Gloucestershire, since 1758, and received several requests to remove to London. The most notable

the request for removal, such as in the case of Ryland Jr., who left the College Lane church in Northampton to pastor the Broadmead Baptist Church and become the principal of the Baptist Academy in Bristol.[252] There was not a universal response among English Particular Baptists to a request for a pastor's removal.

CONCLUSION

In one sense, this whole letter exchange between the Baptist churches of Bourton-on-the-Water and Goodman's Fields was undesirable for both sides. On the part of Goodman's Fields, their strong solicitations were for naught as their request for the Bourton pastor's services was denied. As for Bourton, the village church endured the potential loss of their pastor, who they considered to be an answer to their prayers—both when Beddome initially arrived a decade earlier and more recently when he recovered from a life-threatening illness. The aftermath of this whole episode, though, was sweet for the Bourton church and its pastor. Beddome's memorialist wrote concerning the exchange:

> Few circumstances can be more perplexing than those in which Mr. Beddome was thus placed, or more calculated to try and elucidate uprightness of motive and correctness of principle. The simplicity, disinterestedness, and firmness he displayed on this occasion, speak loudly for his moral and religious character. Thus his conduct was regarded by the members of the church, who became more attached to him than ever, and proved their affection by attempting to increase his comforts, and in removing the debt which had long lain upon the chapel.[253]

Thus, these letters provide an exemplar of the Bourton pastor's conduct.

That a man of Beddome's caliber—with respect to his piety, gifting, and learnedness—ministered for over five decades in the obscure village

---

invitation was from the Carter Lane church to succeed Gill subsequent to Fawcett's refusal recounted above. In their letter to Francis, the Carter Lane deacons indicated that it was Gill's desire that the Horsley pastor would be his successor, and he was willing to retire early if such desire was fulfilled. Despite the approbation of the London divine, Francis remained at Horsley because of his affection for the people. For the details in this paragraph and further information, see Flint, "Rev. Benjamin Francis," 42–43, 42*; Haykin, "Benjamin Francis (1734–1799)," 2:17–18; Nuttall, "Letters by Benjamin Francis," 7–8.

252. For further information on Ryland's removal from Northampton to Bristol, see above.

253. Anonymous, "Memoir," in Beddome, SP, xx–xxi.

of Bourton-on-the-Water was not lost on his early biographers. Given the insignificance of Bourton, it is understandable that Beddome's memorialist wrote, "It will readily be conceived, that the retirement of Bourton would furnish but few incidents for history."[254] Later in the memoir, however, the anonymous writer spoke of Beddome's "eminent usefulness"[255] in Bourton:

> The usefulness of such a man can only be known at the resurrection of the just. In his numerous visits and public labours at Abingdon, Bristol, London, and the circle of the Midland Association, an incalculable amount of good was done in promoting the unity, awakening the zeal, and directing the energies of the people of God, while many sinners were known to be converted to the faith. At Bourton he was highly successful. When he went there the church consisted only of about seventy members; in 1751 they had increased to one hundred and eighty; and in 1766, since his residence amongst them, one hundred and ninety-six persons had been added to the church. During that period, six were called to the work of the ministry.[256]

That memoir was written in 1835, forty years after Beddome's death. G. Hester also wrote a sketch in 1865 for *The Baptist Magazine*. Though writing seventy years after Beddome's death, Hester remembered the Bourton pastor's usefulness:

> In 1740, or at the age of twenty-three, he became the pastor of the Baptist church at Bourton on-the-Water, a village in Gloucestershire. The celebrated John [Collett] Ryland became a minister of this church soon after Mr. Beddome's retirement. Here he lived a retired, studious, pious, and useful life. Like some of his notable contemporaries he refused to change his sphere of labour. He was often invited to supply other churches much larger and more influential in position than his own, but he always declined to accede to the efforts put forth to draw him away from the people whom he loved. Among the churches which invited his services was the church in Goodman's Fields, then one of the largest and most important in London. He lived in the affection and esteem of his own people. They were near his heart; he dwelt in their hearts. They were married in the Lord, and refused to be separated.[257]

---

254. Anonymous, "Memoir," in Beddome, *SP*, xxi.

255. This phrase is borrowed from Fuller, "Qualifications and Encouragement," in *WAF*, 1:143.

256. Anonymous, "Memoir," in Beddome, *SP*, xxvi.

257. Hester, "Baptist Worthies," 443.

Hester's terse statement that in Bourton, Beddome "lived a retired, studious, pious, and useful life" rebutted any notion that a Christian minister could only be useful in the most prominent and influential places.

By way of conclusion, we turn to the words of Robert Hall Jr., who wrote a recommendatory preface to a large volume of Beddome's hymns, which Hall published in 1818. In the preface, Hall captured the peculiar yet beautiful picture of an educated and gifted minister who spent his life ministering in a rural village in the Cotswolds of England: "Though he spent the principal part of a long life in a village retirement, he was eminent for his colloquial powers, in which he displayed the urbanity of the gentleman, and the erudition of the scholar, combined with a more copious vein of attic salt than any person it has been my lot to know."[258] These early biographers spoke with one voice that there were lessons to be learned from this letter exchange between Bourton and Goodman's Fields.

The letters penned by the Bourton church and Beddome provided a visible pastoral theology, that is, *pastoralia* in action. Beddome's example provided future pastors with counsel if they found themselves in a circumstance akin to Beddome's, namely, needing to consider a pastoral move. More significantly, though, Beddome's decision to remain in Bourton demonstrated to posterity the beauty and legitimacy of a pastor remaining in a station to which God had called him, even if it was a less glamorous and influential place. In other words, bigger was not always better.

Further, the manner in which Beddome chose to remain in Bourton and not relocate to London stands in stark contrast to how pastors today would make such a decision. Put simply, most contemporary pastors would not consult their current church when considering a pastoral move, let alone submit to the will of his congregation on the matter. This, however, appears to have been standard practice in Beddome's day as richly demonstrated in the letter correspondence between Bourton and London. A retrieval of wisdom from these letters will be explored in the final chapter of this book.

In his own day, Beddome was well known as a gifted and effective minister, as indicated by the quotations given above. Having considered his letters, we turn to the sermons of the Cotswolds divine. As with the letters, where the focus was on the correspondence that demonstrated his pastoral theology, in the following chapter, attention will be given to those discourses that yield Beddome's view of pastoral ministry, namely, his ordination sermons.

---

258. Hall, "Recommendatory Preface," vi.

CHAPTER 4

Pastoral Ministry According to Benjamin Beddome's Ordination Sermons

ROBERT HALL JR. WAS a renowned preacher in the British Isles during the later eighteenth and early nineteenth centuries. In his dissertation on Hall, Cody Heath McNutt remarked, "He was one of the most celebrated figures among the Baptists of the Regency era, yet his fame extended far beyond Baptist circles."[1] According to McNutt, Hall was referred to as the Prince of Preachers. The title, of course, has since come to belong to Charles H. Spurgeon, but it was applied to Hall prior to Spurgeon's birth.[2] Hall's extemporaneous preaching was so effective that, on occasion, those in the congregation leaned forward in the pews to ensure they caught his every word.[3] In light of his abilities and fame as a preacher, it is significant that Hall commended Benjamin Beddome with these words, which have already been cited:

> Mr. Beddome was on many accounts an extraordinary person. . . . Favoured with the advantages of a learned education, he continued to the last to cultivate an acquaintance with the best writers of antiquity, to which he was much indebted for the chaste, terse, and nervous diction, which distinguished his compositions both in prose and verse. Though he spent the principal part of a long life in a village retirement, he was eminent for his colloquial powers, in which he displayed the urbanity of the gentleman, and the erudition of the scholar, combined with a more copious vein of attic salt than any person it has been my

---

1. McNutt, "Robert Hall, Jr.," 2.
2. McNutt, "Robert Hall, Jr.," 2.
3. Brackney, "Hall, Robert, Jr.," 285.

lot to know. As a preacher, he was universally admired for the piety and unction of his sentiments, the felicity of his arrangement, and the purity, force, and simplicity of his language; all which were recommended by a delivery perfectly natural and graceful.[4]

BEDDOME AND ORDINATION SERVICES

Hall wrote this in the preface to a volume of Beddome's hymns, published in 1818. It is to be expected that Hall would commend Beddome since the Bourton pastor was nearly fifty years his senior. In this case, though, we also have record of the reverse: Beddome's approbation of Hall. In July 1779, Thomas Skinner (1752–1795) was ordained to the pastorate of the Clipstone church in Northamptonshire.[5] Present on the occasion were Beddome, Hall Jr., and his father, Robert Hall Sr. (1764–1831). Beddome and Hall Sr. conducted the main parts of the day's proceedings; Hall Sr. gave the first address and Beddome was to give the evening lecture. However, Beddome insisted that Hall Jr. preach in his place, having been impressed with the appearance and conversation of the young man. Though he initially resisted, Hall Jr. complied and ably preached from 1 John 1:5. The event displayed to those in attendance the clear proofs of the younger Hall's call to the pastoral office. Though Beddome relinquished his opportunity to preach on this occasion, this account gives evidence that the Bourton pastor participated in ordination services.

Three years prior, on August 7, 1776, Beddome attended the ordination of John Sutcliff (1752–1814) to the pastorate of the Baptist church in Olney.[6] Beddome had been invited to participate in the service, but he declined. However, after some urging, he agreed to preach during the evening service.[7] John Newton (1725–1807)—an Anglican minister and composer

---

4. Hall, "Recommendatory Preface," v–vi. Hall himself was a learned minister like Beddome. Hall trained at the Bristol Baptist Academy, then studied at King's College, University of Aberdeen, graduating with an MA. Brackney remarks that Hall was "one of the best-educated Baptists of his era." Brackney, "Hall, Robert, Jr.," 284.

5. For the details in this paragraph, I am indebted to Gregory, "Rev. Robert Hall," 3:8; MacLeod, "Robert Hall"; Morris, *Rev. Robert Hall*, 38–39.

6. For the details in this paragraph, I am indebted to Haykin, "Benjamin Beddome (1717–1795)," 4:259; Haykin, *One Heart*, 118–20.

7. John Fawcett was present on the occasion and delivered the charge to the ordinand. His son, John Fawcett Jr., recorded how his father

> often mentioned, in the subsequent periods of his life, the high gratification he enjoyed, by becoming personally acquainted with many eminent ministers who were

of the hymn "Amazing Grace"—was present on the occasion. He wrote of Beddome that "he is an admirable preacher—simple, savoury, weighty. His text [Zech 11:12] he used chiefly as a motto."[8] For Newton to speak of Beddome's preaching in this way was significant since the Anglican pastor had heard many of the great preachers of the day, including George Whitefield (1764–1831).[9]

There was a further connection between Beddome and Sutcliff that gives insight into what the Bourton pastor valued in his colleagues. Just a year before Sutcliff's ordination to the Olney church, there was an attempt to make him Beddome's assistant in Bourton-on-the-Water.[10] The plan was devised by their mutual friend, Thomas Purdy (d. 1820), who lived a short distance away in Chipping North. However, Sutcliff ended up in Olney and not in Bourton, as noted above.[11] The reason Sutcliff was not called to Bour-

---

assembled there on that occasion. Among the rest, the Rev. Benjamin Beddome particularly attracted his attention. He was strongly solicited to take part in the public services of the day; but through that timidity which is often attendant on genius and talent, he declined it; he was, however, by entreaties, and almost compulsion, induced to deliver a sermon in the evening, with which the audience was greatly delighted." (Fawcett, *Rev. John Fawcett*, 216)

8. Newton, "Wednesday 7 August 1776." In his diary, Newton recorded an earlier time when he heard Beddome preach. On June 27, 1775, Beddome preached from 2 Cor 1:24 at a midweek evening service; Caleb Evans also preached on the occasion from John 3:3. Of the two sermons, Newton wrote, "The latter [that is, Evans's sermon] was a good sermon, but the former [that is, Beddome's sermon] gave me a pleasure I seldom find in hearing. It was an excellent discourse indeed, and the Lord was pleased to give me some softenings and relentings of heart. It is long since I had such an opportunity. O Lord soften me yet more and enable me to rejoice in thy peace." Newton, "Tuesday 27 June 1775"; Haykin, "Benjamin Beddome (1717–1795)," 4:258.

9. Michael A. G. Haykin observed that Newton "had the opportunity to meet and hear many of the leading evangelicals of his day.... For one who often heard the greatest preacher of the day, George Whitefield, these words are high praise indeed." Haykin, "Benjamin Beddome (1717–1795)," 4:258.

10. For the details in this paragraph, I am indebted to Haykin, *One Heart*, 95–96.

11. Purdy had been made aware of Beddome's aging condition and need for an assistant. Beddome had heard positive reports about Sutcliff and so inquired of Purdy if Sutcliff could come and be his assistant in Bourton. There was, however, a small obstacle in that Hugh Evans—the principal of the Baptist Academy—was due to preach at Bourton on Sunday, April 23, 1775. Evans would certainly have recommended one of his students at the Academy, and Sutcliff would have been edged out. Knowing this, Purdy devised a plan that would have Sutcliff happen to arrive in Bourton on Saturday, April 15, eight days before Evans was due to preach at Beddome's church. In this way, Purdy thought, Sutcliff's preaching would be fresh on Beddome's mind during Evans's visit. Purdy's plan did not come to fruition, though a modified version may have. Haykin—who has analyzed the correspondence between Purdy and Sutcliff during these months—says that "a letter which Purdy wrote to Sutcliff on 9 June clearly indicates that Beddome did hear Sutcliff preach, though when the latter went to Bourton

ton was given in a letter he wrote to Purdy. Sutcliff informed his friend that he measured up in every way in Beddome's eyes except in the all-important area of preaching.[12] The Bourton pastor clearly valued preaching and appears to have viewed the task as a central part of a minister's calling.

These connections between Beddome and his contemporaries were significant for at least two reasons. First, they demonstrate Beddome participated in ordination services. In this chapter, the ordination sermons of Beddome will be examined to construct his pastoral theology. Since the discourses deemed as ordination sermons were not labeled as such by Beddome or the publisher, it is helpful to note that Beddome—like many eighteenth-century English Particular Baptist ministers—participated in the ordination of his brothers to the pastorates of local churches.[13] Second, these connections with men like Hall, Newton, and Sutcliff demonstrate Beddome was a respected and renowned preacher, both in his own day and in the generations following his death.

BEDDOME'S ABILITIES AS A PREACHER

John Rippon was the successor to John Gill at the Carter Lane church in London. He was also the author of *The Baptist Annual Register* and Beddome's first biographer. In his obituary of the Bourton pastor, Rippon captured the respect Beddome enjoyed among his Baptist brethren:

> The labours of this good man among his charge were unremitted and evangelical. He fed them with the finest of the wheat. No man in all his connexions wrote more sermons, nor composed them with greater care—and this was true of him to the last weeks of his life. In most of his discourses the application of a student, and the ability of a divine were visible. . . . Indeed sermonizing was so much his forte, that at length when knowledge had received maturity from years, and composition was familiarized by habit, he has been known, with a wonderful facility of the moment, to sketch his picture at the foot of the pulpit stairs, to colour it as he was ascending, and, without turning his

---

remains unclear. He may well have suggested a modification of Purdy's plan, and gone to Bourton after Hugh Evans' visit." Haykin, *One Heart*, 96–97.

12. See Haykin, *One Heart*, 58.

13. Beddome also participated at the ordination of John Collett Ryland to the pastorate of the Baptist church in Warwick. Collett Ryland had been saved at the Bourton church and was a member there until he went to pastor the Warwick church. Newman, *Rylandiana*, 5.

eyes from the canvas, in the same hour, to give it all the finish of matter.[14]

To illustrate Beddome's abilities as a preacher, Rippon recorded a well-circulated anecdote of the Bourton pastor.[15] Beddome was at a minister's meeting in Fairford, Gloucestershire, and was scheduled to preach. Once the service began, Beddome forgot what he had intended to preach. Since he did not preach from notes, he could not consult them and so asked the host pastor, Thomas Davis (d. 1784), "Brother Davis, what must I preach from?" Taken back by Beddome's question, Davis replied, "Ask no foolish questions." The Bourton pastor was relieved and took Titus 3:9, "Avoid foolish questions," as his text and, according to Rippon, "preached a remarkably methodical, correct, and useful discourse on it."[16]

Beddome was a gifted and committed preacher. Toward the end of his life, he was carried to the church and preached from a seated position. Rippon recounted, "It had been his earnest wish not to be long laid aside from his beloved work of preaching the gospel, and his prayer was remarkably answered, as he was ill but one Lord's-day."[17] Reflecting upon the Bourton pastor's relentless commitment to preaching, Michael A. G. Haykin said, "He simply refused to give up preaching. At the heart of this refusal lay a deeply held conviction about the vital importance of preaching."[18]

PUBLICATION OF BEDDOME'S SERMONS

Beddome was tireless as a preacher and delivered a few thousand sermons during his fifty-five-year ministry in Bourton. He had the habit of selecting on Sunday evening the topics for the following week's sermons and "composing a hymn to be sung after each sermon."[19] Rippon said Beddome

14. Rippon, "Rev. Benjamin Beddome," 320.

15. For the details in this paragraph, I am indebted to Rippon, "Rev. Benjamin Beddome," 320–21.

16. Rippon, "Rev. Benjamin Beddome," 321. The anecdote and the sermon were published as Rippon, "Sketch of a Sermon," 415–21. The sermon was also published as Beddome, "Sermon 10," TSD, 5:81–89. Haykin recounts these events as an example of how "many of the best preachers of this community [the English Particular Baptists of the long eighteenth century] were, of course, able to preach with little preparation, if the need arose." Haykin, "Those Who Plead," 3–5.

17. Rippon, "Rev. Benjamin Beddome," 326.

18. Haykin, "Beddome and the Bible," 15.

19. Anonymous, "Memoir," in Beddome, SP, xxvii. Thomas Brooks said of his predecessor, "In the pulpit he is said to have been emphatically at home. And in some sort he was always there, the pulpit was 'in all his thoughts.' The goal of one duty was the

composed more sermons than he preached: "no man in all his connexions wrote more sermons, nor composed them with greater care" than Beddome, "and this was true of him to the last weeks of his life."[20] He added, "Though he had a multitude of sermons which had never been preached, he kept on composing, and was lively in his ministry to the very last."[21] Toward the end of his ministry, though, Beddome generally destroyed his sermons on the Monday after he had preached them.[22]

Rippon said the Bourton pastor had left behind "numerous sketches of sermons."[23] In 1795, when Rippon wrote Beddome's obituary, none of the sermons had been published. It was his hope that they would be made available through publication, though that decision needed to be made by Beddome's progeny.[24] Rippon's wish was granted with the publication of eight volumes of Beddome's sermons, which were printed in the early part of the nineteenth century.[25] These consisted of twenty sermons each, except in the eighth volume, which had eighteen discourses. A final, stand-alone volume of sixty-seven sermons was published in 1835. Affixed to the 1835 volume was a memoir in which the anonymous writer said,

> Of his powers of mind and tone of sentiment, though not of his powers as a preacher, some idea may be formed from the following short sketches of sermons which are taken from his manuscripts. It must not, however be forgotten, that they are the mere skeletons and hints, which he filled out in the pulpit, and preserved without the least design of publication. His invention seemed almost unlimited; while the extent and correctness of his biblical knowledge were evidently great. His diligence must have been incessant, as he generally selected each Sabbath evening the topics for the discourses of the next.... he wrote several hundreds of short discourses besides those that have appeared in print, and those which are here given.[26]

Thomas Brooks, writing a few decades later in 1861, said of the printed sermons, "And yet, we must not forget, that the author had not dreamed that

---

starting point of the next. We are told that he generally selected on the sabbath evening the topics for the discourses for the next." Brooks, *POTP*, 61.

20. Rippon, "Rev. Benjamin Beddome," 320.
21. Rippon, "Rev. Benjamin Beddome," 325.
22. Rippon, "Rev. Benjamin Beddome," 325–26.
23. Rippon, "Rev. Benjamin Beddome," 326.
24. Rippon, "Rev. Benjamin Beddome," 326.
25. For publication details, see bibliography.
26. Anonymous, "Memoir," in Beddome, *SP*, xxvi–xxvii.

they would be given to the public through the press. They were mere channels dug for his thoughts to flow in, skeletons to be clothed with flesh and receive the breath of life as spoken from the pulpit."[27] Given the sermons were but mere sketches, they were short and compact.[28]

Beddome was an able and committed preacher, recognized as such by his contemporaries and posterity. Given his involvement in the ordinations of Skinner and Sutcliff, it is clear the Cotswold divine participated in the ordination of men to the pastorate of other Baptist churches. The process by which his sermons were published has been recounted to give the reader a sense of the nature of the primary sources in question, namely, that they are the sketches of Beddome's sermons. In this final introductory section, it will be shown that some of the extant discourses were likely preached in the context of an ordination service.

BEDDOME'S ORDINATION SERMONS

Beddome was devoted to ministerial training and raising up the gifts of Christ so they could be sent to other churches. During his pastorate at Bourton, several men were called to the ministry and sent to pastor other churches. Pope Duncan remarked in his autobiography how Beddome "ran a kind of seminary for young preachers out of his home in Bourton-on-the-Water. In the process he collected hundreds of books and pamphlets of the Puritans and Separatists."[29] The Bourton pastor was also heavily involved in the Midland Association. One key aspect of associational life was the gathering of ministers, which took place over two to three days annually

---

27. Brooks, *POTP*, 61.

28. In John Greene's reminiscences of Hall Jr., he recounted a time when he had lent Hall a copy of Beddome's sermons during a visit. This was Hall's estimation of the sermons:

> They are very evangelical, and there is a good choice of subjects: there is a bone, and sinew, and marrow, in them, that shows a great mind. I like them, sir, because they are so full of thought; they furnish matter for the mind to dwell upon. It is true that they are very short; but it must be remembered that they are posthumous, and were never intended for publication: they are little more than skeletons. I like them better for their compactness.... In short, sir, I do not know any sermons of the kind in the English language. I believe they are destined to be much more extensively read and appreciated. (Greene, *Rev. Robert Hall*, 105)

Greene had also lent out the sermons to others and found Beddome's sermons to be useful. He sought for their use in families and in visiting the sick, where the sermons could be read in twenty minutes so as to not exhaust the patient. Greene, *Rev. Robert Hall*, 105.

29. Duncan, "President Pope Duncan's Autobiography," chap. 10.

and consisted of preaching and fellowship.[30] That Beddome was selected to deliver the annual address seventeen times demonstrated his commitment to strengthening his brother pastors and their esteem of him.[31] These biographical details, as well as the above recounting of Beddome's involvement at ordination services, suggest he was involved in training and strengthening fellow pastors during his half-century of ministry.

In his dissertation, "'Eminent Spirituality and Eminent Usefulness': Andrew Fuller's (1754–1815) Pastoral Theology in His Ordination Sermons," Nigel Wheeler researches the pastoral theology of the English Particular Baptists according to their ordination sermons, with a particular focus on those of Andrew Fuller.[32] The goal of this chapter is to do the same with Beddome's ordination sermons. Fuller's body of ordination sermons and that of Beddome's, however, differ in two significant ways. First, Fuller's corpus of ordination sermons is the largest of any eighteenth-century English Particular Baptist pastor; thus, there are more sermons to examine. There are thirty-one extant ordination sermons of Fuller compared to the approximate ten of Beddome. Second, Fuller's sermons are more easily identified as those delivered at an ordination because of editorial notes and their inclusion in a section of ordination sermons. In contrast, most of Beddome's sermons were not marked with any provenance or occasion and thus are harder to identify as ordination sermons in any conclusive way.

This lack of identification was likely the reason Wheeler did not include any of Beddome's sermons in his analysis of thirty-two extant ordination sermons published by English Particular Baptists of the long eighteenth century (other than Fuller's).[33] In 2019, Haykin, Brian Croft, and Ian H.

---

30. Haykin, *Holy Spirit Now Descend*, 89.

31. Rippon said that Beddome preached

> 17 times in 46 years; this, on average, was as frequently as he could have been chosen to the service—for it has long been a rule in the Midland Assembly, that no person shall be chosen to preach at the Association oftener than once in three years—but, perhaps, on examination it will appear, in the instance of Mr. Beddome, that this has not been always strictly adhered to from the year 1740, and it seems there was no such limitation at that time. (Rippon, "Rev. Benjamin Beddome," 325)

Jason C. Montgomery says on this point, "This would have exceeded the allowable times a minister was permitted to preach. The standing policy of the Midland Association was to permit a minister to preach no more than one time every three years. A simple doing of the math from Beddome's first appearance as preacher in 1743 to his last in 1789, clearly shows the rule was stretched where Beddome was concerned." Montgomery, "Benjamin Beddome," 146–47.

32. Wheeler, "Eminent Spirituality."

33. Wheeler, "Eminent Spirituality," 13, 13n17; 247–52.

Clary published *Being a Pastor: A Conversation with Andrew Fuller*.[34] Their work, like Wheeler's, focused on the ordination sermons of Fuller, with an aim of retrieving wisdom for contemporary pastors. In that work, Haykin, Croft, and Clary identified four of Beddome's discourses as ordination sermons.[35] These will be considered to demonstrate how they, as well as a few others, bear the marks of an ordination sermon.

As noted, Beddome usually composed a hymn to accompany his Sunday morning sermon.[36] Accordingly, many of his printed sermons had a hymn attached to them. This leads to the first piece of evidence that at least one of Beddome's sermons was delivered at an ordination service. The sermon, "Ministerial Subordination to Christ," had the hymn "Pastors the Gift of Christ" affixed to it.[37] The hymn spoke of the appointment of pastors to local churches and would have been fitting for an ordination service. The hymn was included in a section titled "Times and Seasons," in the collection of Beddome's hymns published by Hall Jr. The hymns before and after "Pastors the Gift of Christ" dealt with opening a place of worship, the meeting of ministers, ordinations, and the parting of ministers.[38]

Moreover, the Bourton pastor directly addressed ministers in two of the sermons identified by Haykin, Croft, and Clary. In "The Nature and Authority of Christian Ministry," Beddome exhorted his fellow pastors, "Remember, *my dear brethren in the ministry*, that your business is like that of your great Master, to seek and to save that which is lost [Luke 19:10]."[39] Using the same phrase in "On the Duty of Ministers to Promote Their People's Joy," he urged his hearers, "Hear, *my brethren in the ministry*, those awful words of God, by the prophet Ezekiel," before quoting a conglomeration of Ezek 34:4 and 10.[40]

A third piece of evidence was that Beddome instructed the church in all four sermons. This was, of course, not unique to ordination sermons. However, in three of the identified sermons, the minister of the Bourton church exhorted the church with respect to its duties toward its pastor. For example, in "On the Sources of Ministerial Delight," Beddome taught how

---

34. Haykin et al., *Being a Pastor*.

35. Haykin et al., *Being a Pastor*, 251. They identified the following as ordination sermons: "Ministerial Subordination to Christ," "Nature and Authority," "Duty of Ministers," and "Sources of Ministerial Delight." These sermons were printed in Beddome, *SP*, 269–73, 302–9, 356–362, and 260–68, respectively.

36. Rippon, "Rev. Benjamin Beddome," 322.

37. Beddome, *Hymns*, #736.

38. Beddome, *Hymns*, #731–37.

39. Beddome, "Nature and Authority," in *SP*, 309 (emphasis added).

40. Beddome, "Duty of Ministers," in *SP*, 361 (emphasis added).

members of a church brought joy to their minister when their character and conduct adorned "their profession." He then directly addressed the church with these words: "Your stability is our felicity."[41] Later in that sermon—as well as in the conclusion to "The Nature and Authority of the Christian Ministry"—Beddome spoke to the church concerning its responsibilities toward its pastor.[42] Similarly, Beddome drew two inferences in "Ministerial Subordination to Christ," namely, that the church not ascribe to ministers any more than is due and that it looks from the minister unto Christ.[43]

As noted, Fuller left behind the largest corpus of ordination sermons from any English Particular Baptist pastor. His sermons are a good representation of this genre of discourse from the long eighteenth century. In his ordination sermons, Fuller took a principle and applied it to the various tasks of the pastor. For instance, in a sermon to a young minister at his ordination, Fuller exhorted the ordinand to maintain the qualities of "spiritual light and holy love" as a minister. He then applied that principle to the different branches of the pastor's work—preaching the gospel, presiding over the church, visiting the people—and to his demeanor throughout life.[44] This relates to the fourth piece of evidence that some of Beddome's discourses were ordination sermons. Like Fuller, Beddome took the principle—that a minister is a helper of his people's joy—and then applied it to three areas of pastoral ministry. Ministers, according to Beddome, were to promote their people's joy, "by the doctrine they preached," "by their private counsels and instructions," and "by their example, which is indeed the most forcible way of instruction."[45]

Last, these discourses resembled ordination sermons simply by their content. In all four ordination sermons identified by Haykin, Croft, and Clary, the principal subject is the nature, qualifications, duties, and joys of the minister or the duties of the church, particularly in relation to its pastor. When we employ this final criterion to determine what might be an ordination sermon, several others could be included. In addition to the four

---

41. Beddome, "Sources of Ministerial Delight," in *SP*, 266.

42. Beddome, "Sources of Ministerial Delight," in *SP*, 268; Beddome, "Nature and Authority," in *SP*, 309.

43. Beddome, "Ministerial Subordination to Christ," in *SP*, 272–73.

44. Fuller, "Spiritual Knowledge and Love," in *WAF*, 1:479–82. Similarly, in "Ministers Fellow Labourers," Fuller taught the Christian ministry to be a labor, and demonstrated this by considering the various aspects of the pastor's work: becoming acquainted with God's mind through his Word, communicating the mind of God, private conversations with people through visitation, and presiding over the church. Fuller, "Ministers Fellow Labourers," in *WAF*, 1:491–93.

45. Beddome, "Duty of Ministers," in *SP*, 360–61.

ordination sermons identified in *Being a Pastor*, this author has identified several more sermons dealing with *pastoralia* in Beddome's corpus.[46] Some were directed to ministers and others were addressed to the church. There is some difficulty in conclusively identifying these as ordination sermons. The charge to ministers could have been given at an ordination service or a ministers' meeting.[47] Similarly, sermons addressed to the church could have been preached to the congregation in Bourton or as the address to the church at an ordination.[48] Even lacking their provenance, however, these sermons provide insight into Beddome's pastoral theology. These discourses will be examined for the *pastoralia* of the Bourton pastor, with insights drawn from the remaining corpus of his sermons, hymnody, and catechism. The significance, qualifications, duties, and motivations of a pastor will be considered first, followed by the duties of the church. At appropriate points, Beddome's pastoral theology will be compared with that of the English Particular Baptists that was outlined in chapter 2.

THE SIGNIFICANCE OF A PASTOR

In the conclusion to his sermon "The Nature and Authority of the Christian Ministry," Beddome said that ministers "transact the most important matters between God and man. This is no trifling employment, nor ought it to

---

46. Beddome, "Happy Results of Repentance," in *SP*, 135–42; Beddome, "Reconciliation to God," in *TSD*, 1:116–24; Beddome, "Sermon 1," in *TSD*, 3:1–7; Beddome, "Sermon 9," in *TSD*, 4:71–80; Beddome, "Sermon 5," in *TSD*, 7:39–45; Beddome, "Sermon 5," in *SD*, 8:45–54. Also, see three other sermons that dealt heavily with *pastoralia*: Beddome, "Sermon 5," in *TSD*, 5:39–47; Beddome, "Sermon 3," in *TSD*, 6:23–29; Beddome, "Sermon 2," in *TSD*, 7:14–21.

47. The lack of provenance with the sermons makes this task more difficult. To illustrate, even one of the sermons identified by Haykin, Croft, and Clary as an ordination sermon—"The Nature and Authority of the Christian Ministry"—is conjectured to have been preached at a meeting of the Midland Association by Montgomery. Montgomery, "Benjamin Beddome," 196.

48. In the introduction to a sermon preached at the ordination of Thomas Morgan to the pastorate at Cannon Street, Birmingham, Andrew Fuller said,

> It is not usual, I believe, for ministers in their ordinary labours to dwell upon the obligations of the people of their charge towards them. They feel, probably, that on such a subject they might be suspected of partiality to themselves; and if such a suspicion were indulged, however just and proper their admonitions might be, they would be but of little use, and might operate to their disadvantage. (Fuller, "Obedience of Churches," in *WAF*, 1:196)

Fuller's comment indicated that some ministers may have been reticent to preach to their own people concerning the church's duties toward its pastor. Whether Beddome thought similarly to Fuller in this regard is uncertain.

be trifled with."⁴⁹ He added in another sermon how ministers were a "wonder, both to themselves and others" since they were aware of their weakness and sinfulness, yet God chose to

> employ them in so sacred and important a work as that of publishing articles of peace between heaven and earth, of bringing messages of grace from the offended Deity to a lost and ruined world. . . . that they who took part in the transgression should be thus employed, can be owing to nothing but the most stupendous grace. Infinite wisdom saw fit to lodge this treasure in earthen vessels that the excellency of the power might be of God, and not of us [2 Cor 4:7].⁵⁰

Beddome was impressed with the gracious nature of pastoral work and knew of its divine origin. According to the Bourton pastor, ministry was not rooted in the ingenuity and industry of man, but rather in the wisdom, power, and grace of God.

As noted, Beddome was an English Particular Baptist pastor during the long eighteenth century. For pastors in this tradition, an oft-cited passage to elucidate the significance of the pastor was from the fourth chapter of Paul's letter to the Ephesians, which said that Christ "gave gifts unto men. . . . And he gave some, apostles; and some, prophets; and some, evangelists; and some, pastors and teachers" (Eph 4:8, 11 KJV). Samuel Pearce preached on this text at the ordination of W. Belsher to the pastorate of the Baptist church in Worcester. Similarly, Andrew Fuller preached on the same theme at the ordination of William Carey to the pastorate of the Baptist church at Moulton.⁵¹ The concept of the pastor being a gift of Christ to the church also featured in Beddome's thought. His hymn "Pastors the Gift of Christ" was based on the text in the Ephesian letter, and it was affixed to his ordination sermon "Ministerial Subordination to Christ." The first three stanzas of the hymn were:

> Jesus ascends above the skies,
> And pours his blessings down;
> Tis thence his church receives supplies,
> From him and him alone.

---

49. Beddome, "Nature and Authority," in *SP*, 308. Though it is beyond the scope of this chapter for a comparative analysis, it appears that "Nature and Authority" was related to Thomas Boston's sermon *Art of Man-Fishing*. For a modern reprint of this sermon, see Boston, *Art of Man-Fishing*.

50. Beddome, "Sermon 7," in *TSD*, 5:59.

51. Pearce, *Duty of Churches*, 50–62; Fuller, "Importance of Christian Ministers," in *WAF*, 1:521–22. The text cited at the top of Fuller's sermon was Ps 68:18, but this was the text quoted in Eph 4:8, and Fuller proceeded to explain Eph 4:9–10 in the sermon.

> The various gifts on men bestowed,
> And by his power ordained,
> Are all the purchase of his blood,
> The trophies he has gained.
>
> He sits a sovereign to command,
> His heralds know his voice:
> They in obedient posture stand,
> And in his strength rejoice.[52]

The "blessings," "supplies," and "various gifts" were all a reference to ministers. These gifts were purchased by the blood of Christ and were the "trophies" he gained in his victory. These were dispensed by the sovereign Lord to his church to advance "his glorious cause" in this world.[53]

The teaching that Christ sent ministers to his churches was underscored in a hymn written on the occasion of a church having lost its pastor. In such a condition, a church would rightly cry out, "Oh send a messenger of peace, / A pastor of thy choice."[54] This same principle can be seen in a sermon on the coming judgment in which Beddome warned, "Did he not send his ministers, one after another, rising up early and sending them? Did he not stand at the door and knock?"[55] Beddome made clear—whether in a hymn seeking to comfort a bereaved church or in a sermon sounding an alarm of judgment—that it was Christ who sent ministers to do his bidding.

When Christ, for example, desired to save an individual or group of people, he would set up a gospel ministry in that place. In "The Hidden Design of Christ's Ministry," Beddome said that when God had "designs of mercy to any, he will either bring the means of grace to them, or them under the means of grace." To illustrate the latter, he alluded to Onesimus—the runaway slave who went to Rome and came under Paul's preaching through which he was converted (Phlm 10–11, 15–16). To demonstrate the former,

---

52. Beddome, *Hymns*, #736.

53. Beddome, *Hymns*, #736.

54. Beddome, *Hymns*, #662. Conversely, upon the occasion of a church calling a pastor, the membership could praise God for his provision of a minister:

> Lord, we adore thy sacred name,
> And sing the wonders of thy grace;
> From thee our timely succour came,
> When overwhelmed in deep distress.
>
> Accompanied with fervent prayer,
> We sought a pastor of thy choice,
> One who should heavenly tidings bear,
> And cause thy people to rejoice. (Beddome, *Hymns*, #663)

55. Beddome, "Justice of Future Punishment," in *TSD*, 2:183.

he pointed to the account of Peter being sent to preach the good news to Cornelius (Acts 10:1–48).[56] The principle for Beddome was: "Where God has a work to do he will set up a gospel ministry, and introduce gospel ordinances."[57] Christ has done this in perpetuity throughout the church age, as argued by Beddome elsewhere, in another discourse: "By raising up a constant succession of ministers to propagate and defend it, the Lord is still giving testimony to the word of his grace."[58] He added, "He who sends the message, can be at no loss for want of messengers.... As soon as one earthen vessel is broken, the heavenly treasure is put into another [2 Cor 4:7]."[59]

Given that Christ sent ministers and he was the one who orchestrated their placement in his churches, the ministry was bestowed with his glory. In "The Mutual Glory of Christ and His People," Beddome spoke of the glory given to Christ by the Father during his earthly ministry. The Bourton pastor said that Christ, in turn, imparted glory to others: the glory of working miracles to the disciples and the glory of sonship to all the saints. There was also the glory of preaching that Christ bestowed on his ministers.[60] This theme of glory in preaching was echoed in another sermon, "On the Dignity of the Christian Church." Beddome compared the glory a king displayed from his throne to the glory that God displayed through his church. It was in the church he received intercessions, homage, and adoration from his subjects and where he displayed his glorious perfections. Though the glory dwelt in a cloud in the old covenant temple, God's glory "[broke] forth in a blaze" in the church—in the preaching of ministers and in the private lives of Christians.[61]

By way of conclusion on the significance of the pastor, Christ's presence in and through ministers will be considered. Drawing on Pauline language in "Reconciliation to God," Beddome said ministers were ambassadors, or representatives, of Christ (2 Cor 5:20). Their authority originated with him, and their commission came from him. A minister needed to look to Christ for direction if he was to faithfully discharge his duties as his ambassador. Ministers stood in Christ's place "as if he were personally present" through his ministers. It was this reality concerning the minister's role that gave dignity to the pastoral office.[62]

---

56. Beddome, "Hidden Design," in *SP*, 374.
57. Beddome, "Hidden Design," in *SP*, 374.
58. Beddome, "Sermon 9," in *TSD*, 5:76.
59. Beddome, "Sermon 9," in *TSD*, 5:77.
60. Beddome, "Mutual Glory," in *SP*, 83.
61. Beddome, "Christian Church," in *SP*, 419.
62. Beddome, "Reconciliation to God," in *TSD*, 1:116–17.

The idea of ministers representing Christ was echoed in several of Beddome's ordination hymns, though with a shift in metaphor. In the sermon "Reconciliation to God," ministers were said to be ambassadors for God with an emphasis on carrying out the work of reconciliation between God and men. In the ordination hymns, however, the dominant imagery was that of a shepherd and his flock. For example, in a hymn written for an ordination service, Beddome exhorted the elders,

> Ye elders feed the flock
> Committed to your care,
> The solemn charge you now receive,
> The voice of Jesus hear.
>
> Let purest motives guide,
> And sacred zeal enflame;
> The oversight you freely take,
> In your great Master's name.[63]

In another hymn, written also for an ordination, Beddome wrote:

> Oh bless the Lord, our souls,
> Our shepherd and our head;
> Though in a weary barren land,
> We still are richly fed.
>
> He under-shepherds gives,
> His little flock to guide;
> And by his faithful tender care,
> Will constant food provide.
>
> Then may they watch for souls,
> And see when danger's near,
> That they a true account may give,
> When Jesus shall appear. . . .
>
> With such a shepherd, Lord,
> Oh may we now be blessed;
> Be sweetly fed and nourished here,
> And in thy pasture rest.[64]

Christ, the Great Shepherd of the sheep, desired to feed his flock and lead them to greener pastures (Heb 13:20; Ps 23:2), and he would achieve this through his ministers, particularly through their preaching. Thus,

---

63. Beddome, *Hymns*, #735.
64. Beddome, *Hymns*, #734.

ministers played a vital role in the lives of God's people. So closely did Christ identify with his ministers and their preaching that, according to Beddome, the Lord Jesus "speaks to us in the preaching of the word; the voice of ministers is the voice of Christ."[65] In another hymn, occasioned by the serious illness of a pastor, as was the case for Beddome for six weeks shortly after his marriage to Elizabeth Boswell on December 21, 1749,[66] he wrote,

> Long have we heard his lips proclaim,
> The gospel's joyful sound,
> Still may he live to bless thy name,
> And spread thy truth around.
>
> *Still may we hear his cheering voice,*
> *And find thee in the word*;
> Our grateful hearts shall then rejoice,
> And bless our living Lord.[67]

THE QUALIFICATIONS OF A PASTOR

In "The Nature and Authority of the Christian Ministry," Beddome expanded the metaphor of fishing—drawn from the dominical words "I will make you fishers of men (Matt 4:19)"—to describe the ministry. The unfolding of the metaphor will be examined below under the duties of a pastor. The character of the minister, which was the second heading of the sermon, will be the focus here, and this reveals Beddome's understanding of what qualified a man for the ministry.[68]

First, ministers were given their natural abilities by Christ, who freely dispensed them according to his will. The capacities Beddome had in mind were "the clear understanding, accurate judgment, lively genius, sprightly

---

65. Beddome, "Heavenly Stranger Received," in *TSD*, 2:46.

66. Rippon, "Rev. Benjamin Beddome," 318–19.

67. Beddome, *Hymns*, #661 (emphasis added).

68. Beddome, "Nature and Authority," in *SP*, 306–8. A similar list of qualifications is found in "Sacred Word." Beddome spoke of how ministers will be measured, or evaluated:

> Ministers who go before others in the worship of God. These we are to measure with respect to their qualifications; whether partakers of grace, endued with gifts, knowing and intelligent themselves, and apt to communicate that knowledge to others. As to their call—their call by the church, and their call by God—whether called by his grace to the work, and by his providence to us. And, further, as to their conduct, whether it is suitable to the profession they have made, and the character they sustain, as being an example to believers; in a word, in conversation, in charity, in spirit, in faith, in purity. (Beddome, "Sacred Word," in *SP*, 57)

imagination, and retentive memory, with the diligent improvement of all these, [were] as the Lord [gave] to every man."[69] Though the provision of natural abilities was not limited to the fishers of men, ministers needed these particular qualities to discharge their duties. Beddome added that ministers tended to have "a liberal education" and "other advantages," which they enjoyed in their youth.[70]

Second, a minister owed his participation in grace to Christ.[71] The Lord Jesus made men Christians before he called them to be ministers, not only placing "the light of divine knowledge in their heads, but [implanting] the seeds of holiness in their hearts."[72] Thus, an unconverted minister was an absurdity to Beddome. A minister who had not experienced grace could not represent the message of Christ accurately or genuinely. This was because, according to Beddome, such a person "preaches what he has not felt, and prescribes what he does not practise."[73] Beddome made the same argument in "Christ Manifested to the Soul," in which he proclaimed, "Certainly that man is not fit to preach Christ who has not experimental knowledge of him."[74] He added that it was this experiential knowledge of Christ that formed a "minister's mind for his work, and [rendered] him superior to all the difficulties attending it."[75]

Then, the Bourton pastor told fellow ministers that they received their qualifications and desires for the ministry from Christ.[76] This included zeal for God and love for souls,[77] as well as abilities like "improving the understanding, touching the conscience, and moving the affections."[78] Some men

69. Beddome, "Nature and Authority," in SP, 306.
70. Beddome, "Nature and Authority," in SP, 306.
71. Beddome, "Nature and Authority," in SP, 306.
72. Beddome, "Nature and Authority," in SP, 307.
73. Beddome, "Nature and Authority," in SP, 306.
74. Beddome, "Christ Manifested," in SP, 125. Cf. Beddome, "Sermon 14," in TSD, 4:117.
75. Beddome, "Christ Manifested," in SP, 125. In "Excellence of the Law," Beddome said, "Experience is the best help to the work of the ministry. A man cannot speak freely, feelingly, boldly and faithfully, or with any probability of success, what he does not believe himself. We believe, says the apostle, and therefore speak [2 Cor 4:13]." Beddome, "Excellence of the Law," in TSD, 1:149.
76. In another sermon, Beddome said, "To the great Head of the church [ministers] owe both their qualifications and success." Beddome, "Sermon 9," in TSD, 5:77.
77. Concerning a minister's love for souls, Beddome said in another sermon, "The apostle Paul was a lover of souls; and so are all faithful ministers, or even good men. The genuine spirit of Christianity is a spirit of philanthropy and benevolence." Beddome, "Grace of Christ," in SP, 220.
78. Beddome, "Nature and Authority," in SP, 307.

would be called to more obscure places and others to prominent locations. Even those who were qualified and used for extensive usefulness, however, owed their qualifications and inclinations to the Lord, as evidenced by the great apostle, who said, "By the grace of God I am what I am" (1 Cor 15:10 KJV), though he had trained under the respected Gamaliel (Acts 22:3).[79]

Fourth, Christ called men into the ministry and provided opportunities for them to exercise their gifts. The external call came from the church, but the internal call came from God. Even with the former, it was God who superintended the desires and decisions of people in the calling of a minister to a church. In general, if God had secretly called a man to the ministry, it was accompanied by the external declaration of the church. This was not foolproof, however, since there were men who assumed the pastoral "office when Christ [had] neither qualified them for it, nor by his church called them to it."[80] This is why the apostle Paul—as with all genuine ministers—expressed gratitude to Christ for enlisting him in ministry.[81]

Last, ministers depended upon Christ in their work, and he gave them success. The effectiveness of a sermon depended not upon the moral argumentation of the preacher "or the energy of the word itself, but the irresistible influence of the Spirit of Christ."[82] Christ gave ministers strength to endure difficulties and to overcome opposition; he supported ministers when they were faint, bolstered them when they were weary, bore charges against them, and would reward their pastoral efforts in the end.[83]

THE DUTIES OF A PASTOR

There are several ordination sermons from the English Particular Baptists that provide a list of the duties, or the branches, of pastoral ministry. In chapter 2, the sermons of Caleb Evans, Gill, and Benjamin Wallin demonstrated a remarkable consistency among the Particular Baptists with respect

---

79. Beddome, "Nature and Authority," in *SP*, 307.

80. Beddome, "Nature and Authority," in *SP*, 307. Beddome's phrasing here is insightful. He does not say that men assumed the pastoral office when neither *Christ had not internally called them* nor had the church externally called them. Rather, he says *Christ had not qualified these men for the ministry*. In other words, the external call should not be understood in a mystical and entirely subjective sense; there is an objectivity to God's call upon a man for the ministry, namely, that he has qualified him for the work.

81. Beddome, "Nature and Authority," in *SP*, 307–8.

82. Beddome, "Nature and Authority," in *SP*, 308.

83. Beddome, "Nature and Authority," in *SP*, 308.

to the various duties of a pastor.[84] Though the three men enumerated the duties differently, the core duties of the pastor were similar. Gill gave a charge to his nephew and four ordinands; in that sermon, he listed four duties of a minister typical for Particular Baptists of the day: ministration of the Word, administration of the ordinances, governance of the church, and visitation of members.[85]

Though Beddome did not enumerate the branches of the pastoral ministry in the same way, that he thought such duties were essential is demonstrable from his sermons and catechism. In his sermon "The Nature and Exercises of True Fidelity," Beddome said faithful ministers were "dispensing the word with boldness, administering the ordinances of God's house in their purity, and maintaining the discipline of it with impartiality."[86] In another discourse, Beddome sought to apply a principle—that ministers are to promote the joy of their people—to various areas of a pastor's life: his preaching, his visitations, and his example.[87] In his catechism, Beddome outlined the means of grace thus: "The outward and ordinary means whereby Christ communicateth to us the benefits of redemption are his ordinances, especially the word, baptism, the Lord's Supper, and prayer; all which means are made effectual to the elect for salvation."[88] In that same section of the catechism, Beddome mentioned that pastors were given for the building up of the church, and the implication was that ministers would accomplish this through preaching and administering the ordinances.[89] Thus, according to Beddome, pastors were vital to the spiritual growth of God's people. Clearly, Beddome was in accord with his Particular Baptist brethren regarding the duties of a pastor.

However, in his ordination sermons, as noted above, he did not enumerate the branches of the ministry in the way that Evans, Gill, or Wallin had done. In the sermons that will be examined below, the great focus of the Bourton pastor was on the work of preaching. Even in this, Beddome was in accord with his Particular Baptist brethren. Evans, Gill, and Wallin each listed preaching as first in their catalog of duties, as did Fuller and

84. Evans, *Charge*, 4–14; Gill, "Gospel-Minister," in *S&T*, 2:16–22; Wallin, *Charge*, 35–42.

85. Gill, "Gospel-Minister," in *S&T*, 2:16–22.

86. Beddome, "True Fidelity," in *SP*, 180.

87. Beddome, "Duty of Ministers," in *SP*, 360–61.

88. Beddome, *Scriptural Exposition*, 156. Unless otherwise indicated, the 2006 reprint of *Scriptural Exposition* will be cited.

89. The sub-question was: "But are God's word and ordinances the ordinary means of salvation?" The answer was: "Yes. He hath given pastors and teachers for the edifying of the body of Christ. Ephesians 4:11, 12." Beddome, *Scriptural Exposition*, 157.

Samuel Stennett when they provided similar lists.⁹⁰ The words of Evans, in his charge to Thomas Dunscombe at his ordination, are fitting here: "Thus we find in the solemn charge of the apostle Paul to his son Timothy (2 Tim 4:2) the first thing mentioned is preaching the word."⁹¹ Evans added,

> The ministers of Christ are to be preachers, public heralds; and the subject of their preaching or heraldry, if I may be allowed the expression, is to be the word, the gospel, the word of life and salvation. You are not, therefore, my dear brother, to entertain your people with florid pompous declamations on the power of reason, the dignity of man, and the beauty of virtue; but you are to preach the word [2 Tim 4:2].⁹²

Beddome was a man committed to being such a herald and exhorted his brethren in ministry to the same, as will be evident in an examination of the following sermons.

The Pastor Is a Lesser Light

The first sermon that will be considered concerning the duties of a pastor is "Ministerial Subordination to Christ."⁹³ It appeared as Sermon 39 in *Sermons Printed* and was based on John 1:8, "He was not that light." As noted above, attached to the sermon was the hymn "Pastors the Gift of Christ."⁹⁴ Beddome's thesis for the sermon was based on the biblical description of John the Baptist, of whom it was said, "He was a light, but not *that* light"; the former statement was implied and the latter explicitly stated in the text. These statements served as the outline of the discourse. The Bourton pastor took what was true of the Baptist and applied it to his contemporary brethren in ministry.⁹⁵ In the sermon, Beddome addressed several topics with respect to *pastoralia*, namely, the minister's identity, task, and relation to Christ.

First, Beddome asserted ministers were a kind of light. More pointedly, they were "a burning and shining light," with burning a reference to

---

90. Fuller, "Spiritual Knowledge and Love," in *WAF*, 1:479–81; Stennett, *Charge*, 58–62.

91. Evans, *Charge*, 4.

92. Evans, *Charge*, 5.

93. Beddome, "Ministerial Subordination to Christ," in *SP*, 269–73.

94. Beddome, *Hymns*, #736. The version in *SP* was missing the last stanza of the version in *Hymns*.

95. Beddome, "Ministerial Subordination to Christ," in *SP*, 269 (emphasis added).

zeal and shining to his exemplary character.⁹⁶ There were four ways that the Baptist and all faithful ministers were lights. First, (1) "on account of their station." Ministers were lights in the world (Matt 5:14), thus, their virtues and vices were observable by others in a way that was not true of those in a more "private station."⁹⁷ (2) The minister's task was to give knowledge to humanity and proclaim the message of salvation. Beddome took the imagery of Matt 5:15 and applied it to ministers who were "compared to candles not put under a bushel, but set on a candlestick, which [gave] light to all that [were] in the house."⁹⁸ (3) The conduct of ministers shined before others (Matt 5:16), so they needed to guard their behavior as to remove all occasions of reproach and not undermine their exhortations.⁹⁹

Ministers were lights (4) because of "their extensive usefulness. Their commission . . . [was] to open blind eyes and turn sinners from darkness to light [Acts 26:18]." Beddome's insights here are helpful in understanding the duty of the pastor in relation to the work of God in a sinner's life. Beddome declared that God performed the work of salvation "efficaciously," while ministers did so "instrumentally."¹⁰⁰ Ministers were helpers of their people's joy, while God was the object and author of their faith. Though they played a secondary role in the conversion of sinners, ministers could rightly be called lights. Illumination was necessary for the conversion of sinners, which was the great aim of ministry, and pastors played an instrumental role in the illumination of blind and darkened eyes that led to conversion.¹⁰¹

Second, Beddome explained the second part of his argument, namely, "he was not *that light*."¹⁰² The Baptist, as well as every minister in following generations, was not the light. The Bourton pastor demonstrated this point in three ways: (1) the Baptist was not the light predicted in the Old Testament; (2) he was not the fulfillment of the anticipation of both the Jews and the gentiles of a figure who would be the benefactor of all humanity. Beddome mentioned the prophecy of Balaam (Num 24:17) that captured the longing of the Jews and "the writings of the sybils" as an example of the gentiles' yearning;¹⁰³ (3) John was not the light that brought salvation to this

---

96. Beddome, "Ministerial Subordination to Christ," in *SP*, 269.
97. Beddome, "Ministerial Subordination to Christ," in *SP*, 269.
98. Beddome, "Ministerial Subordination to Christ," in *SP*, 270.
99. Beddome, "Ministerial Subordination to Christ," in *SP*, 270.
100. Beddome, "Ministerial Subordination to Christ," in *SP*, 270.
101. Beddome, "Ministerial Subordination to Christ," in *SP*, 270.
102. Beddome, "Ministerial Subordination to Christ," in *SP*, 271 (emphasis original).
103. According to *Encyclopedia Britannica*, "The sibyl came . . . to be regarded by some Christians as a prophetic authority comparable to the Old Testament." Editors, "Sibyl."

dark world. Beddome put the matter well: "If we had no other light than that of John, we should have sat in darkness to this day."[104] The Baptist had the unique privilege of preparing the way for the Lord; "he was the harbinger to the Prince of Peace [Isa 9:6], [and] the friend of the bridegroom [John 3:29]," but he was not the bridegroom, the Prince, or the Messiah.[105]

Therefore, John was inferior to the greater light in the following ways: (1) Christ was the source of light and life, whereas John was a "created and reflected light";[106] (2) the Baptist's ministry was only to the Jews, but Christ's was to all nations; (3) John was tainted with sin and corruption, whereas Christ was without any admixture of darkness; and (4) John would soon expire out of this world, but Christ would remain forever as a fixed star.[107] Beddome concluded the discourse with two inferences; these will be considered below in the section on the duties of the church.

The Pastor Is a Fisher of Men

In the Gospel of Matthew, the Lord Jesus called two sets of brothers to follow him: Andrew and Peter, and James and John, the sons of Zebedee. These four men had been fishermen, and in the case of James and John, the biblical text made clear that fishing was the family business. Matthew recorded the brothers' decisive response to the Lord's call. Andrew and Peter "left their nets and followed him," and James and John "left the boat and their father and followed him." For these four brothers, following Jesus entailed leaving behind the business of catching fish for another type of work, namely, the fishing of men (Matt 4:18–22).

It is this metaphor Beddome used as the basis for his sermon "The Nature and Authority of the Christian Ministry." The text for the sermon was Matt 4:19, "I will make you fishers of men," and it was Sermon 44 in *Sermons Printed*. In contrast to the previous discourse, there was no hymn affixed to "Nature and Authority." The sermon was outlined with two major points: the metaphor of fishing applied to Christian ministry and the character befitting the fishers of men. Beddome gave three practical applications at the end. The focus here will be the unfolding of the metaphor since this describes the duties of a minister.

In the introduction, Beddome made helpful remarks concerning pastoral ministry. From the order of the injunctions—"Follow me" and "I will

---

104. Beddome, "Ministerial Subordination to Christ," in *SP*, 271.
105. Beddome, "Ministerial Subordination to Christ," in *SP*, 271.
106. Beddome, "Ministerial Subordination to Christ," in *SP*, 272.
107. Beddome, "Ministerial Subordination to Christ," in *SP*, 272.

make you fishers of men"—Beddome asserted that Christ called men to be Christians first and then made them ministers. Further, when he summoned these four, it was a call not so much to leave their careers as fishermen and accompany him in his travels, but rather a spiritual call involving obedience to Christ's commands, the exercise of faith in him, and the imitation of his example. Beddome preached, "They would be fishers still, but in a different sense."[108]

Beddome proceeded to teach on the pastor's duty by unfolding the metaphor through five sub-points. The Bourton pastor began his first sub-point by comparing unconverted humanity to fish in the sea. Before conversion, the natural man was immersed in sin and took delight in fulfilling his lusts. Like fish, sinful humanity relished being in the sea as if there was "no ruler over them."[109] When brought under conviction of sin—like fish that were caught in a net—they struggled and sought to be set free, though they often entangled themselves further. It was only by God's power that men and women were made subject to Christ.[110]

Second, Beddome likened the fisherman letting down his nets to the minister preaching the gospel. In other words, ministers caught men through their preaching. This net of preaching the gospel was carefully planned by God's wisdom, built by his power, and perfectly suited for "the purposes for which it [was] designed."[111] Ministers were to lower their nets and to "open the doctrines of the divine word, display its terrors, unfold its mysteries, and beseech men, in Christ's stead, to be reconciled to God [2 Cor 5:20]."[112] If ministers discovered they had propagated some error, they should "mend their nets, [and] adhere more closely to the divine standard."[113]

Moreover, Beddome noted that the nature of ministry required three virtues in the minister.[114] Since pastors dealt with all kinds of people in various spiritual states, it required *wisdom*. For instance, he needed to discern if the person to whom he was ministering would be helped by correction or comfort. Beddome argued against a uniform approach to ministry and contended that different people required different approaches or strategies. Like men who fish for a living and not a hobby, pastors needed to be *diligent*.

---

108. Beddome, "Nature and Authority," in *SP*, 302.
109. Beddome, "Nature and Authority," in *SP*, 303.
110. Beddome, "Nature and Authority," in *SP*, 303.
111. Beddome, "Nature and Authority," in *SP*, 303.
112. Beddome, "Nature and Authority," in *SP*, 303.
113. Beddome, "Nature and Authority," in *SP*, 303.
114. This could have fit above under the qualifications of a minister, but since it depended upon the fisherman metaphor, it is included here.

Their labor involved the mind as well as the affections; their ministry was public through the pulpit and private in people's homes; and their congregation consisted of the ignorant, inquirers, the weak, and the wandering. A pastor needed also to subdue the corruption in his own heart and exercise grace in his life. He was required to do this "in season and out of season [2 Tim 4:2], [and] not only spend, but be spent [2 Cor 12:15]."[115] The third virtue Beddome listed was *patience*. He referred to the husbandman and the fisherman since they were presented in Scripture as metaphors of the minister (1 Cor 9:10; 2 Tim 2:6). This quality of patience was highlighted because of the difficulties and mistreatment that often accompanied the work of ministry. Such trials should not lead a minister to complain to God, be angry at others, or become overwhelmed with affliction.[116]

Beddome's fourth sub-point was that such patience was required because, similar to fishing, the success of ministry was precarious and uncertain. Sometimes the gospel made remarkable progress, such as when three thousand souls were added to the Jerusalem church on the day of Pentecost (Acts 2:31). On that occasion, fishing was done with a large net. More often, however, ministers employed "an angling rod" and saw people converted to Christ intermittently.[117] Beddome added, "The most faithful and zealous, the most skillful and industrious, are not always the most useful," citing the prophet Isaiah as an example of this principle.[118] While Beddome believed in the importance of usefulness and employing one's gifts for the advancement of Christ's kingdom, there was no direct correspondence between a minister's godliness and giftedness and the visible fruit of his ministry.[119] The theological conviction underlying Beddome's thinking here was that while ministers were the instrumental cause in the salvation of sinners, God was the efficient cause. Concerning the precarious nature of ministry, Beddome opined how some had been initially caught, but since the net or hook sometimes broke, certain persons escaped.[120]

---

115. Beddome, "Nature and Authority," in *SP*, 304.
116. Beddome, "Nature and Authority," in *SP*, 304–5.
117. Beddome, "Nature and Authority," in *SP*, 305.
118. Beddome, "Nature and Authority," in *SP*, 305.

119. Concerning the importance of usefulness, Beddome preached in another sermon, "Now, where much is given, much is required: a greater improvement is expected from the man who has five talents, than from him who is possessed of two [Matt 25:14–30]." This was in reference to the natural and mental capacities of a person. Speaking about a person's spiritual gifts later in the sermon, Beddome exhorted, "Where an extraordinary measure of faith, or any other grace is bestowed, eminent returns of service are required." Beddome, "Motives to Usefulness," in *TSD*, 1:89–90.

120. Beddome, "Nature and Authority," in *SP*, 305.

The final way Beddome compared the fisher of aquatic creatures and the fisher of souls was in the great change wrought in the catch. When fish were brought out of the water, they died, and so it was for those saved by the gospel—they died "to sin, the law, and the world."[121] Rather than living a life of sin, profaneness, and error that led to eternal death, Christians were those who had died to the governing power of sin, the condemning penalty of the law, and the ensnaring allure of the world. They had been made alive by the grace of God to live for him, and they had never been truly alive until they were caught in the net of the preaching of the gospel.[122]

The Pastor Is an Ambassador of God

In the sermon just considered, Beddome said ministers were to let down their nets at Christ's command and to "open the doctrines of the divine word, display its terrors, unfold its mysteries, and beseech men, in Christ's stead, to be reconciled to God."[123] That final phrase was drawn from 2 Cor 5:20, which served as the basis for the next discourse, "Reconciliation to God," which was Sermon 17 in *Twenty Short Discourses*.[124] There was no hymn affixed to this sermon. The topic of the sermon was the preaching of a minister and thus was likely delivered at an ordination service or a ministers' meeting. Beddome spoke of the kind of preaching through which pastors were to fish for men, to borrow the metaphor from "Nature and Authority." The outline for "Reconciliation to God" was simple: after a longer introduction, Beddome expounded on what ministers were to do, the manner in which ministers were to do it, and three truths gleaned from the discourse.

Beddome began the sermon by introducing the subject of reconciliation. He said, "Reconciliation . . . is a harder work than salvation." In reconciliation, there was enmity between two parties, and thus "it [was] more difficult to reconcile an enemy, than to save a friend." Beddome then distinguished between the state of reconciliation and reconciliation with respect to "the habitual frame and temper of mind." The former—taught in Rom 5:10—was brought about by Christ, whereas the latter—taught in 2 Cor 5:20—was "attempted by his ministers."[125] Since ministers were

---

121. Beddome, "Nature and Authority," in *SP*, 306.
122. Beddome, "Nature and Authority," in *SP*, 305–6.
123. Beddome, "Nature and Authority," in *SP*, 303.
124. Beddome, "Reconciliation to God," in *TSD*, 1:115–24.
125. Beddome, "Reconciliation to God," in *TSD*, 1:116. It should be noted that Paul had spoken of the state of reconciliation a few verses prior in 2 Cor 5:18–19: "And all things *are* of God, who hath reconciled us to himself by Jesus Christ, and hath given to

commissioned and authorized by Christ, they were his royal messengers and ambassadors. Ministers stood in Christ's place, and it was, in the words of Beddome, "as if he were personally present amongst us."[126] Thus, even though ministers may have considered themselves lowly and unworthy, they were nonetheless to be regarded as representatives of Christ.[127]

Beddome said "the chief business" of ambassadors was "to carry on the great work of reconciliation."[128] The work of the minister was to bring about this work of reconciliation, as Paul had by imploring the Corinthians to be reconciled to God.[129] In other situations where reconciliation was required, it was often the weaker party who sought peace. In the gospel, however, it was God who stooped down to the creature. Rather than crushing sinners in his righteous anger, God entreated them to surrender to his love.[130]

A further word on the roles of Christ and ministers in the work of reconciliation is helpful here. In another sermon, commenting on 2 Cor 5:18–19, Beddome said, "The word of reconciliation is committed to ministers, and by them it is dispensed; but the work of reconciling sinners unto God, belongs to Jesus only." Concerning the work of bringing sinners into a reconciled state, the Bourton pastor said, "Here our prayers and our tears have no influence; neither our own work, nor the work of the Holy Spirit on our hearts, contribute any thing toward making our peace with God. There is no admission to the divine favor, without a satisfaction to divine justice; and Christ made that satisfaction by his offering on the cross."[131] Sinners contributed nothing to the reconciling work of God through Christ on the cross, and neither did ministers. In the application of that reconciling work, however, ministers were involved through the proclamation of

---

us the ministry of reconciliation; To wit, that God was in Christ, reconciling the world unto himself, not imputing their trespasses unto them; and hath committed unto us the word of reconciliation" (KJV; emphasis original).

126. Beddome, "Reconciliation to God," in *TSD*, 1:116.

127. Beddome, "Reconciliation to God," in *TSD*, 1:116–17.

128. Beddome, "Reconciliation to God," in *TSD*, 1:117.

129. Montgomery wrote on Beddome's perspective on the modern question. The modern question was put forth in 1737 by Matthias Maurice, who asked "whether or not it was 'the duty of unconverted sinners, who hear the gospel, to believe in Christ." According to Montgomery, Beddome would have answered in the affirmative, claiming it was the duty of sinners to repent and believe in Christ. He said it was in "Reconciliation to God" where this teaching could be most clearly seen in Beddome's sermons. Montgomery, "Modern Question," 142–43, 167. For a full discussion on Beddome and the modern question, see Montgomery's dissertation: Montgomery, "Benjamin Beddome," 182–220.

130. Beddome, "Reconciliation to God," in *TSD*, 1:117.

131. Beddome, "Sermon 1," in *TSD*, 4:7.

the word of reconciliation. In other words, sinners needed to respond to the reconciling work of God in Christ, and it was ministers who implored humanity to be reconciled to God. Beddome also believed that the gospel was to be preached to all and sundry, against the High Calvinism of his day.[132] Commensurately, Beddome's hearers had a "duty" to respond to the gospel.[133] In the rest of "Reconciliation to God," Beddome elaborated on the content of this word of reconciliation and the way it was to be preached.

The Bourton pastor began, explaining that as ambassadors of Christ, ministers were to "not be silent but to speak [see Acts 18:9]." Since they represented Christ, he should be the dominant theme of their ministrations, study, and preaching. Since he was "the author of their ministry," he should be the content and reason for it. Christ was to be central because "in him all the doctrines of the gospel centre; to him all the invitations of it lead; by him all the promises of it are confirmed, and all the blessings of it bestowed."[134]

---

132. Concerning Beddome's perspective on this issue, Montgomery says, "Calling upon men under the sound of his voice to the duty of trusting in the saving mercy of God was part and parcel of the preaching of Beddome." Capturing the thought of High Calvinists, Montgomery continued, "This general call to trust in the mercy of Christ, freely offered in the gospel to all, was not characteristic of the preaching of high-Calvinism. Free offers of grace were frowned upon at best, if not openly denied." Montgomery, "Benjamin Beddome," 198.

133. Beddome, "Reconciliation to God," in *TSD*, 1:124. In the sermon, Beddome said, "We use no coercive measures; we do not endeavour to frighten, but to draw you to your duty." Commenting on this sentence, Montgomery says, "Beddome notes that we clearly have a 'duty' in this work," that is, of being reconciled. Montgomery, "Modern Question," 169. Montgomery also demonstrates how Beddome disagreed with a High Calvinist such as Joseph Hussey (1660–1726) on this issue. Commenting on the text that Beddome preached from in "Reconciliation to God," Hussey concluded that there was "no invitation [or] earnest exhortation to accept of Christ in the sinner's first reconciliation to him." Hussey, *God's Operations of Grace*, 322. See Montgomery, "Modern Question," 169.

134. Beddome, "Reconciliation to God," in *TSD*, 1:118. That Beddome preached in this manner was captured by Rippon in his obituary of the Bourton pastor: "In his preaching he laid Christ at the bottom of religion as the support of it, placed him at the top of it as its glory, and made him the centre of it, to unite all its parts, and to add beauty and vigour to the whole." Rippon, "Rev. Benjamin Beddome," 321. Rippon was simply quoting Beddome who, in his 1765 circular letter, wrote to the Midland Association thus:

> Look well, then, to the foundation upon which you are built, and seriously and frequently examine your state God-ward. See that you lay Christ at the bottom of your religion, as the support of it; that you place him at the top of it, as its glory; and that you make him the centre of it, to unite all its parts, and add beauty and vigour to the whole. Remember that growth in Christianity is growth in the knowledge of Christ. Seek that sorrow, that peace, that holiness, that establishment, which flow from Christ; let all your duties begin and end in Christ. (Beddome, *Circular Letter* [1765], 2)

Beddome proceeded to elaborate on the word of reconciliation. First, ambassadors of Christ were to proclaim the enmity of the human heart against God. The picture that Beddome painted with regard to humanity was bleak. The natural man desired to dethrone God and put him out of existence if it were possible. Every act of sin was a rebellion against God, and there was not an act of sin the carnal man would not commit. Humanity was unaware of such enmity in their hearts, either because they were imperceptive to the workings of their own hearts or they lived in the delusion that God did not exist.[135] The proclamation of this enmity of the human heart was needed because, as Beddome said in another place, "There can be no reconciliation, until we are convinced of our estrangement from him. The wound must be opened and searched before it can be healed, the disease must be felt before it can be cured. . . . Peace cannot enter the soul until it has been deeply penetrated with a sense of sin."[136]

Ministers also had the responsibility to teach. While the basis for reconciliation was laid in eternity, the actual reconciliation of sinners to God was brought about in time by the Spirit.[137] On God's part, he sent Christ into the world to fulfill the law and satisfy his justice. This had been completed, and the responsibility of sinners was merely to believe and rejoice in God's work. As it pertained to reconciliation on the part of the sinner, this work was "begun and completed by the grace of the Spirit."[138] It was the Holy Spirit who effectively worked to subdue the natural enmity in the human heart and granted the spiritual ability to see the beauty and loveliness of God. This resulted in a believer's willful submission to him as his faithful Sovereign and cleaving to God as his supreme good. Though he had been an enemy of God, the Christian was now a friend of God, and though he had been hostile to godly practices, he now found joy in them.[139] Those who had experienced this grace of the Spirit were distraught when they found evidence of the old man—such as coldness, indifference, or enmity—still subsisting. With a longing to be freed from such remnants of sin, Beddome ended this section by quoting Paul in Rom 7:24, "Oh wretched man that I am, who shall deliver me from the body of this death!"[140]

The third task of the minister in the work of reconciliation was to declare the necessity "of a further reconciliation in those already reconciled to

---

135. Beddome, "Reconciliation to God," in *TSD*, 1:118–19.
136. Beddome, "Sermon 13," in *SD*, 8:124.
137. Beddome, "Reconciliation to God," in *TSD*, 1:119.
138. Beddome, "Reconciliation to God," in *TSD*, 1:119.
139. Beddome, "Reconciliation to God," in *TSD*, 1:119–20.
140. Beddome, "Reconciliation to God," in *TSD*, 1:120.

God."[141] Beddome instructed preachers to press for deeper reconciliation in the hearts and lives of those who had already been reconciled; this interpretation leaned on the observation that the original hearers of the letter were addressed as "the church of God at Corinth, and the saints in all Achaia [2 Cor 1:1]."[142] Though Beddome believed Christians were already reconciled to God, in another sense, he deemed their reconciliation partial. Thus, further reconciling work was required, which would only be completed in glorification.[143] Beddome spoke of four ways that further reconciliation was needed in those already reconciled to God.

First, Christians needed to come to terms with the sovereignty of God, particularly in the salvation of sinners.[144] Moreover, believers must be reconciled to the providences of God since he acts purposefully with "some gracious end in view."[145] Then, since believers had vestiges of the old

---

141. Beddome, "Reconciliation to God," in *TSD*, 1:120. The notion that an already reconciled person needed to be further reconciled might sound puzzling. However, Beddome was picking up on the words of Paul, who said, "We pray you in Christ's stead, be ye reconciled to God" (2 Cor 5:20 KJV). The Bourton pastor observed that since the recipients were called the church and saints [cf. 1 Cor 1:1], Paul was speaking to an already reconciled group of people.

In contemporary scholarship, however, there is debate on whom Paul was addressing in 2 Cor 5:20. Murray J. Harris says the imperative could have been addressed to (1) unbelievers within, or associated with, the Corinthian church; (2) the Corinthian church, or at least to the subset who were antagonistic to Paul; or (3) any evangelistic audience. Harris prefers the third position. Harris, *Second Epistle to the Corinthians*, 447–48. Colin G. Kruse holds the second position—in Harris's schema—but concedes the language is evangelistic. He says,

> This may reflect the language of Paul's evangelistic preaching, but here the appeal is directed to members of the Corinthian church. Paul can hardly be implying that his audience had not yet responded to the gospel, for they had accepted the message he himself had brought to them. However, Paul's apostolic authority and gospel had been called into question in Corinth, and in succeeding passages he entreats his converts not to accept the grace of God in vain (6:1–13), but to open their hearts to their apostle (6:11–13; 7:2–4). It is perhaps by way of preparation for these appeals that Paul employs the language of evangelistic preaching here. (Kruse, 2 *Corinthians*, 172)

In his sermon, Beddome employed Paul's words in both an evangelistic manner—to declare the sinner's enmity against God, the distinction between the eternal plan of reconciliation and the effecting of it in time, and the terrors awaiting those who rejected the reconciliation of God—and a call to already reconciled believers to be further reconciled to God. Though, there was no sense that Beddome's hearers in Bourton were antagonistic to him as some of the Corinthians had been toward the apostle Paul.

142. Beddome, "Reconciliation to God," in *TSD*, 1:120.

143. Beddome, "Reconciliation to God," in *TSD*, 1:120.

144. Beddome, "Reconciliation to God," in *TSD*, 1:120–21.

145. Beddome, "Reconciliation to God," in *TSD*, 1:121. In another sermon, on Ps 148:14, Beddome said,

man, they needed to be further reconciled to God's requirements in his law. Beddome told his hearers—who struggled with sin and temptation—to seek acquaintance with God's law, "to have [their] temper conformed to it, and [their] actions determined by it."[146] Fourth, those in a reconciled state needed to be further reconciled to the gracious design and method of the gospel. The grace of God was contrary to the corrupted human nature, exceeded human understanding, and repugnant to the flesh. Thus, believers needed to be exhorted to embrace, defend, and, if necessary, be martyred for the sake of the gospel.[147]

The final task of the minister as an ambassador for God was to warn his hearers of the terrible judgment awaiting those who were unreconciled to God. Reconciliation needed to take place in this life and not in the next. Those who died in an unreconciled state would experience everlasting ruin. After death, there would be no opportunities for repentance, and ministers could not intercede for or preach to them. The divine attributes would operate against them, the law which they broke would condemn them, and the word of reconciliation would provide no comfort to those who died in an unreconciled state.[148]

Beddome here provided insight into his views on heaven and hell. Those who resided in heaven were happy in God. He said if those who rejected God could, theoretically, go to heaven, they would remain unhappy because they did not love God. Sarcastically, he quipped, "But depend upon it, he will never suffer you to make the trial!" There was no person who was forced to go to heaven. God would allow those who rejected and remained at enmity with him to fall into judgment, thereby easing "himself of his adversaries."[149] Though sinners were numb to their sinful enmity and guilt, they would be made perceptive of it in the life to come; their guilty consciences would gnaw at them for all eternity. Beddome quoted Stephen Charnock (1628–1680) who said, "The perfection of love in heaven . . . is a part of heaven's happiness; so the perfection," if it could be such called, "of

---

Let us be reconciled to those providences which tend to bring us near. The severest trials are often among the means which God employs to bring us to himself; and had it not been for them we might still have been afar off, and without hope [Eph 2:12–13]. Nor are we likely to be kept near without a similar discipline. Afflictions make us feel our need of mercy, and lead us to seek it. How often, when the Christian has departed from God, is he brought back by means of the rod! (Beddome, "Sermon 6," in *TSD*, 3:51)

146. Beddome, "Reconciliation to God," in *TSD*, 1:121.
147. Beddome, "Reconciliation to God," in *TSD*, 1:122.
148. Beddome, "Reconciliation to God," in *TSD*, 1:122.
149. Beddome, "Reconciliation to God," in *TSD*, 1:123.

enmity in hell, is a part of the misery of the damned."[150] Not wanting such a fate for his hearers, Beddome pled, "Think then, oh, think, how will you escape, if you neglect so great salvation! [Heb 2:3]."[151]

The second major heading of the sermon concerned the way ministers should speak to "sinners about their reconciliation to God."[152] First, all ministers, as ambassadors of Christ, were perfectly agreed as to the subject and aim of their ministrations, namely, their hearers' reconciliation to God. Moreover, those entrusted with the word of reconciliation were to preach "with warmth and affection." Beddome used the image of a preacher falling on his knees to plead with his hearers to be reconciled to God.[153] Third, since ministers were representatives of God, they were to speak with "spiritual power and authority." Last, gospel ministers did not coerce their hearers but rather sought to persuade them in meekness and gentleness.[154]

Beddome concluded the sermon with three applications. He highlighted the depravity of the human nature. Then, he spoke of the necessity of God to effect the conversion of a sinner, which he said, was "a greater miracle than the dividing of the sea . . . the casting down of the walls of Jericho, or raising the dead body of Lazarus." Finally, he commended Christ to whom all believers were indebted, for without him, there was no reconciliation, since it was his grace that had brought it about.[155]

The Pastor Is a Persuader of Men

The next sermon was Sermon 5 in the eighth volume of Beddome's discourses. It was based on 2 Cor 5:11, "Knowing therefore the terror of the Lord, we persuade men."[156] To the sermon was attached the hymn "The Giving of the Law."[157] The outline consisted of two main headings: the foundation of the gospel ministry and the object of the gospel ministry; this was followed by two inferences.

---

150. The quotation is found in Charnock, *Two Discourses*, 252–53. For the location of this source, I am indebted to Brady, "References to Other Writers."
151. Beddome, "Reconciliation to God," in *TSD*, 1:123.
152. Beddome, "Reconciliation to God," in *TSD*, 1:123.
153. Beddome, "Reconciliation to God," in *TSD*, 1:123.
154. Beddome, "Reconciliation to God," in *TSD*, 1:124.
155. Beddome, "Reconciliation to God," in *TSD*, 1:124.
156. The text quoted at the beginning of the sermon was 2 Cor 5:11, but the biblical reference was wrongly printed as 2 Cor 5:2. Beddome, "Sermon 5," in *SD*, 8:45.
157. Beddome, *Hymns*, #357.

Beddome asserted the importance of pastors having experiential knowledge of the truths they preached. Pastors who were personally comforted by the gospel could provide that same comfort to others (2 Cor 1:4). Since their task was to awaken careless and carnal Christians, ministers were also required to have acquaintance with "the terror and vengeance of the law."[158] It was acquaintance with "the terror of the Lord" that formed the basis for "the foundation of a gospel ministry," the first major heading of the discourse.[159]

Beddome began with the terror of the Lord because sinners needed to be made aware of their sin and danger before they would run to the gospel for salvation and refuge.[160] If gospel ministers were to "persuade their hearers to receive the gospel," they needed to be "well acquainted with their danger."[161] Beddome listed four ways a pastor could be acquainted with the terror of the Lord.

First, there was "the terror of his attributes." Though God was lovely, he was also dreadful. He was "a consuming fire [Deut 4:24; Heb 12:29], both to the persons of the wicked and to the sins of the righteous." As the omniscient and omnipresent one, God knew the conduct of every person, even those things done in secret, and he was able to "discern the thoughts and intentions of the heart [Heb 4:12]." No one could stand in his sight; thus even Job, a good and blameless man, was made to "abhor himself and repent in dust and ashes [Job 42:6]." Ministers needed to embrace the terror of his attributes since they were to warn sinners of danger and to urge "them to flee from the wrath to come [Matt 3:7]."[162]

Second, gospel ministers needed to be acquainted with "the terror of his threatenings." Such threatenings were, in a sense, akin to God's promises in that they signaled or predicted a future event.[163] If the prophet Habakkuk was alarmed by the impending destruction of the physical Jerusalem (Hab 3:16), how awful would be the eternal destruction awaiting those who rejected the gospel? Beddome was clear that the threatenings of destruction were not aimed at God's people, but such warnings should have induced a healthy fear for God and greater obedience to him. As for a minister, such warnings ought to have provoked a deeper concern for the sinners who

---

158. Beddome, "Sermon 5," in *SD*, 8:45.
159. Beddome, "Sermon 5," in *SD*, 8:45.
160. Beddome, "Sermon 5," in *SD*, 8:45–46.
161. Beddome, "Sermon 5," in *SD*, 8:46.
162. Beddome, "Sermon 5," in *SD*, 8:46.
163. Beddome, "Sermon 5," in *SD*, 8:46.

heard his preaching and more earnestness and animation in the pulpit to the degree he felt compassion for their awful plight.[164]

Moreover, a knowledge of the terror of the Lord included apprehension of "the terror of his rod." The Lord had the ability to punish the wicked and to discipline his own people.[165] God was able to humble the loftiest of men, "embitter [the] sweetest [of] comforts," and remove the most helpful counsel from friends.[166] Beddome brought up Paul as one who had been acquainted with the terror of the Lord's rod of discipline. The apostle underwent many perils, assaults, persecution, and threats, but was restored so he might more zealously and effectually persuade men and women to flee from the wrath to come and find refuge in Christ.[167]

Finally, Beddome said ministers needed to be acquainted with "the terror of the judgment day." This was chiefly in Paul's view in the broader context of 2 Cor 5. The Bourton pastor was particularly impassioned in this section. The day of judgment would be an awful day for the earth and much of humanity. He warned, "The sun shall be turned into darkness, and the moon into blood [Joel 2:31; Acts 2:20]; and all those things which now delight our eyes and engross our affections shall become heaps of ruin and desolation. . . . The meek, the lowly, the lovely Jesus will appear in all the majesty of a God; and to the wicked, with all the fury of an Avenger."[168] He then quoted Ps 50:3, Dan 7:9–10, and Mal 4:1 in succession to demonstrate the Old Testament witness to this great day of judgment.[169]

He then reproved sinners for their callousness. How could they hear such warnings and not be bothered to seek peace with God? The Bourton pastor also corrected ministers who were not moved by "the consideration [of judgment day] to become anxiously solicitous for the salvation of souls." Beddome lifted his voice to the congregation "like a trumpet" to show his hearers their sin and transgression. If they died and perished, having been warned of the danger, their blood would be on their own heads since Beddome had faithfully discharged his duty (Ezek 33:1–4; Acts 18:6).[170] Having expounded on the foundation of a gospel ministry, Beddome transitioned to the second heading: "The object of the gospel ministry."

---

164. Beddome, "Sermon 5," in *SD*, 8:47.
165. Beddome, "Sermon 5," in *SD*, 8:47.
166. Beddome, "Sermon 5," in *SD*, 8:47–48.
167. Beddome, "Sermon 5," in *SD*, 8:48.
168. Beddome, "Sermon 5," in *SD*, 8:48.
169. Beddome, "Sermon 5," in *SD*, 8:48–49.
170. Beddome, "Sermon 5," in *SD*, 8:49.

Beddome explained the constitution of man and what that meant for preaching. Human beings, as creatures endowed with "reason and understanding," had the capacity to be persuaded, though God needed to make the "motives effectual." Concerning a pastor's labor, Beddome said, "The word 'persuade' is very expressive of the work of a gospel minister."[171] Therefore, ministers should not resort to "external force or violence" since men and women would become Christians "not by coercion, but conviction."[172]

For a minister to persuade, he needed to aim his preaching at the understanding and not the emotions. Beddome warned that the stimulation of emotions, without understanding, was fleeting and impermanent. The Bourton pastor turned to the example of Paul, who reasoned out of the Scriptures and put forth evidence that Jesus was the Christ (Acts 17:2–3). By emphasizing the understanding, Beddome was not suggesting pastors deliver dispassionate discourses since the apostle felt the truths he preached.[173] Certainly, Paul made "his appeal to the heart," but it was "founded on evidence presented to the understanding."[174] To clarify how an emphasis on the understanding was not dispassionate, Beddome listed three elements required in the work of "persuasion": warm affection for the hearers in addressing eternal matters, earnest and passionate manner of speaking,[175] and persistence and a willingness to use various methods. Concerning the last element, Beddome said, "If one argument will not prevail, we must try another."[176]

Having described the nature and characteristics of persuasion in gospel ministry, Beddome laid out the content of the preaching. First, a minister needed to persuade their hearers "of their guilt and danger." God's Word was at the minister's disposal because it was directed against the ungodly and impenitent. On the day of judgment, neither an honorable reputation nor a claim to religion would be advantageous. Like John the Baptist, preachers

---

171. Beddome, "Sermon 5," in *SD*, 8:49.

172. Beddome, "Sermon 5," in *SD*, 8:49.

173. Beddome, "Sermon 5," in *SD*, 8:49–50.

174. Beddome, "Sermon 5," in *SD*, 8:50.

175. Beddome said, "To persuade men supposes earnestness of expression. Hence the apostle varies the phrase, and sometimes uses the word beseech," as Paul did in 2 Cor 5:20. Beddome, "Sermon 5," in *SD*, 8:50. As noted above, 2 Cor 5:20 was the text for the sermon Beddome, "Reconciliation to God," *TSD*, 1:116–24.

176. Beddome, "Sermon 5," in *SD*, 8:50–51. In his sermon "Heavenly Stranger Received," Beddome said of ministers, "Knowing the terrors of the Lord, they persuade men, and use every means to fix conviction upon their hearts; urging every motive, and addressing every passion of the human mind, to bring them to serious reflection and concern about their eternal interests." Beddome, "Heavenly Stranger Received," in *TSD*, 2:39.

were to employ striking words to warn sinners of the impending judgment.[177] Hearers would never come to Christ unless they were convicted of sin, and thus to strike the conscience through "the terrors of the law [was] the first work of the gospel minister."[178]

Furthermore, ministers were to hold forth Christ as "the remedy" and "way of escape." Specific warnings were to be issued to people in different spiritual states. The *awakened* should not flee to false refuges or delay embracing Christ. *Enquirers* were to be warned "against depending on uncovenanted mercy." There was a temptation for enquirers to place their assurance of conversion in their sense of guilt, rather than in Christ the Mediator. *Sinners* needed to be persuaded against despondency through invitations of the gospel, promises of divine assistance and acceptance, and examples of mercy toward the vilest sinners. Most of all, the gospel minister was to "hold forth Christ," his character, threefold office, and atoning blood. Christ could "soften the hardest heart," and he could subdue the most obstinate will.[179] He was "able to save to the uttermost all that [came] unto God by him (Heb 7:25)," and this was enough to silence the objections of the human heart—based on a sense of "their guilt and unworthiness"—to come to him.[180]

In third place, ministers were to preach to Christians. Though they had taken refuge in Christ, believers needed to be persuaded to gratitude and obedience if they were to continue in "their present happy state." Beddome's church members were to live in a way that pleased the Lord by denying ungodliness and pursuing righteousness. The motivation for this behavior could be found in the gospel itself. If they were currently in a peaceful frame of mind, Christians were to fight future sin and temptation by "their past terrors." By this, Beddome was instructing his hearers to invoke the terrors of the law and judgment—which they had been relieved of—to battle sins and temptations that would arise in the future. Believers could exchange the fear a slave had for his master for the fear a son had for his father. They were to evidence their religion with a righteous life and persevere to the end. Christians were to draw others to the gospel, by their life and instruction, so that outsiders would be constrained to say, as in the prophecy of Zechariah, "We also will go with you, for we have heard that God is with you (Zech 8:23)."[181]

---

177. Beddome, "Sermon 5," in *SD*, 8:51.
178. Beddome, "Sermon 5," in *SD*, 8:51–52.
179. Beddome, "Sermon 5," in *SD*, 8:52–53.
180. Beddome, "Sermon 5," in *SD*, 8:53.
181. Beddome, "Sermon 5," in *SD*, 8:53.

Beddome concluded the sermon with two inferences. The first was that men who had not experienced the gospel were unfit to be ministers since that would be like the blind leading the blind, with the result of both falling into the ditch (Matt 15:14).[182] The second inference gives insight into how Beddome viewed the dynamic between the role of the minister and that of God in the conversion of sinners. He said, "All that ministers can do is to persuade; God must do the rest. Without his efficacious influence, all the force of reasoning, and all the charms of eloquence will be lost."[183] This, of course, was a fitting end to a sermon that strongly emphasized and elucidated the responsibility of a minister to persuade men to believe in the gospel.

The Pastor Is a Promoter of Joy

The final sermon concerning the duty of ministers is "On the Duty of Ministers to Promote Their People's Joy." It was Sermon 52 in *Sermons Printed* and based on 2 Cor 1:24, "Not that we have dominion over your faith, but are helpers of your joy." The hymn affixed was "Life of His People," though there were some variations in the version attached to the sermon.[184] As customary, Beddome took his outline from the constituent parts of the verse. The headings for this sermon were the character of the minister stated negatively, then positively. He also included two concluding thoughts.

The first major heading of the sermon was the "negative character" of the minister. By this, Beddome was not speaking of some deficient qualities in a pastor but rather defining what a pastor was not. The phrase "Not that we have dominion over your faith" could have referred to the subjective faith exercised by individuals. In this sense, pastors had no dominion over their people's faith. Though ministers explained the object, nature, and necessity of faith, they could not produce it.[185] This conviction was aligned

---

182. Beddome, "Sermon 5," in *SD*, 8:53–54.

183. Beddome, "Sermon 5," in *SD*, 8:54.

184. Beddome, *Hymns*, #104. Here is a brief comparison of the two versions of the hymns. Stanza 1 was nearly identical, with a minor difference in line 3. Stanza 2 has lines 1/2 swapped out with lines 3/4, with a few pronoun changes from first person to third person in the version in *SP*. Stanza 3 of the version in *Hymns* is missing from the version in *SP*. Stanza 4 has similar concepts but divergent wording: in the *Hymns* version, Beddome wrote about daily grace and living to God's glory in this life, whereas in the *SP* version, he wrote of pardoning grace and the hope of glory to reign with God in the future.

185. Beddome said, "The most masterly reasonings, the most flowing eloquence, and the most pathetic expostulations, will not avail to the putting forth of any act of faith without a divine influence." Beddome, "Duty of Ministers," in *SP*, 356.

with Beddome's thinking considered thus far—for instance, pastors were called to persuade, but God needed to work in the heart to effectually call a man to Christ. Even the measure of faith, said Beddome, was according to the divine will. If pastors had the power to dispense faith, then all his hearers would "[be] not only believers, but strong believers."[186]

The sense of faith employed in the verse, however, was not the subjective faith of individual Christians but rather the doctrines of the faith. With respect to doctrine, ministers did not have the authority to propose "new articles of faith" or to bind men's consciences on matters the Scriptures did not speak to.[187] Ministers were allowed to hold "private judgments"; they were not permitted, though, to teach these judgments as law.[188] If they were to impose their preferences upon the congregation, they were to do so "with meekness and modesty, and not with heat and violence." Beddome cited the examples of the apostles and the Lord Jesus as men who, though possessing certain knowledge, encouraged their hearers to use their minds in discerning truth.[189]

To ensure that his hearers understood him rightly, Beddome provided three situations in which the principle of private judgment was not violated. First, a person was permitted to persuade others of what he thought to be the truth. However, this needed to be accomplished without corruption, deceit, or coercion because of the free agency of human beings and the way Christianity was designed.[190] Moreover, it was not a violation of private judgment for a man to impose certain rules in his sphere. Beddome gave the example of a man prescribing a particular form of family worship and requiring those in his home to attend.[191] Third, Beddome spoke of religious societies, or local churches. It was permissible for a local church to require a person to adhere to a confession of beliefs prior to admitting him into membership.[192] This was necessary for the local church to praise God with

---

186. Beddome, "Duty of Ministers," in *SP*, 356.
187. Beddome, "Duty of Ministers," in *SP*, 356.
188. Beddome, "Duty of Ministers," in *SP*, 356–57.
189. Beddome, "Duty of Ministers," in *SP*, 357.
190. Beddome, "Duty of Ministers," in *SP*, 357.
191. Beddome, "Duty of Ministers," in *SP*, 357.
192. Though Beddome changed his position on communion during his pastorate in Bourton, here, he was arguing for a closed communion position. Peter Naylor remarks that Beddome held to a closed communion view in his earlier years at Bourton, and this was evidenced in the respective sections in his catechism. Naylor observed, "But in later years Beddome shifted his position, his assistant, William Wilkins, appointed in 1777, introducing to the Lord's Table some who had been sprinkled in infancy." Naylor, *Calvinism, Communion*, 54.

one voice (Rom 15:6). Even in this, however, force and punishment were to be avoided, though the community could rightly exclude those who may have posed a threat to its witness or unity.[193]

The second heading for the sermon was the minister's "positive character," based on the latter half of the verse: "But are helpers of your joy." Beddome compared the Christian's joy with the varied ingredient perfume of the Old Testament Law (Exod 32:23-24, 34-35). Joy consisted of contentment in one's circumstances, longsuffering amid trials, a clean conscience, and a hopeful trust in God. When these qualities existed in abundance, joy increased, whereas when they decreased in the believer, so did his joy. Since joy was a fruit of the Spirit (Gal 5:22), "ministers [were] not the authors of [believers'] joy" but rather "helpers of it."[194] Beddome proceeded to give two sub-headings describing the various aspects of joy and an explanation of how the minister promoted joy.

The first sub-heading described four aspects of joy. First, joy came from contemplation upon: the being, attributes, works, and promises of God; "the unparalleled love and loveliness of the Lord Jesus Christ," his person, humiliation, and exaltation; and "the beauties of holiness," and the advantages of a pious life, both in this age and in the age to come.[195] To underscore the advantages of meditation, Beddome cited Augustine of Hippo thus: "'Lord,' saith St. Austin, 'the more I meditate on thee, the sweeter thou art to me.'"[196] Next, joy came from reflection upon what God had done in the believer's life. In every true believer, it was God who had wrought change, outwardly and inwardly. Beddome explained that the Christian need not look about the earth for happiness because of the gracious and good change that God

---

193. Beddome, "Duty of Ministers," in *SP*, 358.

194. Beddome, "Duty of Ministers," in *SP*, 358.

195. Beddome, "Duty of Ministers," in *SP*, 358-59.

196. Beddome, "Duty of Ministers," in *SP*, 359. The author could not find the quotation in Augustine's writings. However, an almost exact rendering is found in Thomas Brooks, who wrote, "Lord! saith Austin, the more I meditate on thee, the sweeter thou art to me." Brooks, "Epistle Dedicatory," 291. Given the similitude between Brooks and Beddome, the latter was likely depending on the former. For the sake of clarity, the Thomas Brooks in question was the seventeenth-century English Puritan; he should not be confused with a later Thomas Brooks who features prominently in this book since he pastored the Bourton church and wrote its history in the nineteenth century.

had worked in his own heart. This, he clarified, was not "inconsistent with rejoicing in Christ, and having no confidence in the flesh [Phil 3:3]."[197]

Third, joy arose from the spiritual blessings a believer possessed, such as God's goodwill, a good reputation in society, and—borrowing the dominical words spoken to Martha—"that good part that shall never be taken from him" (Luke 10:42).[198] Because he had "inward peace, and a good hope through grace," the believer "would be happy [even] if all the world about him was miserable."[199] Last, true believers experienced joy in the prospect of the future, even though they may have been "poor, tempted, afflicted, or deserted" in the present. Though they experienced trials without and imperfections within, believers were already partakers of grace and on their way to glory. Every instance of divine blessing was an installment of the fullness of blessings to come in the eschaton.[200] Even if they experienced little of such favor now, believers had "enough in reversion," that is, the right to inherit the divine favor in the future. There was coming a day for believers when "their happiness [would] be unalloyed, uninterrupted, and everlasting."[201] These gems of truth were in the arsenal of ministers who were the promoters of the joy of their people.

Under the second sub-heading, Beddome explained three ways how the minister could promote the joy of his people. First, a pastor could promote his people's joy through preaching. The main work of a pastor was to proclaim Christ, "the way of pardon and reconciliation . . . through him," and to present him as "a complete and all-sufficient Saviour." Beddome also spoke of the minister's responsibility "to reveal the Spirit in all his operations."[202] By this, he referred to the work of the Spirit in the application of redemption. The minister was to continually depend upon the Spirit and explain "the covenant of grace, and promises of the divine word."[203]

There were many instances in ministry, though, where preaching would not go far enough. The second way a pastor could promote joy was through "private counsels and instructions." At times, there were obstructions to his people's joy that ministers needed to remove. This was more effective in personal conversations than from the pulpit since a minister

---

197. Beddome, "Duty of Ministers," in *SP*, 359.

198. In the Lukan account, of course, the Lord says *of Mary* that she "hath chosen that good part, which shall not be taken away from *her*" (Luke 10:42 KJV; emphasis added).

199. Beddome, "Duty of Ministers," in *SP*, 359.

200. Beddome, "Duty of Ministers," in *SP*, 359–60.

201. Beddome, "Duty of Ministers," in *SP*, 360.

202. Beddome, "Duty of Ministers," in *SP*, 360.

203. Beddome, "Duty of Ministers," in *SP*, 360.

could address fears and take note of spiritual decline among his people.[204] Last, Beddome remarked, "The most forcible way of instruction" was by the example of the minister. As a pastor walked with his people, it would comfort and sharpen his people, since "iron sharpens iron, so the countenance of a man his friend [Prov 27:17]."[205]

THE MOTIVATIONS OF A PASTOR

In the second chapter of this book, the motivations of a pastor according to eighteenth-century English Particular Baptists were considered. In that section, attention was given to the encouragements for the arduous work of ministry and the promise that a watchful minister would save both himself and his hearers (1 Tim 4:16). In the present chapter, motivation refers to the sources of joy in ministry and are derived from the sermon, "On the Sources of Ministerial Delight." In this discourse, Beddome preached on 1 Thess 2:20, "Ye are our glory and joy." The Bourton pastor began thus: "Glory is one of the greatest, and joy one of the sweetest, words in any language."[206] Beddome remarked how the words "glory" and "joy" particularly applied to the Thessalonian church, which Paul had planted, but also that they could be applied to any faithful church.[207] He preached, "Happy the minister who can say this; happy the people concerning whom it may be said!"[208] Furthermore, these words could be said of an entire church or to particular individuals within it, and these categories served as the outline for the rest of the sermon.

Beddome enumerated six ways that an entire church could be the "glory and joy" of a minister.[209] First, a church could be reckoned as such when it consisted of those who had been converted and gave themselves to the Lord.[210] Second, a minister could glory and take joy in the church when it was increasing in numbers.[211] Though it was God who added to the church, ministers could rejoice when they saw "the lost sheep found, and

---

204. Beddome, "Duty of Ministers," in *SP*, 360–61.
205. Beddome, "Duty of Ministers," in *SP*, 361.
206. Beddome, "Sources of Ministerial Delight," in *SP*, 260.
207. Beddome, "Sources of Ministerial Delight," in *SP*, 261–62.
208. Beddome, "Sources of Ministerial Delight," in *SP*, 262.
209. The six ways in which a church could be the minister's glory and joy, admittedly, could have been placed in the section on the duties of a church. Since, however, the sermon addressed the joys of *the minister*, its explanation is included here.
210. Beddome, "Sources of Ministerial Delight," in *SP*, 262.
211. Beddome, "Sources of Ministerial Delight," in *SP*, 262.

the dead son made alive [Luke 15:6, 32]."²¹² Then, Beddome spoke of how "the purity of principles of the church [was] also a matter of joy to faithful ministers." By this, he meant the church's unity in and commitment to the truth.²¹³ Fourth, Beddome praised the strictness of discipline in a church. Christ invested the church with his authority to exclude scandalous people and to dismiss the heterodox. When the church exercised this authority, happy was its minister.²¹⁴

The internal peace and unity of a church was the fifth way a church could be a minister's glory and joy. Such qualities brought the pastor comfort and satisfaction.²¹⁵ These qualities existed among the Thessalonians to a considerable degree. Timothy gave a good report of the church at Thessalonica concerning their faith in the Lord Jesus and of their love and affection toward one another (1 Thess 3:6). Beddome also cited Ps 133:1 to extol unity in the church: "Behold, how good, how pleasant a thing it is for brethren thus to dwell together in unity!"²¹⁶ Last, ministers were comforted as their churches were characterized by holiness and circumspection rather than immorality and carelessness.²¹⁷ This principle was demonstrated in Paul's confidence that the Thessalonians walked in his commands (2 Thess 3:4) and the apostle John's rejoicing that his children walked in the truth (3 John 3–4).²¹⁸ The lowly Christian who was "tenderhearted," trembled at God's Word (Isa 66:2), and was watchful over his life caused the minister more joy than the showy profession of hypocrites whose lives were devoid of grace and good works.²¹⁹

The Bourton pastor proceeded to talk about four ways that individual Christians were the "glory and joy" of ministers. First, ministers rejoiced at the "first awakening" of converts. In a somewhat paradoxical manner, ministers rejoiced as a person was brought to a state of godly sorrow, since

---

212. Beddome, "Sources of Ministerial Delight," in *SP*, 263.
213. Beddome, "Sources of Ministerial Delight," in *SP*, 263.
214. Beddome, "Sources of Ministerial Delight," in *SP*, 263.
215. Beddome, "Sources of Ministerial Delight," in *SP*, 263.
216. Beddome, "Sources of Ministerial Delight," in *SP*, 264.
217. Beddome, "Sources of Ministerial Delight," in *SP*, 264.
218. Beddome, "Sources of Ministerial Delight," in *SP*, 264.

219. Beddome, "Sources of Ministerial Delight," in *SP*, 264. Beddome was quoting an anonymous author; the full quotation is,"'The church' says one, 'is more honoured, and ministers more rejoiced, by the conduct of one poor, meek, tenderhearted Christian, who trembles at God's word [Isa 66:2], and maintains a constant watch over his heart and actions, than by all the splendid professions of the artful hypocrite, whose knowledge is unattended with grace, and whose life is barren of good works.'" Quoted in Beddome, "Sources of Ministerial Delight," in *SP*, 264.

that led to his salvation. Such was the case when three thousand people were pierced to the heart and responded to Peter's sermon on the day of Pentecost (Acts 2:37–41).[220] This theme was expanded in "The Happy Results of Repentance," in which Beddome said,

> Ministers often rejoice at the sorrow of others. They are first the means of making them sorrowful, by showing them the sinfulness of their ways, and exhibiting the terrible judgments of God against their evil doings. And when sinners are roused of their carnal security, and excited to flee from the wrath to come, and saints are quickened, then faithful ministers ... rejoice.[221]

Second, joy was brought to a minister when a person was espoused to Christ. This necessarily proceeded from the previous point concerning the sinner's awakening. Ministers rejoiced at the breaking in of comfort for Christ's sake since his purposes were fulfilled and sufferings rewarded; they rejoiced on their people's account since they saw anew the worth of their souls; and they rejoiced for their own sakes because conversions were "fresh seals" upon their ministry and signs of "divine approbation."[222] Beddome cited Barnabas and John the Baptist as positive examples of ministerial rejoicing. Barnabas was glad to see the grace of God at Antioch and was not envious of other instruments God had used (Acts 11:20–24).[223] In the case of the Baptist, he rejoiced that he and others had heard the voice of the Bridegroom (John 3:29).[224] Moreover, these awakened converts would be the "glory and joy" of their minister as they walked circumspectly and in a manner that adorned their profession. The spiritual stability of his people was the source of the minister's happiness and strength. The conscientious

---

220. Beddome, "Sources of Ministerial Delight," in *SP*, 265.

221. Beddome, "Happy Results of Repentance," in *SP*, 136. In this sermon, Beddome referred to the results of Peter's preaching at Pentecost as the cause for much thanksgiving, evidently due to the three thousand hearts that were pricked that day.

222. Beddome, "Sources of Ministerial Delight," in *SP*, 265–66.

223. Beddome, "Sources of Ministerial Delight," in *SP*, 266. Beddome said in another sermon,

> Barnabas was only a visitor at Antioch, and had not been the instrument of this great work; it was effected chiefly by the preaching of the men of Cyprus and Cyrene; yet he rejoices in it, and afterwards abides with them, and much people were still added unto the Lord [Acts 11:20–24]. He rejoiced on their account who had received the grace of God, on his account who bestowed it, and also on his own account, as affording a prospect of success in his future labours among them. (Beddome, "Sermon 9," in *TSD*, 3:121)

224. Beddome, "Sources of Ministerial Delight," in *SP*, 266.

and godly person—regardless of her circumstances or mental capacities—brought joy to a minister.[225]

Last, Beddome preached that true converts would be the "glory and joy" of their ministers on judgment day. Beddome quoted 2 Cor 1:14—"We are your rejoicing, even as ye also are ours in the day of the Lord Jesus"—to demonstrate that a minister and his people would mutually rejoice over each other on the last day.[226] From the perspective of a minister, as his people were "won to Christ by his ministry, and kept faithful to the end," it would be demonstrated that he had neither run nor labored in vain (Phil 2:16). The people he had sought to "feed, guide, and watch over" in this life would be his joy and crown on that day (1 Thess 2:19).[227]

THE DUTY OF A CHURCH TOWARD ITS PASTOR

In four of the addresses identified as ordination sermons, Beddome gave applications to his hearers. These practical remarks, or inferences, provide the Bourton pastor's views on the duties of the church toward its minister. Each sermon will be considered in turn.

In the conclusion to his sermon "On the Sources of Ministerial Delight," Beddome addressed both sinners and saints. Beddome first rebuked the unconverted in the congregation for being the cause of their minister's grief rather than his joy. Such people caused weeping in the minister in his intercessions for them and trembling as he conceived of the day of judgment, at which he would need to witness against his hearers. Human nature was such that while sinners could be allured toward sin and hell by Satan,

---

225. Beddome, "Sources of Ministerial Delight," in *SP*, 266.

226. Beddome, "Sources of Ministerial Delight," in *SP*, 266–67.

227. Beddome, "Sources of Ministerial Delight," in *SP*, 267. An eschatological understanding of ministry could also be seen in one of Beddome's ordination hymns, where he wrote,

> The Shepherd soon will come,
> To whom the sheep belong;
> Oh may you then with joy appear,
> Amidst the happy throng.

> He Lord of all below,
> His heritage will claim;
> Will bless the steward, faithful found,
> His honours loud proclaim.

> He on his head shall place
> A bright unfading crown,
> And then before assembled worlds,
> Will he his servant own. (Beddome, *Hymns*, #735)

ministers did not have the capacity to draw them to God and heaven.[228] Then, Beddome exhorted the saints to give thanks to God for having turned them away from sin and destruction and caused them to be "the glory and joy of [their] ministers."[229] It was their "conversion, comfort, and establishment" that would be a joy to their ministers and, even more, to themselves. As the saints increased in "gifts, graces, and usefulness," they fulfilled the joy of their ministers. The Bourton pastor spoke of ministers being prey to despondency due to the remnant corruptions in their own hearts and the difficulty of ministerial work. The church could encourage its pastor by praying for and loving him. Particularly by living in a godly and upright manner, the church could strengthen its pastor and ensure that his present sorrows would be mingled with pleasures.[230]

Beddome also spoke of the importance of the church praying for its minister in "Christ the Subject of Prayer." The Cotswold minister said, "It is certainly our duty to pray for our ministers; and their wants require it . . . and it is but a grateful return for the pains and the labour they bestow upon us."[231] He explained that when a church prayed for its pastor, it was acting in its own interest since a pastor's increase in abilities would result in the comfort and building up of the church. Increased help through prayer or any other means by the church would result in greater usefulness of the pastor.[232] Beddome said in another sermon, "A prayerless people, and an unsuccessful ministry generally go together."[233]

---

228. Beddome, "Sources of Ministerial Delight," in *SP*, 267.
229. Beddome, "Sources of Ministerial Delight," in *SP*, 267–68.
230. Beddome, "Sources of Ministerial Delight," in *SP*, 268.
231. Beddome, "Christ the Subject," in *SP*, 240–41.
232. Beddome, "Christ the Subject," in *SP*, 241.
233. Beddome, "Sermon 8," in *TSD*, 4:64. In one of his hymns, Beddome captured the kind of prayer a church should utter on behalf of its pastor:

> Father of mercies, bow thine ear,
> Attentive to our earnest prayer;
> We plead for those who plead for these,
> Successful pleaders may they be! . . .
>
> Clothe thou with energy divine
> Their words, and let those words be thine;
> To them thy sacred truth reveal,
> Suppress their fear, enflame their zeal.
>
> Teach them aright to sow the seed,
> Teach them thy chosen flock to feed;
> Team them immortal souls to gain,
> Nor let them labour, Lord, in vain. (Beddome, *Hymns*, #700)

In the next ordination sermon, "Ministerial Subordination to Christ," after establishing that the Baptist was a vastly inferior light to Christ, Beddome gave two inferences. First, he reminded his hearers that even the most trained, experienced, popular, and successful ministers were not *the* light. That title, of course, belonged only to the Lord Jesus, and so the church should "not ascribe to any man more than is his due."[234] Second, any church would be wise to look from their pastor to Christ, "from the lesser to the greater light" who would become a light in us and, as Paul said, "Christ in you . . . the hope of glory [Col 1:27]."[235]

Building on the fishing metaphor, Beddome gave three practical remarks in the conclusion to "The Nature and Authority of the Christian Ministry" and began each with a question. Though the first two remarks did not address the duty of churches toward their pastors, they will be included here, nonetheless. First, he rhetorically asked, "Are they fishers?" Given that such was their office, ministers were not to be prideful concerning it. Ministers were exhorted to help one another, lacking envy and disdain for other ministers, praying for and encouraging them instead.[236] Second, Beddome asked, "Are they fishers of men?" Since ministers were engaged in catching men, theirs was a dignified and important work. Since the people with whom they dealt would exist eternally, ministers needed to "exert themselves to the utmost" and have compassion for the lost condition of sinners.[237]

Third, he asked, "Are they fishers of men, and does Christ make them so?" Their office as the fisher of men required a church to properly value its minister. Since they were but *fishermen*, they were not to be overvalued; yet, because they were the fisher *of men*, they were not to be undervalued.[238] When ministers were properly esteemed, it was on account of their office and not their person. Since God had used their minister to catch them in "the gospel-net," the church ought to appropriately value and esteem him.[239]

---

234. Beddome, "Ministerial Subordination to Christ," in *SP*, 272.

235. Beddome, "Ministerial Subordination to Christ," in *SP*, 272–73.

236. Beddome, "Nature and Authority," in *SP*, 308.

237. Beddome, "Nature and Authority," in *SP*, 308–9.

238. In "Danger and Sin of Idolatry," Beddome spoke of how "young converts, and imprudent professors" were prone to idolize their ministers, "expecting too much from them, and ascribing too much to them." Such wrongheadedness stemmed from a failure to understand that God was the one who gave the success in ministry. The Bourton pastor brought up the examples of Paul, Apollos, and Cephas who, he said, "were three of the best preachers that ever lived upon earth, yet were not the authors, but only the means, made use of by God for their conversion and salvation." Beddome, "Danger and Sin," in *SP*, 391.

239. In another sermon, Beddome said, "It teaches us especially to cherish a high esteem for the ministers of Christ, and to love and honour them for their work [sic] sake." Beddome, "Sermon 12," in *TSD*, 5:100. Cf. Beddome, "Sermon 4," in *TSD*, 6:34–35.

Failure to do so would weaken his hands; to do so excessively, however, would grieve the heart of the minister and God alike. Even the minister was to be aware of the source of his strength, namely Christ, so "that the excellency of praise might be to him also." In this final practical remark, the Bourton pastor briefly mentioned the cheerful financial support of its minister as one of the church's duties.[240]

In the ordination sermon "On the Duty of Ministers to Promote Their People's Joy," the Bourton pastor provided two concluding remarks. The first was brief and said that churches should not seek to have dominion over the faith of their ministers.[241] Second, since ministers were "helpers of their people's joy," Beddome exhorted the church to share burdens with their pastors during times of distress. On the part of the minister, he was to welcome this from his people and not do anything to discourage it.[242] Beddome concluded this section and the sermon by appealing to his "brethren in the ministry." He issued a warning from Ezekiel's prophecy that God was against shepherds who failed to heal the sick, bind up the broken, and gather the scattered sheep. God would hold his ministers accountable for how they cared for his people.[243] Contrary to the false shepherds, the Lord Jesus, the Great Shepherd, "gathers the lambs with his arm, and carries them in his bosom," providing a model for his under-shepherds to imitate.[244] "A tender heart," said Beddome, "is as necessary a qualification for a minister as a clear head."[245]

---

240. Beddome, "Nature and Authority," in *SP*, 309. Beddome preached elsewhere on Matt 22:21, which says, "And [render] unto God the things that are God's." In the sermon, he exhorted his hearers to render various aspects of themselves to God. In the section on rendering to wealth to God, Beddome said, "We should honour him with our substance, and devote a considerable part of our worldly estate to works of piety and charity. His interest should be supported, his ministers maintained, and his poor provided for by us according to our ability." Beddome, "Entire Surrender to God," in *SP*, 254.

241. Beddome, "Duty of Ministers," in *SP*, 361.

242. Beddome said something similar in another sermon: "Let us now inquire, Are we those who fear God? Manage this inquiry with caution, pursue it with diligence, crave the help of your ministers, but above all, beg the divine assistance." Beddome, "Fear of God," in *SP*, 213.

243. Beddome, "Duty of Ministers," in *SP*, 361.

244. Beddome, "Duty of Ministers," in *SP*, 361–62.

245. Beddome, "Duty of Ministers," in *SP*, 362.

THE DUTY OF A CHURCH TOWARD THE PREACHING

When considering Beddome's thoughts concerning the duties of a pastor, preaching featured prominently. According to Beddome, preaching was a central aspect of the minister's work, and through preaching, God nourished the flock and established his people in their faith.[246] In the chapter on the pastoral theology of the denomination to which Beddome belonged, it was observed that the pastor's duties were mirrored by those of the church. Since preaching was an important aspect of the pastor's duties, the proper reception of that preaching by the church would be an important element of their duties as well. This is also what we find also in the sermons of the Bourton pastor. In what follows, two sermons will be considered that address the church's duty with respect to the preaching of the Word.

The first sermon was based on the phrase "Consider what I say," from 2 Tim 2:7. The basic premise was that hearers ought to seriously consider what they heard so that they would be spiritually benefited and the preaching would not be in vain. The discourse contained two headings and some applications. The hymn attached to the sermon was "Impenitence Deplored."[247]

Under the first heading, Beddome gave four ways in which hearers were to hear the Word. First, hearers were exhorted to "consider well the matter or import of what [was] spoken."[248] Beddome spoke against the practice of listening to a sermon until some obstacle was reached—such as an offensive statement, careless remark, or contrarian view—and then rejecting the sermon as a result.[249] Second, hearers were to evaluate and discern "the truth and propriety" of what was preached. Beddome upheld the Bereans of the book of Acts as a positive example since it was their custom "to search the scriptures daily, whether these things be so or not [Acts 17:11]." What the preacher said needed to accord with the Scriptures, which was "the unerring word." Beddome also exhorted his hearers to exercise "the right of private judgment," which was too often being neglected.[250]

---

246. Beddome wrote in a hymn, from which the title of this book is derived, "Long may thy servant feed they sheep, / And lead them to the pastures fair." Beddome, *Hymns*, #663. He said in a sermon, "Every Christian will die safely; but the established Christian dies joyfully and triumphantly. In a word, this is the perfection of religion, the end of divine providences and ordinances; that for which ministers preach, and you hear." Beddome, "Gracious Character," in *SP*, 162.

247. Beddome, *Hymns*, #470.

248. Beddome, "Sermon 1," in *TSD*, 3:1.

249. Beddome, "Sermon 1," in *TSD*, 3:2.

250. Beddome, "Sermon 1," in *TSD*, 3:2.

Then, the Bourton pastor instructed his hearers to "consider the weight and importance" of what they heard. The truths which pertained to salvation were the most significant and, thus, should have received the most attention. Beddome said, "Hearing the word is a divine ordinance, and the manner of hearing should correspond with its end and design; and this is not to gratify our curiosity, nor merely to inform the understanding, but to purify our hearts and regulate our lives."[251] If sinners failed to respond to the gospel and be saved, preaching would only "justify and aggravate [their] condemnation."[252] Last, hearers were to consider how the truths applied to them individually.[253] Beddome asserted, "The minister is as much addressing himself to every particular person in the assembly, as if there were only one individual to address."[254]

The second heading was "the motives which should induce [hearers] well to consider what [they] hear,"[255] and there were three sub-headings. First, people needed to remember whom their ministers represented. The minister was a servant of God and an ambassador for Christ. Beddome said, "They act by his authority, receive their commission from him, and in his stead beseech you to be reconciled to God [2 Cor 5:20]."[256] He went on, "The apostle's description of the work and office of a faithful minister is very impressive: it is not only he who speaks to us, but God also by him."[257] A second motivation was to consider the aim of their pastor's ministry. The under-shepherds of the flock sought people rather than their possessions. Pastors labored to convert sinners and struggled until Christ was formed in his people (Gal 4:19) with the hope that they would be his "glory and joy [1 Thess 5:20]."[258] Third, the Bourton pastor motivated his hearers with the reality that they would be measured on judgment day according to the preaching they heard.[259] Hearers needed to consider, respond to, and improve the words spoken to them by their ministers. They failed to do so to their own peril.[260]

---

251. Beddome, "Sermon 1," in *TSD*, 3:3.
252. Beddome, "Sermon 1," in *TSD*, 3:3.
253. Beddome, "Sermon 1," in *TSD*, 3:3–4.
254. Beddome, "Sermon 1," in *TSD*, 3:4.
255. Beddome, "Sermon 1," in *TSD*, 3:4.
256. Beddome, "Sermon 1," in *TSD*, 3:4.
257. Beddome, "Sermon 1," in *TSD*, 3:4–5.
258. Beddome, "Sermon 1," in *TSD*, 3:5.
259. Beddome, "Sermon 1," in *TSD*, 3:5.
260. Beddome, "Sermon 1," in *TSD*, 3:6.

The second discourse was part of a series of eight sermons on 1 Thess 5:16–22.[261] The sermon was based on 1 Thess 5:20, "Despise not prophesyings." There were three headings and a concluding paragraph. The hymn attached to the sermon was "Efficacy of the Gospel."[262] The discourse will not be considered in its entirety, but only the section which addressed the way a person was to attend the preaching of the Word.

Beddome explained that, in context, prophesyings meant not the prediction of future events but "the expounding of the scriptures, or giving public instruction in the church of God."[263] Each minister had his own particular gifting—some to improve understanding, others to convict the conscience, and yet others to move the affections—and could benefit his hearers. Thus, no prophet, in the broader sense of the term, or his prophesyings were to be despised.[264] Beddome exhorted, "We are neither to despise the work nor the workman, the message nor the messenger. For our own sakes we are to receive the message."[265] The discourse's three headings were an explanation of despising God's Word, the causes of despising God's Word, and the danger of despising God's Word. It is the first of these that will be considered here.

The exhortation "despise not prophesyings" was aimed at hearers who were "required to reverence and esteem the messages which God [sent] them by his servants." This was true even of the maturest saints since no one had yet attained or become perfect, to borrow the words of the apostle (Phil 3:12).[266] Therefore, it was the hearer's duty, said Beddome, "to guard against a sickly stomach, which rejects the most wholesome food" that could nourish the soul.[267] Beddome listed three ways a hearer could despise prophesyings.

First, a person could despise prophesyings by refusing to attend the preaching of the gospel, motivated by either indifference or contempt. Beddome chastised those who engaged in "worldly business, amusement, or fleshly indulgence" on the Sabbath.[268] Others were overfull of the gospel and wrongly conceived that praying and meditating at home would more greatly profit them. The Bourton pastor recalled darker times in the history

---

261. These eight sermons are in Beddome, *TSD*, 4:36–106.
262. Beddome, *Hymns*, #697.
263. Beddome, "Sermon 9," in *TSD*, 4:71.
264. Beddome, "Sermon 9," in *TSD*, 4:71–72.
265. Beddome, "Sermon 9," in *TSD*, 4:72.
266. Beddome, "Sermon 9," in *TSD*, 4:72.
267. Beddome, "Sermon 9," in *TSD*, 4:72.
268. Beddome, "Sermon 9," in *TSD*, 4:73.

of the church when Christians chose to not gather. Those ancestors avoided assembling for fear of persecution, but Beddome's hearers were guilty of "slothful indifference, the love of carnal ease, ignorance and conceit, and enmity against the truth."[269] Whatever the motivation, said Beddome, those who failed to attend the preaching of the Word would be famished and contributed to their own destruction. Evidently, there were some in his parish who thought that time spent "in private devotion" was sufficient. Such thinking was wrongheaded, though, because preaching was a divinely instituted ordinance, and thus the hearing of it was also divinely appointed.[270]

Beddome's thought about preaching as a divine ordinance, or means of grace, is laid out in his catechism. Question 93 asked, "What are the outward means whereby Christ communicateth to us the benefits of redemption?" The answer: "The outward and ordinary means whereby Christ communicateth to us the benefits of redemption are his ordinances, especially the word, baptism, the Lord's Supper, and prayer; all which means are made effectual for salvation."[271] The catechism conceded that some had been converted through spiritual conversations, visions, severe trials, and miraculous encounters. A follow-up question was, "But are God's word and ordinances the ordinary means of salvation?" The answer: "Yes. He hath given pastors and teachers for the edifying of the body of Christ, Ephesians 4:11, 12." Thus, people should attend the preaching of the Word and do so diligently and regularly.[272] Question 94 asked, "How is the word made effectual to salvation?" The answer: "The Spirit of God maketh the reading, but especially the preaching of the word, an effectual means of convincing and converting sinners, and of building them up in holiness and comfort through faith unto salvation."[273] In response to question 95, Beddome elucidated the manner in which the preached Word ought to be heard: "That the word may become effectual to salvation, we must attend thereunto with diligence, preparation, and prayer; receive it with faith and love, lay it up in our hearts, and practice it in our lives."[274]

Second, Beddome spoke to the persons who attended the preaching, "yet with improper dispositions." He said such people "still come under the charge in our text."[275] There were two kinds of people Beddome had in view.

---

269. Beddome, "Sermon 9," in *TSD*, 4:73.
270. Beddome, "Sermon 9," in *TSD*, 4:73.
271. Beddome, *Scriptural Exposition*, 156.
272. Beddome, *Scriptural Exposition*, 157.
273. Beddome, *Scriptural Exposition*, 157.
274. Beddome, *Scriptural Exposition*, 159.
275. Beddome, "Sermon 9," in *TSD*, 4:73.

The first was the person who attended church but was entirely unengaged with the worship and preaching.[276] For instance, such a person may have been "reading the Bible" rather than listening to the "public instruction," or worse, "observing the different appearances on their fellow worshipers, when their eyes should [have been] fixed on the preacher, or devoutly lifted up to heaven."[277] Beddome continued, "When they came home they can tell more of what passed in the seats, than of what was delivered from the pulpit."[278] Thus, attendance at church was a lost opportunity. These people attended "out of custom ... to see [others] and be seen, and verily they have their reward [Matt 6:1–2, 5, 16]." The second kind of person in Beddome's mind was the person who was continually seeking after something "novel and entertaining." These people had "itching ears [2 Tim 4:3]" and were not satisfied by the "wholesome food" of God's Word. Such a person had the habit of moving churches to satisfy their appetite but was often disappointed and such frequent relocation benefited them little spiritually.[279]

Third, those who attended the preaching with apparent seriousness, "but who neither [received] it in love, [mixed] it with faith, nor [reduced] it to practice," also came under the censure of the command "despise not prophesyings."[280] Such a person neither showed contempt for the preaching nor neglected it by non-attendance. They did not, however, digest the Word and they simply forgot what they had heard. This characteristic would be evident through their conduct following the preaching. These people were "hearers, but not doers of the word, deceiving their ownselves [Jas 1:22]." They remained frivolous, careless, and unfruitful; they did not mortify even one cherished sin, forsake an evil practice, or begin to perform a formerly "neglected duty."[281] Those who attended the gospel but for unworthy purposes, such as "to hide some iniquity, to silence conscience, to raise our reputation, or promote our worldly interest," were also guilty of despising prophesyings, as were those who brought the gospel "into disgrace by their unworthy conduct."[282]

---

276. Beddome, "Sermon 9," in *TSD*, 4:73.
277. Beddome, "Sermon 9," in *TSD*, 4:73–74.
278. Beddome, "Sermon 9," in *TSD*, 4:74.
279. Beddome, "Sermon 9," in *TSD*, 4:74.
280. Beddome, "Sermon 9," in *TSD*, 4:74.
281. Beddome, "Sermon 9," in *TSD*, 4:75.
282. Beddome, "Sermon 9," in *TSD*, 4:75.

CONCLUSION

When Bernard Foskett died on September 17, 1758, his family invited Beddome to give the "oration" at the funeral. The Bourton pastor, however, passed off the honor to Hugh Evans, who preached from 1 Cor 9:27. Since Foskett never married, he bequeathed a considerable portion of his assets to the Beddome family and to Evans. The latter had served as Foskett's assistant, at the Broadmead Baptist Church and the Bristol Baptist Academy, and took over the leadership of both until his death in 1781. Under Foskett's leadership, approximately seventy students had been trained at the Academy, and several of his former students carried the coffin from the church building to the cemetery on the day of his funeral. Beddome was one of the pallbearers.[283]

What a solemn occasion this must have been for the Bourton pastor. Beddome had known Foskett his entire life, since he and his father, John, were close friends. Foskett had served as John's assistant in Alcester, Warwickshire, from 1711 until 1720 when the former left for Bristol to serve as Peter Kitterell's (d. 1727) assistant at Broadmead.[284] Then, in 1724, John was also called to Bristol to serve as the pastor of the Pithay church. Upon the Beddome family's arrival in the city, Foskett moved into their home; Benjamin was around seven years old at the time.[285] Thus, Foskett had had an enormous influence on the younger Beddome.[286] First, this influence would have been present during Beddome's childhood while Foskett lived in his family's home, and then, during his time at the Bristol Academy

---

283. For the details in this paragraph, I am indebted to Montgomery, "Benjamin Beddome," 119–20; Strivens, "Bernard Foskett (1658-1758)," 4:92–93, 101. Roger Hayden says that Foskett left behind his assets to the Beddome family, his own family, and "smaller amounts to over thirty Baptist ministers of his acquaintance"; for this quotation and more details concerning Foskett's will, see Hayden, *Continuity and Change*, 67n12.

284. Strivens, "Bernard Foskett (1658-1758)," 4:88–90. Foskett had been invited to preach at Broadmead in 1719 but was called to the church to be the assistant minister in 1720; upon Kitterell's death in 1727, Foskett became the senior minister. For these details, see Hayden, *Continuity and Change*, 66; Strivens, "Bernard Foskett (1658-1758)," 4:90.

285. Strivens, "Bernard Foskett (1658-1758)," 4:90; Rippon, "Rev. Benjamin Beddome," 316.

286. Montgomery says that the three formative influences on Beddome were his father, John, his tutor, Foskett, and his "gospel-saturated home." Montgomery, "Benjamin Beddome," 68–69. Derrick Holmes spoke of this relationship thus: "The influence of Bernard Foskett upon Benjamin Beddome was probably considerable. Mr. Foskett came to Bourton to deliver the charge when Beddome was ordained in 1743 and evidence of their continued friendship can be seen from a note which is still held in Bristol Baptist College Library." Holmes, "Early Years (1655–1740)," 22.

where he was trained in the Bristol Tradition.[287] When John died in 1757, it was surely Foskett who now served in that paternal role to Benjamin.[288] The younger Beddome also honored his tutor by naming one of his sons, Foskett, who was born around the time of his namesake's death.[289] What conversations, memories, and exhortations must have been ruminating in Beddome's mind as he carried the casket of his former mentor to his grave, which was also the place where his father had been laid to rest the previous year.[290]

One final connection between Foskett and Beddome will be made by way of conclusion. As noted above, Beddome was ordained to the pastorate of the Bourton church on September 23, 1743. Joseph Stennett preached to the church from Heb 13:17, and the address to the ordinand was given from 1 Tim 4:12 by Foskett.[291] It is safe to presume that the words spoken that day, and the man who spoke them, left an indelible mark on Beddome. The long-standing relationship between the preacher and ordinand that day was unique when compared with other Particular Baptist ordination services.

---

287. Hayden wrote, "A . . . student who owed a great deal to Foskett was John Beddome's son, Benjamin, whom Foskett probably first prepared for medical studies, and then later gave him a theological education." Hayden, *Continuity and Change*, 80.

288. For the date of John's death, see Anonymous, "Memoir," in Beddome, *SP*, ix. Montgomery says, "Foskett was like a second father to Benjamin, having lived in his home since his birth." Montgomery, "Benjamin Beddome," 119. Foskett apparently lived with the Beddome family also in Henley while the two were pastoring in Alcester. Henley-in-Arden was part of the Baptist church in Alcester, and Beddome had bought a large house in Henley, turning part of it into a church and the other part into his home. See Brady, "Being Benjamin Beddome," 5; Hayden, *Continuity and Change*, 64; Montgomery, "Benjamin Beddome," 78.

289. Benjamin's son Foskett was born in 1758 and died on October 28, 1784, in a tragic drowning accident. Rippon said that when he died, he was "in the 26th year of his age," that is, he was twenty-five. Beddome apparently had a habit of naming his children after the significant and influential people in his life. Though the connections are somewhat conjectural, his first son was named John Reynolds after his father, and perhaps one of the Bourton deacons; his next surviving son was named Benjamin after himself; his third son was named Samuel after the late pastor of the Little Prescott Street church where Beddome was baptized and called to the ministry or, perhaps, his brother; his next son was called Foskett after his lifelong tutor; his fifth son was called Boswell Brandon after his wife's and mother's maiden names; his lone daughter was named Elizabeth after his bride; and his sixth son was named Richard, after his father-in-law; and there was a seventh son named Josephus, perhaps, after his brother, Joseph. For the information in this paragraph, see Brady, "Being Benjamin Beddome," 15; Hayden, *Continuity and Change*, 66; Rippon, "Rev. Benjamin Beddome," 323.

290. Brady says, "Beddome senior and Foskett eventually shared the same grave in Redcross Street." Brady, "Being Benjamin Beddome," 5.

291. Rippon, "Rev. Benjamin Beddome," 317.

However, a more seasoned pastor exhorting a younger one concerning the ministry was by no means exceptional.

This chapter began by demonstrating that Beddome participated in ordination services during his ministry; on such occasions, he served as the seasoned pastor to his younger brethren entering the ministry. That his sermons would impact his hearers in a way akin to how Foskett had influenced him was surely the Bourton pastor's aim and petition. An explanation was also given of how several of Beddome's sermons resemble ordination sermons. These discourses were then examined to construct his pastoral theology. When compared with the pastoral theology of his denomination, the Particular Baptists of the long eighteenth century, there is a marked consistency and continuity. The unique contribution of Beddome, perhaps, is the focus on preaching in his ordination sermons. Even in this, though, he aligned with his Particular Baptist brethren, since they too valued and prioritized the sacred desk. Thus far in this study, the works of Beddome and his Particular Baptist ministerial brethren have been the focus. In the next chapter, lessons will be retrieved for contemporary churches and its pastors.

CHAPTER 5

Retrieving Benjamin Beddome's Pastoral Theology for the Contemporary Church

As noted in chapter 1, one of the world's leading experts on Benjamin Beddome is Gary Brady, the current pastor of Childs Hill Baptist Church in London.[1] In a paper presented at the 2021 Westminster Conference, Brady explained his thought behind his devotion to studying Beddome as a historical figure.[2] For Brady, he and his pastoral colleagues are generalists and, as such, need "to know something about a wide range of subjects." He continued, "But there is merit in a generalist specializing to some extent in order to share their knowledge with other generalists." Brady recommended that pastors choose an area to develop as a specialty, be it in biblical studies, systematic theology, or church history. In the area of church history, the obvious choices would be giants like John Owen, Jonathan Edwards, or Andrew Fuller. The Childs Hill pastor challenged such an approach, however, and contended for the value of "studying lesser lights." This way, Brady said to his fellow pastors, you are "studying someone you can hope to emulate, rather than a giant you will only ever admire from afar."[3] Of course, the "lesser light" that Brady has given attention to is Beddome. Given the fact that Beddome can help pastors, this chapter will draw out ways in which contemporary pastors and churches can learn from and emulate the eighteenth-century Bourton pastor.

---

1. Both Jason C. Montgomery and Daniel S. Ramsey, in their respective dissertations on Beddome, acknowledge Brady's expertise concerning the Bourton pastor. Montgomery, "Benjamin Beddome," 140; Ramsey, "Blessed Spirit," 4.
2. Brady, "Benjamin Beddome 1717–1795," 145.
3. Brady, "Benjamin Beddome 1717–1795," 145.

THE PRIMACY OF PREACHING

Preaching was central to the pastoral task according to eighteenth-century English Particular Baptists. A few quotations from representative figures bear out this conviction. In "The Work of a Gospel-Minister," John Gill said, "The ministration of the word . . . is a principal part of the work of a minister of Christ."[4] In agreement with Gill, Andrew Fuller exhorted an ordinand thus: "You must serve the church of God, by feeding them with the word of life—This is the leading duty of a minister."[5] Caleb Evans, preaching at the ordination of Thomas Dunscombe, said that "the ministers of Christ are to be preachers, public heralds." Evans added, "Ministers are sometimes called shepherds, and in this character you may remember they are exhorted to feed their flocks [John 21:15, 17]. . . . It is our business as preachers, not to amuse the fancies of our hearers, but to feed nourish and strengthen their precious souls."[6] Thus, according to men like Gill, Fuller, and Evans, the proclamation of the Word of God was the primary work of pastors.

That Beddome was in hearty agreement with his Particular Baptist brethren is demonstrated by his biographers and the subject of his ordination sermons. His biographers rightly portrayed Beddome as an able and committed preacher. The quotations that demonstrate this were provided in chapter 4; here, two brief comments will establish Beddome's commitment to the sacred desk. Thomas Brooks wrote of his predecessor, "In the pulpit he is said to have been emphatically at home. And in some sort he was always there, the pulpit was 'in all his thoughts.' The goal of one duty was the starting point of the next. We are told that he generally selected on the sabbath evening the topics for the discourses of the next."[7] Toward the end of his life, Beddome was carried to church and preached while seated because of his gout. Reflecting on the Bourton pastor's devotion to the pulpit in the face of such health challenges, Michael A. G. Haykin remarked, "At the heart of this refusal [to give up preaching] lay a deeply held conviction about the vital importance of preaching. Like the eighteenth-century Calvinistic Baptists in general, Beddome believed it was through preaching to the mind that God appealed to the hearts and wills of human beings."[8] Beddome's commitment to preaching is also demonstrated by the subjects addressed in his ordination sermons. Of the approximate ten discourses identified as

---

4. Gill, "Gospel-Minister," in S&T, 2:16.
5. Fuller, "Ministers and Churches Exhorted," in WAF, 1:544.
6. Evans, Charge, 5.
7. Brooks, POTP, 61.
8. Haykin, "Benjamin Beddome and the Bible," 15.

ordination sermons, three have as the focus the minister's preaching and three the church's response to it. In the sections that follow, contemporary applications concerning preaching will be given. Then, the appropriate response of the church to that preaching will be considered.

There has been a recent resurgence in biblical preaching of the expository kind. Many evangelical pastors have embraced the practice of working through entire books of the Bible in their pulpit ministry.[9] This renewal of

> 9. David Jackman (1942–) intimates the opposite in an essay he contributed for a Festschrift in honor of R. Kent Hughes: "The hostility of the culture has always been a 'given,' but the skepticism and rejection of sound biblical teaching at the heart of the local church's life and ministry—from within the congregation itself—is perhaps a defining aspect of the current crisis." Jackman, "Hermeneutical Distinctives," 10. He added,
>
>> That is why a biblical ministry, such as College Church has enjoyed under our esteemed brother Kent these many years, stands as a beacon light in the darkness and crosscurrents of contemporary confusion. . . . At the heart of this ministry lies the conviction that it is the Word of God in the hands of the Spirit of God that accomplishes the work of God—through the preacher, the man of God. (Jackman, "Hermeneutical Distinctives," 11)
>
> Jackman remarked that these convictions also lay at the heart of The Proclamation Trust in the United Kingdom—of which Jackman was the president for several years—and their informal partner organization, the Charles Simeon Trust in America. Jackman said of The Proclamation Trust, "Founded in 1986, the Trust at its inception could already look back over twenty-five years of extraordinary growth and fruitfulness." He was referring here to the fruitful ministry of the Trust's founder, Dick Lucas, who had been the rector of St. Helen's Bishopsgate in London and had a thriving ministry to the business community in the heart of the city. Thus, "over the years, countless numbers of people heard the Word of the Lord." Jackman continued, "The simple purpose of The Proclamation Trust is to train and equip a new generation of biblical preachers to do the same work . . . across the land and around the world." This was accomplished through two programs: preaching conferences throughout the year, which culminated in an annual conference held at St. Helen's Bishopsgate, drawing as many as nine hundred gospel workers from the United Kingdom. The other program was the Cornhill Training Course, of which Jackman was the director; it provided "practical tools for biblical expository ministry" over a longer period. Jackman ended his essay with this hope: "As we thank God for a wonderful example of such apostolic ministry at College Church through our brother Kent, let us dedicate ourselves to that kind of prayer and hard work, so that through the agency of the Simeon Trust and others whom the Lord will yet raise up, this kind of ministry will be multiplied across the world in the coming days far beyond all that we might ask, or even imagine [Eph 3:20], as the Word does the work."
>
> Hughes, together with David Helm and Jon Dennis, founded the Charles Simeon Trust in 2001; the work was inspired by and modeled after the work of The Proclamation Trust. Evidently, both The Proclamation Trust and its sister organization, the Charles Simeon Trust, have enjoyed success since their respective beginnings. For instance, the latter plans to host a total of 150 workshops during the 2024–25 ministry year. Thus, while Jackman's earlier comment that there is hostility toward biblical preaching both from inside and outside the church still stands, there is ample evidence that there has been and continues to be a recovery of such preaching as well. For the information in

expository preaching is connected to the renaissance of Reformed theology and the accompanying emphasis on sound doctrine and biblical fidelity.[10] Influential preachers in the movement, such as D. Martyn Lloyd-Jones (1899–1981), Dick Lucas (1925–), James Montgomery Boice (1938–2000), John Stott (1921–2011), R. C. Sproul (1939–2017), John MacArthur (1939–), R. Kent Hughes (1942–), and John Piper (1946–) have promoted the recovery of biblical preaching.[11] Given this recent resurgence of expository preaching, on the one hand, the lessons retrieved from Beddome will serve contemporary pastors by affirming their commitment to such preaching.[12] On the other hand, Beddome emphasized aspects of preaching that contemporary pastors may tend to ignore, and so he also serves in a corrective and instructive manner.

---

this paragraph and quotations, I am indebted to Jackman, "Hermeneutical Distinctives," 11–12, 21. For information regarding the history of the Charles Simeon Trust, see Charles Simeon Trust, "Brief History."

Bryan Chapell recounts the renewed interest in biblical theology among Protestant evangelicals, which has also resulted in scholars and pastors giving greater attention to biblical preaching. Chapell, preface to *Christ-Centered Preaching*, xiii–xv. Chapell captures the recovery of both biblical theology and preaching thus:

> Only after evangelicalism gained firmer ground in the 1960s and 1970s did key voices begin to remind the Bible-believing church of the far-reaching implications of our conviction that the proper interpretation of any text requires regard for its context. That context includes not only its literary and historical setting but also its place in God's redemptive plan. The exegetical and doctrinal disciplines began to register the importance of the organic unity of Scripture for sound interpretation, and these insights inevitably affected our approach to preaching. . . . In the present context, it is almost unthinkable that a new biblical commentary would be published without contextualizing the book or its contents within the redemptive flow of biblical history. Even if elementary preachers are unsure how to preach a particular passage redemptively, they have now been sensitized to detect sermons that are nothing more than moralistic challenges to straighten up, fly right, and do better. (Chapell, preface to *Christ-Centered Preaching*, xiv–xv)

10. The renaissance of Reformation doctrine has been so significant that *Time* magazine identified Calvinism as one of "10 Ideas Changing the World Right Now" in 2009. Van Biema, "New Calvinism."

11. In his article "History of Expository Preaching," James F. Stitzinger lists several of these men as being in a stream of men throughout church history who were committed to expository preaching. Stitzinger, "History of Expository Preaching," 27–31.

12. Beddome was not an expository preacher in that he did not work through biblical books, from begging to end, in the pulpit. Rather, he was a textual preacher; he selected a verse or two for each discourse and constructed his sermon outline from the constituent parts. As noted above, the Bourton pastor typically chose his texts each Sunday evening for the following Lord's Day. Beddome did, however, deliver a series of eight consecutive sermons from 1 Thess 5:16–22; see Beddome, *TSD*, 4:36–115.

The Significance of Preaching

The English Particular Baptists esteemed both the pastoral office and the work of ministry. In his charge to the church at the ordination of W. Belsher to the pastorate of the Baptist church in Worcester, John Ryland Jr. said that ministers were the gifts of Christ to the church (Eph 4:11) and this demonstrated "the care which the blessed Redeemer [exercised] over his church upon earth."[13] In his sermon "Pastors Required to Feed the Flock of Christ," Fuller similarly connected the love of Christ and the work of a pastor: "There is a close connexion between his having died for them and his desire to have them fed."[14] He added that though under-shepherds did not have the ability to supply the pasture, they could lead their people to it. He went on, "But Christ does more. He not only provides shepherds, but pasture—the gospel, of which he is the subject."[15]

Like his Particular Baptist brethren, Beddome believed in the significance of the pastor and his work. First, Christ sent ministers to local churches to serve as under-shepherds of the flock;[16] thus, a church without a pastor was to pray, "Oh send a messenger of peace, / a pastor of thy choice."[17] Furthermore, Beddome taught that when God desired to save a person, he would "either bring the means of grace to them, or them under the means of grace. . . . Where God has a work to do he will set up a gospel ministry, and introduce gospel ordinances."[18] In another place, Beddome remarked, "In whatever place the Lord stations a faithful and laborious minister, we may reasonably expect that he has some work for him to do."[19] God accomplishes his work in the world by establishing and sustaining local churches and sending pastors to shepherd and oversee those churches.

Moreover, there was a glory to the pastor's work. In "Mutual Glory of Christ and His People," Beddome said that Christ bestowed "the glory of preaching the gospel . . . on his faithful ministers."[20] He spoke of this glory in another sermon, "On the Dignity of the Christian Church," in which the Bourton pastor taught that God displayed his glory in the church during

---

13. Ryland, *Duty of Churches*, 42.
14. Fuller, "Pastors Required to Feed," in *WAF*, 1:477.
15. Fuller, "Pastors Required to Feed," in *WAF*, 1:478.
16. Beddome, "Future Punishment," in *TSD*, 2:183.
17. Beddome, *Hymns*, #662.
18. Beddome, "Hidden Design," in *SP*, 374–75.
19. Beddome, "Sermon 11," in *TSD*, 3:92–93. In a different sermon, Beddome said, "By raising up a constant succession of ministers to propagate and defend it, the Lord is still giving testimony to the word of his grace." Beddome, "Sermon 9," in *TSD*, 5:76.
20. Beddome, "Mutual Glory," in *SP*, 83.

the new covenant era. Through the church, God displayed "the glory of all his perfections, his wisdom, power, holiness, mercy, and faithfulness." Of this glory, Beddome said, "Ministers display it in their sermons, and private Christians in their lives."[21] It was no wonder, then, that the Bourton pastor said of ministers that they transacted "the most important matters between God and man."[22]

Last, it was in the pastor's preaching that Christ's voice was heard. In "Heavenly Stranger Received," Beddome said that the Lord "speaks to us in the preaching of the word: the voice of ministers is the voice of Christ."[23] He remarked similarly in another place: "If we would hear the Saviour's voice, we must go where his gospel is proclaimed."[24] In the hymn "Illness of a Pastor," Beddome penned,

> Long have we heard his lips proclaim,
> The gospel's joyful sound,
> Still may he live to bless thy name,
> And spread thy truth around.
>
> Still may we hear his cheering voice,
> *And find thee in the word*;
> Our grateful hearts shall then rejoice,
> And bless our living Lord.[25]

Of course, a minister's voice and Christ's voice could be distinguished from one another. Beddome said, in "Communion with God Our Security and Bliss," that even if a pastor's sermons were "ever so striking and eloquent, pathetic and evangelical, and his manner of address so engaging, his voice will have but little effect, unless that of his Master also be heard."[26] Thus, the Spirit needed to be operative for preaching to be effective, but the ordinary means through which Christ spoke to sinners and saints was through the preaching of the Word by the minister of the gospel. The interplay between the role of the pastor in preaching and that of God's will be discussed below. In a different hymn written for an ordination service, the Bourton pastor highlighted the spiritual nourishment that Christ gave through the pastor's preaching:

---

21. Beddome, "Christian Church," in *SP*, 419.
22. Beddome, "Nature and Authority," in *SP*, 308.
23. Beddome, "Heavenly Stranger Received," in *TSD*, 2:45.
24. Beddome, "Sermon 13," in *TSD*, 4:114.
25. Beddome, *Hymns*, #661 (emphasis added).
26. Beddome, "Communion with God," in *SP*, 400.

> Oh bless the Lord, our souls,
> Our shepherd and our head;
> Though in a weary barren land,
> We still are richly fed.
>
> He under-shepherds gives,
> His little flock to guide;
> And by his faithful tender care,
> Will constant food provide....
>
> With such a shepherd, Lord,
> Oh may we now be blessed;
> Be sweetly fed and nourished here,
> And in thy pasture rest.[27]

Given the gravitas of his calling and work, Beddome said, "Ministers of the gospel are often a wonder, both to themselves and others."[28] He went on,

> It is indeed wonderful that God should condescend to employ men of like passions with ourselves, weak and sinful creatures, who are ever prone to transgress against him; especially that he should employ them in so sacred and important a work as that of publishing articles of peace between heaven and earth, of bringing messages of grace from the offended Deity to a lost and ruined world; and unto them should be committed the ministry of reconciliation [2 Cor 5:18], and the care of immortal souls. Had the embassy been given to angels, it would have been less surprising, for they have never sinned; but that they who took part in the transgression should thus be employed, can be owing to nothing but the most stupendous grace. Infinite wisdom also saw fit to lodge this treasure in earth vessels, that the excellency of the power might be of God, and not of us [2 Cor 4:7].[29]

Contemporary pastors ought to be encouraged and sobered by Beddome's reflections on the pastor and his work. These reflections provide clarity to the pastor concerning the nature and function of his office. Pastors have been sent to their respective churches by the risen Christ to function as a shepherd and overseer because the Savior desires to do work in and through his ministry there. Contrary to the prevalent notion among evangelical Christians that a believer can be spiritually nourished either through

---

27. Beddome, *Hymns*, #734.
28. Beddome, "Sermon 7," in *TSD*, 5:58.
29. Beddome, "Sermon 7," in *TSD*, 5:59.

personal Bible reading or listening to sermons online or via podcast, a pastor's preaching is needful in the life of a Christian if she is to be fed spiritually. Something unique is happening in the preaching of the Word and the administration of the ordinances whereby Christ meets with and speaks to his people in a way he ordinarily does not do through any other means. Furthermore, if Christ commissioned the pastor, of course, he must look to his Master for both strength and directives. This is particularly pertinent in a time when pastors are expected to be a proficient thinker and leader in many areas, for example, by being a political pundit, a psychology guru, a religious entrepreneur, a Christian influencer, a motivational life-coach, and the like. In such a climate, Beddome and his Particular Baptist brethren remind pastors that they are called to be under-shepherds of the flock on behalf of the Great Shepherd, and their principal task is to guide and feed his people through the preaching of the Word.

The Efficacy of Preaching

Beddome was an heir of the Reformation and English Puritanism. More particularly, Jason C. Montgomery located the Bourton pastor in the stream of Evangelical Calvinism, which was embraced by the Bristol Tradition.[30] Accordingly, Beddome taught that God needed to be operative in the salvation of sinners. Drawing from the sphere of horticulture, he explained,

> Nothing but heavenly culture, nothing but divine influence, can produce in us the fruits of righteousness. Barren trees will still continue so, after all the culture and the care that human labour can bestow, unless those efforts are rendered effectual by the powerful co-operation of the Spirit of God. Parents, friends, and ministers labour but in vain, unless the Lord rears the plant and waters it [1 Cor 3:7].[31]

By emphasizing the sovereign role of God in the salvation of sinners, Beddome was not implying that the pastor's role was unnecessary or insignificant. In another sermon, Beddome listed the various ways in which God called sinners to himself, but preaching was the primary means: "Sometimes God has made use of remarkable providences, personal afflictions, public calamities, the sudden death of others; sometimes startling dreams,

---

30. Montgomery, "Benjamin Beddome," 7. That Beddome believed in the free offer of the gospel and the responsibility of hearers to believe it, over and against the High Calvinism of his day, was the argument of Montgomery's dissertation.

31. Beddome, "Sermon 20," in *TSD*, 5:168.

sometimes the edifying discourse of private Christians, but generally the public ministry of the word, to bring about this wonderful and most desirable change."[32] He said, in another sermon, "Though the reading of the scriptures is a necessary and profitable exercise, yet it is more especially the word preached that is rendered effectual; for it pleaseth God, by the foolishness of preaching, to save them that believe [1 Cor 2:1]."[33] Thus, while God was the efficient cause in salvation, ministers were the instrumental cause, and primarily so, through their preaching.[34]

This dynamic between the roles of God and of the preacher in the salvation of sinners was borne out in several places in Beddome's discourses. For instance, in "The Danger and Sin of Idolatry," he said that though Paul, Apollos, and Peter "were three of the best preachers that ever lived upon earth, yet [they] were not the authors, but only the means, made use of by God for [the people's] conversion and salvation." He added, "The ministry of reconciliation was committed to them [2 Cor 5:18], but the work of reconciliation belonged to another."[35] Beddome also differentiated between the external call made by the preacher and the internal call made by the Savior; Beddome captured this distinction thus:

> Ministers in preaching the word, speak to all their hearers, and not to one more than another.... But Christ speaks to the individual, and does not speak in vain. They [that is, ministers] draw the bow at a venture; but he aims at a certain mark, and never misses his aim.... Ministers speak to the ear only, and can do no more; but he speaks to the heart.[36]

Using yet another metaphor in a different sermon, Beddome said, "Ministers may knock at the door, but it is God alone that can open it."[37]

The distinction between the role of the pastor and that of Christ in the salvation of sinners was undergirded by the different powers that belonged

---

32. Beddome, "Heavenly Calling," in *SP*, 115.
33. Beddome, "Sermon 5," in *TSD*, 5:44.
34. Beddome said of Paul and Apollos, "They are instruments merely; God is the efficient cause." Beddome, "Sermon 13," in *TSD*, 5:109.
35. Beddome, "Danger and Sin," in *SP*, 391.
36. Beddome, "Sermon 12," in *TSD*, 3:102.
37. Beddome, "Sermon 17," in *TSD*, 3:142. Similarly, the Bourton pastor said elsewhere that "ministers stand at the door and knock; the Spirit comes with his key, and opens the door." Beddome, "Heavenly Calling," in *SP*, 116. The Bourton pastor was quoting Thomas Watson here, who wrote, "Ministers knock at the door of men's hearts, the Spirit comes with a key and opens the door." Watson, *Body of Practical Divinity*, 128. For the quotation from Watson, I am indebted to Beeke, *Reformed Preaching*, 156.

to each. The Bourton pastor explained the respective abilities of the minister and the Savior:

> Ministers call by the preaching of the word, and often call in vain: Christ calls by the internal application of the word, and his calls are always effectual. Ministers lift up their voice, but Christ makes bare his arm, and the report of the gospel is believed [Isa 53:1]. Ministers beseech men in his stead to be reconciled to God [2 Cor 5:20], but he alone is the pacificator, and makes them willing to be reconciled.[38]

In a sermon on regeneration, he highlighted these differences thus: "He who gave man his being at first, can alone create him in Christ unto good works [Eph 2:10]. Ministers may be the instruments, but God is the agent. He alone can enstamp his own image, and make us partakers of a divine nature [Col 3:10; 2 Pet 1:4]. He every where assumes this work to himself, and all who are born again ascribe it to him."[39]

Contemporary pastors ought to derive clarity with respect to their role in preaching and be encouraged in their work.[40] The Bourton pastor differentiated the role of the pastor and that of God in the conversion of sinners and sanctification of the saints. Ministers of the gospel are the means, or the instrument, but are not the efficient cause of salvation. That truth should yield a lessening of pressure in the pastor's heart that he must save and transform sinners, because it is not in his power to do so. This, of course, does not imply that preaching is unimportant or that the task can be approached haphazardly because of some skewed emphasis on divine sovereignty. Rather, Beddome's teaching on the external call of the preacher and the internal call of the Savior underscores the vital nature of preaching. In "Heavenly Calling," Beddome said that "ministers call externally by the preaching of the word; and they often call in vain." He added that when "God calls internally," he does so "by the application of the word and the influence of the Spirit."[41] In other words, the sovereign Savior of sinners has designed it so that his saving work is accomplished *through* the preaching of his ministers. Though that is not the singular way in which God draws men and women to himself, it is the chief and ordinary way. Consequently, then, contemporary pastors would do well to give themselves wholly to the

---

38. Beddome, "Sermon 8," in *TSD*, 6:65.
39. Beddome, "Sermon 5," in *TSD*, 3:33.
40. While Beddome would have distinguished between a pastor's preaching and a Christian's evangelism, aspects of this paragraph will apply to church members in their work of evangelism.
41. Beddome, "Heavenly Calling," in *SP*, 111.

preaching of God's Word with the hope that God's Spirit might effectually work through it.

The Content of Preaching

The English Particular Baptists collectively emphasized the need to preach the Word of God. They were also insistent that pastors must preach the gospel of grace and make Christ the central subject of their discourses. Representative of the conviction of his contemporaries, Beddome said that ministers "are not to be silent, but to speak: and as they are ambassadors for Christ [2 Cor 5:20], he should be the principal subject of their ministrations."[42] That Beddome followed his own advice in the course of his ministry was captured by John Rippon in his obituary of the Bourton pastor: "In his preaching he laid Christ at the bottom of religion as the support of it, placed him at the top of it as its glory, and made him the centre of it, to unite all its parts and to add beauty and vigour to the whole."[43]

John Gill, in a charge to John Reynolds at his ordination, provided a ten-point summary of Christian doctrine that the ordinand was to hold fast to in his ministry.[44] Similarly, John Brine, preaching at the ordination of John Collett Ryland to the pastorate of the Baptist church in Warwick, gave a list of seven doctrines that Ryland was to preach to his congregation.[45] Finally, Fuller provided a short, four-point summary of what preaching Christ entailed.[46] Beddome, of course, wrote his catechism, and over two hundred of his sermons and eight hundred of his hymns are extant. Thus, a summation of the Bourton pastor's theology could be derived.[47] The focus

---

42. Beddome, "Reconciliation to God," in *TSD*, 1:118.

43. Rippon, "Rev. Benjamin Beddome," 321. Rippon was quoting the Bourton pastor himself, who said in his circular letter written over thirty years prior,

> Look well, then, to the foundation upon which you are built, and seriously and frequently examine your state God-ward. See that you lay Christ at the bottom of your religion, as the support of it; that you place him at the top of it, as its glory; and that you make him the centre of it, to unite all its parts, and add beauty and vigour to the whole. Remember that growth in Christianity is growth in the knowledge of Christ. Seek that sorrow, that peace, that holiness, that establishment, which flow from Christ; let all your duties begin and end in Christ. (Beddome, *Circular Letter* [1765], 2)

44. Gill, "Form of Sound Words," in *S&T*, 2:53–62.

45. Brine, *Solemn Charge*, 7–21.

46. Fuller, "Preaching Christ," in *WAF*, 1:503.

47. E.g., see the essays on aspects of Beddome's theology in Haykin et al., *Glory to the Three Eternal*.

here, however, will be on Beddome's gospel preaching, mainly drawn from "Reconciliation to God" and a sermon on 2 Cor 5:11.

Beddome preached from Matt 3:10, "The axe is laid to the root of the tree," in "Character Tried by the Word and Providence of God." The axe was "laid ministerially by the preachers of the word." John the Baptist was held up as a model in this regard, since "he was a powerful and awakening preacher, and seems to have had a peculiar talent of touching the consciences of men, exciting their fears, and arousing them from their carnal security."[48] Due to the tendency of humanity to remain in a spiritual slumber, ministers needed to sound an alarm. In a different sermon, Beddome said, "It is evident that the principal design of a trumpet is to sound an alarm; and such is the direct object of the gospel ministry. Men in general, as to their spiritual interests, are in a profound sleep: the whole world is at rest and quiet."[49] Further, in "Reconciliation to God," Beddome said that ministers needed to speak to sinners concerning the natural enmity of their hearts against God and warn of the terrible judgment that awaited those who remained in their unreconciled state.[50]

In another sermon on 2 Cor 5:11, Beddome spoke of the need for ministers to "be acquainted with the terror and vengeance of the law" if they were to awaken the spiritually careless and negligent.[51] The messenger of the gospel must hold forth God as Lawgiver before his hearers can embrace him as Savior; likewise, people must be made aware of the divine vengeance against their sin before they can perceive their need for the gospel's refuge.[52] Later in the sermon, he said,

> The great object of the Christian ministry is to persuade men of their guilt and danger, and of the terror of the Lord, which is ready to fall upon them; to convince them of the evil of sin, the strictness and severity of the divine law, the tremendous power of that God whom they have offended, and the dreadful nature of that destruction which their iniquities have deserved. All the artillery of God's word is pointed against the impenitent.[53]

Having issued such warning to his hearers, the minister of the gospel can "point out the remedy, and persuade them to accept it."[54] Beddome

---

48. Beddome, "Character Tried," in *SP*, 224.
49. Beddome, "Sermon 3," in *TSD*, 6:23.
50. Beddome, "Reconciliation to God," in *TSD*, 1:118, 122.
51. Beddome, "Sermon 5," in *SD*, 8:45.
52. Beddome, "Sermon 5," in *SD*, 8:45–46.
53. Beddome, "Sermon 5," in *SD*, 8:51.
54. Beddome, "Sermon 5," in *SD*, 8:52.

gave different exhortations to the awakened, inquiring, and sinner, but he concluded thus: "Above all it is the object of the gospel ministry to hold forth Christ, to recommend him to our attention in all his endearing characters and offices, as a prophet, priest and king; who by his blood has made full atonement for sin, who by his grace can soften the hardest heart, and subdue the most inveterate enmity."[55] By way of conclusion, the Bourton pastor reiterated that, according to God's design, men would be saved through the preaching of the gospel.[56]

Pastors were to preach, not only for the conversion of sinners, but also for the establishment of the saints. In "The Stability of the Gracious Character," Beddome said, "Every Christian will die safely; but the established Christian dies joyfully and triumphantly. In a word, this is the perfection of religion, the end of divine providences and ordinances; that for which ministers preach, and you hear."[57] In the sermons "Reconciliation to God" and the discourse on 2 Cor 5:11, Beddome focused mainly on evangelistic preaching, but he also exhorted the converted. Those already reconciled were to seek further reconciliation to God by pursuing holiness and seeking to have "every thought brought into subjection to Christ [2 Cor 10:5]."[58] He said, similarly, to those who had already fled the coming judgment and found refuge in the gospel, that they needed to be persuaded unto further thanksgiving and submission to God, denying ungodliness and seeking after godliness instead (Titus 2:12). It was "the gospel," said Beddome, that provided "abundant motives for such a line of conduct."[59]

With the contemporary recovery of Reformed theology, there has also been a revival of focus on the gospel. As such, pastors desire to lead gospel-centered churches, and Christian leaders gospel-centered organizations. Therefore, this reflection on the content of a minister's preaching is unlikely an innovative or fresh concept for many pastors and leaders today. This reality is something to be thankful for, with respect to the revival of the gospel and sound doctrine within evangelicalism. It should be remembered, though, that a pastor can easily drift from having this single-minded focus on Christ and him crucified (1 Cor 2:2). Within the panoply of voices that call for the Christian leader's attention to adopt a trendy method or to proclaim a fashionable idea, Beddome's assertion to pastors that Christ "should be the principal subject of their ministrations" is welcome. One further way

---

55. Beddome, "Sermon 5," in *SD*, 8:52–53.
56. Beddome, "Nature and Authority," in *SP*, 303.
57. Beddome, "Gracious Character," in *SP*, 162.
58. Beddome, "Reconciliation to God," in *TSD*, 1:120.
59. Beddome, "Sermon 5," in *SD*, 8:53.

that Beddome is helpful to modern pastors is in his emphasis on the terrors of the law and coming judgment. Pastors must not be afraid or reticent to speak of the sinner's enmity against God, their spiritual slumber, and God's threatenings against unrepentant sinners, with the hope that they might be persuaded of their plight and flee to the gospel for refuge.

THE PASTOR REMAINING IN HIS STATION

The focus of the third chapter was the seven-letter correspondence between the Baptist churches of Bourton-on-the-Water and Goodman's Fields in London over the pastoral services of Beddome. These letters remained dormant for over a century until Thomas Brooks discovered them while reading the minute books of the Bourton church and submitted them to *The Baptist Magazine* for publication in 1859.[60] Brooks—who had come to the church four years prior—was likely reading the minute books in preparation for writing the church's history, which he published in 1861.[61] The nineteenth-century Bourton pastor rightly deemed the letters as being useful and of interest to his Baptist brethren concerning how churches handled the removal of pastors from one place to another and the relation between a pastor and his people.

Beddome's early biographers spoke univocally of the lessons to be learned from his decision to remain in Bourton and not relocate to the more significant station of London. Of the exchange, Brooks praised his predecessor's character thus: "Comparatively few ministers are ever called to pass through an ordeal as trying as the one disclosed in the above correspondence, and it may be safely affirmed, that none ever came out with more credit to themselves."[62] Brooks seems to have been echoing the words of an anonymous memorialist who wrote twenty-six years prior: "Few circumstances can be more perplexing than those in which Mr. Beddome was thus placed, or more calculated to try and elucidate uprightness of motive and correctness of principle. The simplicity, disinterestedness, and firmness he displayed on this occasion, speak loudly for his moral and religious character."[63]

---

60. Brooks, "Ministerial Changes" (July 1859), 425–29; Brooks, "Ministerial Changes" (Aug. 1859), 482–87.

61. Brooks, POTP. For the date of Brooks becoming the pastor of the church, see Brooks, POTP, 110–11.

62. Brooks, POTP, 47.

63. Anonymous, "Memoir," in Beddome, SP, xxvi.

These quotations, of course, were commending Beddome's godly character throughout the exchange of letters between the churches. The example for contemporary pastors, however, is not limited to the Bourton pastor's upright manner in making and communicating his choice to remain in Bourton, but the very decision itself. Though Beddome was eminently gifted, as Robert Hall Jr. memorably remarked, "he spent the principal part of a long life in village retirement."[64] Such a course of action was inconceivable to the Goodman's Fields church, who desired a learned minister to replace the late Samuel Wilson.[65] They lamented the state of the Baptist denomination since trained pastors were so few, particularly when compared to the Congregationalists and Presbyterians.[66] Beddome had trained at the Bristol Baptist Academy and the Independent Academy in London and was a suitable candidate in the minds of the Goodman's Fields deacons. They relied heavily on the maxim which, to them, applied in every sphere of life: "That the service of all is to be preferred before that of a part. No man ever said that the interest of one member is of equal importance with that of society in general."[67] Given London's prominence in both the nation and the empire during the mid-eighteenth century, it is not surprising that the Little Prescott Street church argued this way.

Now, greater usefulness was important in the minds of English Particular Baptist pastors, including Beddome. Concerning the decision to remove to London, Beddome said in his first letter that he was "in a great strait," that is, he was uncertain of which way to go.[68] He acknowledge that there was the potential for greater usefulness in London and the opportunity to fellowship with "the best of preachers" there.[69] Beddome proclaimed in a sermon, "Motives to Usefulness," that occasionally God fits a man with "intellectual powers fit . . . for a large sphere of usefulness." He went on, "Now, where much is given, much is required [Luke 12:48]: a greater improvement is expected from the man who has five talents, than from him who is possessed of two [Matt 24:14–30]."[70] Later in the sermon, he exhorted his hearers, "Whenever providence opens a door, or furnishes an opportunity for

64. Hall, "Recommendatory Preface," vi.
65. Goodman's Fields Church to Bourton Church, November 11, 1750, in Brooks, *POTP*, 33–34.
66. Goodman's Fields Church to Bourton Church, November 11, 1750, in Brooks, *POTP*, 33.
67. Goodman's Fields Church to Bourton Church, February 3, 1751, in Brooks, *POTP*, 39.
68. Beddome to Goodman's Fields Church, n.d., in Brooks, *POTP*, 36.
69. Beddome to Goodman's Fields Church, n.d., in Brooks, *POTP*, 35.
70. Beddome, "Motives to Usefulness," in *TSD*, 1:89.

usefulness, follow its call, enter immediately upon the business, and never give over till thou hast dispatched it."[71] With such strong injunctions to usefulness to his congregation, why did Beddome choose to remain in Bourton when a more significant station called him? We discover an answer to that question in the response of the Bourton church and its pastor, who together impart wisdom to contemporary pastors.

From the perspective of Bourton, it was not a foregone conclusion that a learned minister needed to automatically relocate to a more influential station. In the case of Beddome, there were legitimate reasons for him to remain. For instance, he had been ordained over the church; the people had become more united under his pastorate; he had been useful in Bourton, as evidenced by the over one hundred people who had been converted through his ministry; and the church expressed affection for their pastor and was willing to provide for him financially.[72] The Bourton deacons also argued for the propriety of their pastor remaining with them. Drawing from the imagery of the biblical book of Revelation, the deacons argued that a star was more needed in the darker parts of the sky (that is, Bourton) than in the regions where God had set up a constellation (that is, London). The stars in this case represented ministers of the gospel.[73] They also pointed out that removals did not always lead to continued usefulness and success; if God appointed a pastor to a place, he should not presume that his usefulness would continue in another place unabated. Contrary to the pragmatic view of usefulness held by the London deacons, their counterparts in Bourton aptly said, "Usefulness consists not barely in preaching to a very great auditory, but in honouring religion by serving God and our generation in that post in which he sets us."[74]

The principle was that God desired to work through his ministers in the place where he had stationed them. Beddome taught this in a sermon, saying, "In whatever place the Lord stations a faithful and laborious minister, we may reasonably expect that he has some work for him to do."[75] Thus, while usefulness was certainly a factor in Beddome's mind, faithfulness in his current station of Bourton was also a biblical priority. He spoke of ministers in another sermon, "The Nature and Exercises of True Fidelity," thus: "Ministers are called stewards, and of such it is required, that they

---

71. Beddome, "Motives to Usefulness," in *TSD*, 1:91.

72. Beddome to Goodman's Fields Church, n.d., in Brooks, *POTP*, 35–36.

73. Bourton Church to Goodman's Fields Church, February 24, 1751, in Brooks, *POTP*, 43.

74. Bourton Church to Goodman's Fields Church, February 24, 1751, in Brooks, *POTP*, 43.

75. Beddome, "Sermon 11," in *TSD*, 3:92–93.

be found faithful [1 Cor 4:1–2]; faithful to God, to their own consciences, and to their people; dispensing the word with boldness, administering the ordinances of God's house in their purity, and maintaining the discipline of it with impartiality."[76]

If the maxim of the London church was carried to its logical end, then it would be impossible for less significant churches to retain their pastors. This would be detrimental to country churches, since the city churches could invoke usefulness as grounds for removal in every case. For an English Particular Baptist pastor such as Beddome, this was of great concern, because the effectiveness of a pastor was helped by his remaining in a place for a long tenure. Benjamin Wallin captured this principle in his charge to Abraham Booth at his ordination: "Scarce any thing is more grievous, or hurtful to social religion, and the welfare of churches, than frequent and unnecessary changes in this near and tender relation among the people of God: so that a steady perseverance in your station is of great importance, and what I earnestly commend."[77]

By way of conclusion, the London church was most concerned with the question: "Where will a pastor be most useful?" Usefulness, to them, was to have the greatest influence on the greatest number of people from the most significant post. This factor trumped all others, as evidenced by their quick dismissal of the Bourton church's desire to retain their pastor based on their affection for him and sense that he had been given in answer to their prayers.[78] For Beddome, this was too simplistic an approach; instead he and the Bourton church asked, "To what station has God called a man?" To determine this, usefulness was a consideration among others, but it was not the only factor. For instance, Beddome learned from his contemporaries and John Owen that a pastoral removal was unadvisable if the pastor's current church did not give their consent.[79] On this point, he wrote, "If my people would have consented to my removal (though I should have had much to sacrifice on account of the great affection I bear them) yet I should then have made no scruple of accepting your call. But, as they absolutely refuse it, the will of the Lord be done [Acts 21:14]."[80] Having determined that the will of God for him was to remain in Bourton, he resolved to be faithful there. Beddome continued, "I am determined that I will not violently rend myself

---

76. Beddome, "True Fidelity," in *SP*, 179–80.
77. Wallin, *Charge*, 35.
78. Goodman's Fields Church to Bourton Church, February 3, 1751, in Brooks, *POTP*, 41.
79. Beddome to Goodman's Fields Church, February 24, 1751, in Brooks, *POTP*, 45.
80. Beddome to Goodman's Fields Church, February 24, 1751, in Brooks, *POTP*, 46.

from them, for I would rather honour God in a much lower station than that in which he hath placed me, than intrude myself into a higher without his direction."[81] All this serves to demonstrate the propriety of a learned, gifted, and useful minister remaining in a more obscure station, even when a more prominent and influential church was demanding his services.

There is much for contemporary pastors to glean from Beddome's response to the invitations from London. Consider, for instance, a pastor who is presented with an opportunity to relocate to a more significant church. The building is larger and has better facilities, the church has more staff, and the budget is twice that of the pastor's current church. The prospective church has more influence in the denomination, is well-positioned to impact other churches in the region, and has a larger membership. In such a scenario, many pastors would likely relocate to the more significant church since he can seemingly have a greater impact for the kingdom. This mindset is captured in Zach Eswine's testimony of his approach to ministry when he was finishing seminary: "It was becoming quite clear to me that if I was to prove successful in ministry, I needed to do something great, and I needed to define something great in terms of how large, famous, and fast I could accomplish it."[82]

For the sake of clarity, there is no moral transgression in relocating to a more influential church. One of Beddome's contemporaries, John Ryland Jr., left the College Lane church in Northampton to pastor the Broadmead Baptist Church and become the principal of the Baptist Academy in Bristol, and this was motivated by a prospect of greater usefulness. Thus, the lesson is not that a pastor should always remain at his current church for the sake of longevity. Rather, Beddome's example provides an alternative perspective to that of Eswine while he was a seminarian.

Granted, it is not the common experience of contemporary pastors to receive such strong summons to a more influential and significant church. The lessons from this correspondence, however, are not constrained to the situations when a minister of the gospel is faced with a decision of whether to relocate to another church. Beddome's life demonstrates the appropriateness and beauty of a pastor remaining in a station where God had called him, even if it was an obscure place like Bourton-on-the-Water in the Cotswolds of England. The twentieth-century apologist Francis Schaeffer spoke of the temptations facing those engaged in ministry: "All of us—pastors, teachers, professional religious workers and nonprofessionals included—are tempted

---

81. Beddome to Goodman's Fields Church, February 24, 1751, in Brooks, *POTP*, 46–47.

82. Eswine, *Imperfect Pastor*, 21.

to say, 'I will take the larger place because it will give me more influence for Jesus Christ.'"[83] Schaeffer continued, "But according to the Scripture this is backwards: we should consciously take the lowest place unless the Lord Himself extrudes us into a greater one. . . . This is the way of the Christian: he should choose the lesser place until God extrudes him into a position of more responsibility and authority."[84] According to Schaeffer and Beddome, bigger is not always better.

THE PASTOR'S RELATIONSHIP WITH HIS CHURCH

As Dissenters, the Particular Baptists maintained that the authority to call a pastor belonged to the local church. In his charge to Booth, Wallin said, "But you know, sir, the office of a pastor, or bishop, is of a more peculiar nature: it is relative to a particular church, gathered according to divine appointment; and results from a solemn contract between a minister and the people of his charge."[85] Beddome remarked in a sermon, "The True Unity of True Believers," that all the saints "have equal authority in managing the affairs of the church, [including] the choice of a minister."[86] Thus, the Bourton pastor instructed Baptist churches, who had "the privilege of choosing their own teachers," to test ministerial candidates before appointing them to the office.[87]

In addition to the call of the church for a man to serve as its pastor, for the English Particular Baptists, there was a need for the candidate's current church to provide consent for release. This is demonstrated by a letter of dismission from the Bourton church addressed to their friends in Warwick concerning John Collett Ryland. Beddome, who wrote the letter, said, "As it was our happiness that God should raise up such a gift as our brother Ryland amongst us, so 'tis our privilege that you have enjoyed his ministry so long . . . and are now likely to have him settled in office amongst you. For

---

83. Schaeffer, *No Little People*, 34. For the quotation from Schaeffer, I am indebted to Eswine, *Imperfect Pastor*, 146. Schaeffer added that both individuals and organizations, whether churches or parachurch ministries, can "fall prey" to this kind of thinking as they rationalize building "bigger and bigger empires." Schaeffer, *No Little People*, 34.

84. Schaeffer, *No Little People*, 34–35. The reasons Schaeffer gave as to why a Christian leader should seek a lower place were different than those of Beddome. Schaeffer said that it was easier to quiet one's soul before God in a lower place, and seeking a higher position can tempt a person toward egotism, which disqualifies him for Christian leadership. Schaeffer, *No Little People*, 35–37.

85. Wallin, *Charge*, 35.

86. Beddome, "True Unity," in *SP*, 332.

87. Beddome, "Sermon 10," in *TSD*, 4:83.

this purpose we dismiss him from his fellowship with us, and recommend him to you."[88] Such practice explains why Beddome constrained himself to the will of the Bourton church with respect to the call from London.[89] The decision to entrust himself to the will of the membership was not a kind gesture but an outworking of Baptist polity whereby a pastor could only relocate with the consent of his current church. This was the instruction that Beddome received both from Owen through his writings and several counselors through conversations and correspondence when the invitation came from the Little Prescott Street church.[90]

While it is commonplace for Baptist churches today to cast their vote in the calling of a pastor to a church, for most it is unthinkable that a pastor would submit to the will of his current congregation concerning a potential relocation.[91] Many of these pastors would consider themselves as having entered a covenantal relationship with the church, whereby both pastor and church would fulfill their duties to one another.[92] It is notable, then, that when it comes to the decision to leave, the contemporary pastor does not involve the church in establishing his plans, let alone submit to a congregational vote on the matter.[93]

---

88. Bourton Church to Warwick Church, July 8, 1750, in Newman, *Rylandiana*, 6.

89. Beddome to Goodman's Fields Church, n.d., in Brooks, *POTP*, 36; Beddome to Goodman's Fields Church, February 24, 1751, in Brooks, *POTP*, 46.

90. Beddome to Goodman's Fields Church, February 24, 1751, in Brooks, *POTP*, 45.

91. For instance, in *What to Look for in a Pastor*, Brian Biedebach provides counsel to search committees in finding their next pastor. In the first five chapters, he talks about the qualities of an ideal candidate and covers the areas of a pastor's preaching, shepherding, character, theology, and practical theology. In the sixth and final chapter, Biedebach instructs a church on how it can find its next pastor. After examining the pros and cons of four contemporary models adopted in a pastoral search, he provides a few points of general advice. In a section concerning reference checks, Biedebach says that the goal is to dig deeper and "to find a common friend—someone who knows your church and who knows your candidate." A committee may opt to contact the candidate's former church, but seemingly more with a view to finding a common point of contact. The point here is that in a book about the pastoral search process, there is little said about contacting the candidate's former church, let alone anything about securing its consent for the pastor's dismission to another congregation. Biedebach, *What to Look for in a Pastor*, 167–68.

92. Andrew Fuller said on this point: "The connexion of pastor and people, in dissenting churches, is altogether voluntary. There are no bonds to bring them together, or to keep them together, but love." Fuller, "Churches Walking," in *WAF*, 1:529.

93. For the sake of clarity, the present author is not putting forth this practice in a prescriptive manner, but rather describing how the practice of eighteenth-century Particular Baptist churches differed greatly from that of contemporary evangelical churches with respect to pastoral removals.

Nonetheless, even for the eighteenth-century Dissenters, there were legitimate reasons for a pastor to leave a church. Beddome acknowledged this in his second letter to Goodman's Field: in general, a pastor was unjustified in leaving his people "without their consent, unless there be something on their side,—such as want of love, a wilful deficiency in their contributions, divisions, dissensions, or the like."[94] Later in the letter, Beddome referenced John Gill's funeral sermon for the late Samuel Wilson, noting how Gill did not cite greater usefulness as a legitimate reason for pastoral removal. The reasons that justified the relocation of a pastor from one church to another, according to Gill, were: heretical doctrine infected a church and could not be unrooted; immorality was pervasive, and the people would not submit to discipline or Christ's laws; the church could not financially provide for the pastor; or there was such strong dissatisfaction between the pastor and the church that peace and fellowship was impossible to maintain, and the ministry of the Word and ordinances was stifled.[95]

The love between a pastor and his people was vital for the Particular Baptists. The Bourton deacons lamented the prospect of country churches continually needing to give up their pastors to those in London: "If the churches in the country must lose their ministers, whom God has fixed over them, and *whom they dearly love*, is not this the way to stir up animosities and divisions?"[96] In their first letter to Goodman's Fields, they wrote that their "great love and esteem" for their pastor would be sufficient reason to refuse the request for Beddome's removal.[97] Fuller spoke of the corresponding need for a pastor to love the flock under his charge. Of Barnabas, who was a model minister, he said, "As he loved Christ, so he loved his people."[98] In another sermon, Fuller remarked how Christ's appointment of a pastor over a church demonstrated his love for the sheep, and thus, as the undershepherd, a pastor needed to love those committed to his charge since he represented the Great Shepherd.[99]

A pastor was called to love the church, and the church, in turn, was instructed to love its pastor. Additionally, the people were exhorted to esteem their ministers for their work. Beddome said in a sermon that Christians are "to cherish a high esteem for the ministers of Christ, and to love and

94. Beddome to Goodman's Fields Church, February 24, 1751, in Brooks, *POTP*, 45.
95. Gill, "Reverend Mr Samuel Wilson," in *S&T*, 1:484.
96. Bourton Church to Goodman's Fields Church, February 24, 1751, in Brooks, *POTP*, 44 (emphasis added).
97. Bourton Church to Goodman's Fields Church, December 16, 1750, in Brooks, *POTP*, 38.
98. Fuller, "Qualifications and Encouragement," in *WAF*, 1:135.
99. Fuller, "Pastors Required to Feed," in *WAF*, 1:477–78.

honour them for their work [*sic*] sake [1 Thess 5:12]."[100] In his ordination sermons, Beddome spoke of the church's responsibility toward its pastor. For instance, in "On the Sources of Ministerial Delight," he instructed the church to strengthen their ministers through their prayers, "affectionate conduct," and upright conversations.[101] In another sermon, "The Nature and Authority of the Christian Ministry," Beddome warned of thinking too highly of ministers, yet Christians were to hold them in high regard and contribute financially to their support.[102] Negatively, believers could quench the Spirit by neglecting and despising a minister's efforts, for example, by not attending the preaching or lacking affection for the other members.[103] In the hymn "Bereaved Church," Beddome captured the proper lament of a church that had taken for granted their late pastor's labors:

> Now we lament our errors past,
> With sighs and groans and tears
> The numerous moments spent to waste,
> Amidst our perplexing cares.
>
> The labours of thy servant, Lord,
> By us were misimproved;
> Too little have we read thy word,
> Too much the world have loved.[104]

A pastor had duties toward the church which had called him and the church toward the man they had invited to minister among them. As noted in the section concerning the responsibilities of the church in chapter 2, the Particular Baptists observed a correspondence between the responsibilities of the church and those of the pastor. In other words, a pastor was called to preach the Word to his flock and they, in turn, were to engagingly receive his preaching. Similarly, a pastor was given to a people to guide them concerning spiritual matters; accordingly, it was prudent for members to seek and heed their pastor's counsel.

To return to Gill's funeral sermon for Wilson, the London divine's final reason that a pastor could lawfully remove from one location to another was when "disaffection between him and the people rises so high, on one account or another, that peace and fellowship cannot be maintained, nor the ends of the ministration of the word, and administration of the ordinances

---

100. Beddome, "Sermon 12," in *TSD*, 5:100.
101. Beddome, "Sources of Ministerial Delight," in *SP*, 268.
102. Beddome, "Nature and Authority," in *SP*, 309.
103. Beddome, "Sermon 8," in *TSD*, 4:64.
104. Beddome, *Hymns* (1818), #662.

be answered."[105] The call for mutual love between a pastor and the church was not merely for the friendship between the two but for the sake of the effectiveness of the means of grace in the life of the church. This seems to be an underlying assumption on the part of the Bourton church and Beddome as they penned their letters to Goodman's Fields. The love that existed between the church and its pastor was a strong argument for the latter to remain in Bourton since that allowed for an effective ministry there. Concerning this dynamic, Nigel Wheeler wrote, "Since the church's success rests on a mutual love between the pastor and the church, this affection must be guarded and developed constantly."[106]

For a contemporary pastor to heed the call to love his flock is difficult in that it requires him to walk by the Spirit, deny the flesh, and daily die to self (Matt 16:24; Gal 5:16, 24). It is easy, however, in that he can simply heed the instruction. It is more challenging, from a pastor's perspective, to issue a call to the flock to love the under-shepherd. For a pastor to call his church to their responsibility to show affection toward, have esteem for, and contribute financially for the sake of their minister can be undoubtedly difficult in its own way. Fuller captured the potential awkwardness of a pastor calling his people to fulfill their duties toward him as their pastor:

> It is not usual, I believe, for ministers in their ordinary labours to dwell upon the obligations of the people of their charge towards them. They feel, probably, that on such a subject they might be suspected of partiality to themselves; and if such a suspicion were indulged, however just and proper their admonitions might be, they would be but of little use, and might operate to their disadvantage. Nor is it a subject that a humble and holy man would ordinarily choose, even though there were no danger of misconstruction; he had rather inspire in his people the love of Christ and of one another, hoping that if this prevailed, it would constrain them to whatever was proper towards himself.[107]

There is wisdom in Fuller's words here. He continued, "It does not follow, however, that this species of Christian duty ought never to be insisted on; the glory of God, the success of the church, and the spiritual advantage of individuals will be found to be involved in it."[108] So while a contemporary pastor would be well-advised not to dwell continually on these duties on

---

105. Gill, "Reverend Mr Samuel Wilson," in *S&T*, 1:484.
106. Wheeler, "Eminent Spirituality," 209.
107. Fuller, "Obedience of Churches," in *WAF*, 1:196.
108. Fuller, "Obedience of Churches," in *WAF*, 1:196.

the part of his people or have it be a constant subject of his expositions, it would serve Christ, the church, and himself well to teach on these matters from time to time, perhaps, as they arise in the text under consideration. The Particular Baptists' observation that love between pastor and people is for the effectiveness of the means of grace, and not ultimately for the sake of friendliness or the pastor's comfortability, is helpful in this regard.

CONCLUSION

When Benjamin Beddome died on September 3, 1795, at the age of seventy-eight,[109] he had ministered in Bourton-on-the-Water for fifty-five years. The Bourton pastor had indicated his wish that no funeral sermon be preached for him, but the note was only discovered after his interment. Thus, Benjamin Francis of the Baptist church in Horsley, Gloucestershire, preached at Beddome's funeral from Phil 1:21, "To me to live is Christ, and to die is gain." After speaking of the worthy life and "gainful death" of the apostle, Francis applied the words to "his affectionate friend." The Horsley pastor then urged the large audience to improve "the labours of this great man of God."[110] These words give evidence of Francis's esteem of Beddome, as does the large number of people that gathered on the day of his funeral. The significance of the Bourton pastor's impact on the Midland Association is seen in the appointment of a day of fasting and prayer upon his death.[111]

Beddome had, of course, been useful in Bourton, but he was also respected in his own association and beyond for his preaching and ministerial labors.[112] His impact was extended through the publication of *A Scriptural Exposition of the Baptist Catechism by Way of Question and Answer*, which was widely used by Particular Baptists in their churches and at their principal training center, the Bristol Baptist Academy.[113] After his death in

---

109. Rippon said that "Mr. Beddome had arrived at the good old age of 79 years, 55 of which he ministered at Bourton." Rippon, "Rev. Benjamin Beddome," 326. Beddome's tombstone says, "He died Sep 3rd 1795 / Aged 79." Brady, "Being Benjamin Beddome," 5. It appears that the engravers of the tombstone and Rippon meant that Beddome died in his seventy-ninth year, which would have made him seventy-eight at the time of his death. This is corroborated by the anonymous memorialist who said, that Beddome died "in the 79th year of his age." Anonymous, "Memoir," in Beddome, *SP*, xxv.

110. Rippon, "Rev. Benjamin Beddome," 326. The words "his affectionate friend" referred to Francis in the original; here, I used the phrase to refer to Beddome instead.

111. Stokes, *Midland Association*, 95.

112. Anonymous, "Memoir," in Beddome, *SP*, xxvi.

113. For the information here and the publication details of the various editions of the catechism, see Haykin, "Benjamin Beddome (1717–1795)," 4:268, 273.

1795, Beddome's influence continued, primarily through the posthumous publication of his hymns and sermons and reprintings of his catechism. Even at the beginning of the twentieth century, Beddome was the most significant Baptist hymnwriter, and thus his hymns were widely used in Britain and America.[114]

During the majority of the twentieth century, however, only a few studies on the Bourton pastor emerged, with a master's thesis by Derrick Holmes being the only significant work.[115] The last thirty years has witnessed a resurgence in Beddome studies, with both biographical works and those on his thought having been published.[116] This book has sought to contribute to the discussion by analyzing the life and writings of Beddome to construct his pastoral theology. Throughout, Beddome has been considered against the backdrop of his communion, the English Particular Baptists of the long eighteenth century. While Beddome was not identical in his theology to his brethren, he was, overall, consistent with Particular Baptist *pastoralia*, with his own emphases. In this chapter, the author has retrieved some key lessons for today since it is his conviction that the Bourton pastor has much to teach the contemporary church and its pastors.

---

114. Haykin says, "It is noteworthy that close to one hundred of these hymns were still appearing in hymnals at the end of the nineteenth century, though today, only a handful are still being sung." Haykin, "His Hymns," 106. Roger Hayden states, "The quality of Beddome's work has been undervalued among Baptist hymn writers, but when it is set against the overall assessment which Julian in his Dictionary of Hymns applied to all hymn writers, Beddome was the most prolific of Baptist hymn writers still in use in Britain and America. Over one hundred of his compositions were listed as in regular use, significantly more than his closest rival, Anne Steele." Hayden, *Continuity and Change*, 172. As noted, Hayden is leaning on John Julian, who wrote, "Beddome is thus seen to be in [common usage] to the extent of about 100 hymns. In this respect he exceeds every other Baptist hymn-writer; Miss Steele ranking second." Julian, "Beddome, Benjamin," 124.

115. Holmes, "Early Years (1655–1740)."

116. See Seki, "Resurgence," 45–60.

Bibliography

Anderson, Courtney. *To the Golden Shore: The Life of Adoniram Judson.* Valley Forge, PA: Judson, 1987.

Anonymous. "Memoir." In *Sermons Printed from the Manuscripts of the Late Rev. Benjamin Beddome, A.M. of Bourton-on-the-Water, Gloucestershire; with a Brief Memoir of the Author*, by Benjamin Beddome, ix–xxviii. London: William Ball, 1835.

Anonymous. "Memoir of the Late Mr. Boswell Beddome, of Weymouth." *Baptist Magazine* 27 (1835) 77–83.

Anonymous. "Memoir of the Rev. Samuel Wilson; Formerly Pastor of the Church in Goodman's Fields, London." *Baptist Magazine* 11 (Apr. 1819) 141–45.

Arnold, Richard, ed. *English Hymns of the Eighteenth Century: An Anthology.* American University Studies Series 4, English Language and Literature 137. New York: Peter Lang, 1991.

Arrell, Alex. "The Laying Aside of 'Empty Hands': John Gill and His Theology of Ordination." *JAFS* 7 (Sept. 2023) 45–64.

Auld, Stephen Roy. "'Eminent Spirituality and Eminent Usefulness': Andrew Fuller's Contribution to the Revitalization of the Particular Baptists in the Long Eighteenth Century." Master's thesis, The Southern Baptist Theological Seminary, 2023.

Ballor, Jordan J., et al., eds. *Church and School in Early Modern Protestantism: Studies in Honor of Richard A. Muller on the Maturation of a Theological Tradition.* Studies in the History of Christian Traditions 170. Leiden: Brill, 2013.

Bebbington, David W. "The Significance of Bristol Baptist College." *BQ* 53.4 (Oct. 2022) 149–66.

Beddome, Benjamin. *The Circular Letter from the Elders and Messengers of the Several Baptist Churches [. . .] Met in Association at Bourton on the Water.* Worcester, UK: R. Lewis, 1765.

———. *The Circular Letter from the Elders and Messengers of the Several Baptist Churches [. . .] Met in Association at Pershore.* Pershore, UK: R. Lewis, 1759.

———. "Extracts from Six Letters Written by Benjamin Beddome in 1759 and 1760." Edited by Gary Brady. *JAFS* 1 (Sept. 2020) 59–65.

———. *Hymns Adapted to Public Worship, or Family Devotion: Now First Published, from the Manuscripts of the Late Rev. B. Beddome, A. M.* Edited by Robert Hall. London, 1818.

———. *Hymns Adapted to Public Worship or Family Devotion: A New Edition Including Hymns Not in 1818 Book and Hymns Published Earlier*. 1818. Edited by Barry C. Johnston. Reprint, N.p.: London, 2020.

———. "Letter of Proposal from Benjamin Beddome (1717–1795) to Anne Steele (1717–1778), 23 December 1742." Steele Papers, 1712–1789. Angus Library and Archives, Regent's Park College, Oxford University. https://theangus.rpc.ox.ac.uk/?media-bank-object=letter-of-proposal-from-benjamin-beddome-1717-1795-to-anne-steele-1717-1778-23-december-1742.

———. "Letter to the Association 1789." Transcribed by Gary Brady. *Benjamin Beddome 1717–1795* (blog), Sept. 20, 2011. https://benbeddome.blogspot.com/2011/09/letter-to-association-1789.html.

———. "Original Poetic Epistle to John Collett Ryland." In *The Christian's Elegant Repository*, 41–43. London: Button and Son, 1800.

———. *A Scriptural Exposition of the Baptist Catechism*. 1776. Reprint, Birmingham, AL: Solid Ground Christian Books, 2006.

———. *A Scriptural Exposition of the Baptist Catechism by Way of Question and Answer*. London: J. Ward, 1752.

———. *A Scriptural Exposition of the Baptist Catechism, by Way of Question and Answers by Benjamin Beddome, M.A.* Richmond, VA: Harold & Murray, 1849.

———. *The Sermons of Benjamin Beddome*. Vol. 1. Knightstown, IN: Particular Baptist Heritage Books, 2022.

———. *Sermons Printed from the Manuscripts of the Late Rev. Benjamin Beddome, A.M. of Bourton-on-the-Water, Gloucestershire; with a Brief Memoir of the Author*. London: William Ball, 1835.

———. *Short Discourses, Adapted to Village Worship or the Devotions of the Family*. Vol. 8. London: Samuel Burton; Simpkin and Marshall, 1825.

———. *Twenty Short Discourses, Adapted to Village Worship or the Devotions of the Family*. Vol. 1. 2nd ed. Dunstable, UK: J. W. Morris, 1807.

———. *Twenty Short Discourses, Adapted to Village Worship or the Devotions of the Family*. Vol. 2. Dunstable, UK: J. W. Morris, 1807.

———. *Twenty Short Discourses, Adapted to Village Worship or the Devotions of the Family*. Vol. 3. 6th ed. London: Samuel Burton; Simpkin and Marshall, 1824.

———. *Twenty Short Discourses, Adapted to Village Worship or the Devotions of the Family*. Vol. 4. 4th ed. London: Burton and Smith, 1822.

———. *Twenty Short Discourses, Adapted to Village Worship or the Devotions of the Family*. Vol. 5. London: W. Simpkin and R. Marshall, 1833.

———. *Twenty Short Discourses, Adapted to Village Worship or the Devotions of the Family*. Vol. 6. 5th ed. London: W. Simpkin and R. Marshall, 1834.

———. *Twenty Short Discourses, Adapted to Village Worship or the Devotions of the Family*. Vol. 7. London: Samuel Burton; Simpkin and Marshall, 1825.

Beeke, Joel R. *Reformed Preaching: Proclaiming God's Word from the Heart of the Preacher to the Heart of His People*. Wheaton, IL: Crossway, 2018.

Beeley, Christopher A. *Gregory of Nazianzus on the Trinity and the Knowledge of God: In Your Light We Shall See Light*. Oxford Studies in Historical Theology. New York: Oxford University Press, 2008.

Belcher, Joseph. *Historical Sketches of Hymns, Their Writers, and Their Influence*. Philadelphia: Lindsay & Blakiston, 1859.

Biedebach, Brian. *What to Look for in a Pastor: A Guide for Pastoral Committees.* Leominster, UK: Day One, 2011.
Booth, Abraham. "Advertisement." In *The Difficulties and Supports of a Gospel Minister; and the Duties Incumbent on a Christian Church*, by John Ryland and James Swinton, 2–5. Bristol: Harris and Bryan, 1801.
Boston, Thomas. *The Art of Man-Fishing: How to Reach the Lost.* Fearn, UK: Christian Focus, 2012.
Brackney, William H. "Hall, Robert, Jr." In *Biographical Dictionary of Evangelicals*, edited by Timothy Larsen et al., 284–86. Downers Grove, IL: InterVarsity, 2003.
Brackney, William H., et al., eds. *Pilgrim Pathways: Essays in Baptist History in Honour of B. R. White.* Macon, GA: Mercer University Press, 1999.
Brady, Gary. "Being Benjamin Beddome: A Biographical Study." In *Glory to the Three Eternal: Tercentennial Essays on the Life and Writings of Benjamin Beddome (1718–1795)*, edited by Michael A. G. Haykin et al., 1–33. MBH 13. Eugene, OR: Pickwick, 2019.
———. "Benjamin Beddome 1717–1795." Paper presented at the 2021 Westminster Conference for Theological and Historical Study, December 7, 2021.
———. *Benjamin Beddome 1717–1795* (blog). https://benbeddome.blogspot.com/.
———. "Benjamin Beddome on Friendship (Part 1)." *Banner of Truth Magazine*, October 2023, 9–13.
———. "Benjamin Beddome on Friendship (Part 2)." *Banner of Truth Magazine*, November 2023, 9–13.
———. "A Red Letter Day in Bourton On The Water, August 1765." *Foundations* 85 (Winter 2023) 65–83.
———. "References to Other Writers." *Benjamin Beddome 1717–1795* (blog), Jan. 16, 2022. https://benbeddome.blogspot.com/2022/01/references-to-other-writers-in-sermons-1.html.
Breed, David R. *The History and Use of Hymns and Hymn-Tunes.* Chicago: Fleming H. Revell, 1903.
Briggs, John H. Y., ed. *Pulpit and People: Studies in Eighteenth-Century Baptist Life and Thought.* SBHT 28. Eugene, OR: Wipf & Stock, 2009.
Brine, John. *The Solemn Charge of a Christian Minister Considered.* London: John Ward, 1750.
Brooks, Thomas. "The Epistle Dedicatory." In *The Mute Christian Under the Smarting Rod: With Sovereign Antidotes Against the Most Miserable Exigents*, 287–93. 8th ed. London: John Hancock, 1684.
Brooks, Thomas. "Ministerial Changes a Hundred Years Ago." *Baptist Magazine* 51 (Aug. 1859) 482–87.
———. "Ministerial Changes a Hundred Years Ago." *Baptist Magazine* 51 (July 1859) 425–29.
———. *Pictures of the Past: The History of the Baptist Church, Bourton-on-the-Water.* London: Judd & Glass, 1861.
Brown, Raymond. *The English Baptists of the Eighteenth Century.* A History of the English Baptists 2. London: Baptist Historical Society, 1986.
Chandler, Samuel. *A Sermon Preached at the Ordination of the Reverend Mr. Thomas Wright.* London: J. Waugh, 1759.
Chapell, Bryan. *Christ-Centered Preaching: Redeeming the Expository Sermon.* 3rd ed. Grand Rapids: Baker Academic, 2018.

Charles Simeon Trust. "A Brief History." https://simeontrust.org/about/a-brief-history/.
Charnock, Stephen. *Two Discourses: The First, of Man's Enmity to God [...]. The Second, of the Salvation of Sinners*. London: Tho. Cockerill, 1699.
Church Records of Bourton-on-the-Water Baptist Church, Gloucestershire, 1701–1950. Angus Library and Archive, Regent's Park College, Oxford University.
The Christian's Elegant Repository. London: Button and Son, 1800.
Connell, R. Scott. "'Such Wondrous Grace Demands a Song': The Hymns of Benjamin Beddome." In *Glory to the Three Eternal: Tercentennial Essays on the Life and Writings of Benjamin Beddome (1718–1795)*, edited by Michael A. G. Haykin et al., 118–41. MBH 13. Eugene, OR: Pickwick, 2019.
Cook, Joshua Hawkins. "Benjamin Wallin: A Respectable Minister's Proclamation of the Gospel in Eighteenth-Century London." PhD diss., The Southern Baptist Theological Seminary, 2021.
Copson, Stephen L., and Peter J. Morden, eds. *Challenge and Change: English Baptist Life in the Eighteenth Century*. Didcot, UK: Baptist Historical Society, 2017.
Cramp, J. M. *Baptist History from the Foundation of the Christian Church to the Close of the Eighteenth Century*. Philadelphia: American Baptist Publication Society, 1869.
Crocker, Christopher W. "The Life and Legacy of John Ryland Jr. (1753–1825): A Man of Considerable Usefulness—an Historical Biography." PhD diss., Bristol Baptist College, University of Bristol, 2018.
Cross, Anthony R. *Useful Learning: Neglected Means of Grace in the Reception of the Evangelical Revival Among English Particular Baptists*. Eugene, OR: Wipf & Stock, 2017.
Culross, James. *The Three Rylands: A Hundred Years of Various Christian Service*. London: Elliot Stock, 1897.
Daley, Brian E. *Gregory of Nazianzus*. Early Church Fathers. London: Routledge, 2006.
David, Luke. "Biographical Preface: The Life and Times of Benjamin Beddome (1717–1795)." In *The Sermons of Benjamin Beddome*, by Benjamin Beddome, xi–xxix. Knightstown, IN: Particular Baptist Heritage Books, 2022.
Dix, Kenneth. "'Thy Will Be Done': A Study in the Life of Benjamin Beddome." *Bulletin of the Strict Baptist Historical Society* 9 (1972) n.p.
Doddridge, Philip. *The Works of the Rev. P. Doddridge*. 10 vols. Leeds: Edward Baines, 1803.
Duncan, Pope. "President Pope Duncan's Autobiography (draft, circa 2003)." Stetson University. https://library.stetson.edu/ld.php?content_id=76998453.
The Editors of Encyclopedia Britannica. "Sibyl." *Encyclopedia Britannica*, July 4, 2022. https://www.britannica.com/topic/Sibyl-Greek-legendary-figure.
Eswine, Zach. *The Imperfect Pastor: Discovering Joy in Our Limitations Through a Daily Apprenticeship with Jesus*. Wheaton, IL: Crossway, 2015.
Evangelical Magazine for 1800. Vol. 8. London: T. Chapman, 1800.
Evans, Caleb. "A Confession of Faith." In *A Charge and Sermon [...] Delivered at the Ordination of the Rev. Mr. Caleb Evans*, by Samuel Stennett and John Thomas, 13–45. 2nd ed. Bristol: S. Farley, 1767.
Evans, Caleb, and Hugh Evans. *A Charge and Sermon; Delivered at the Ordination of the Rev. Thomas Dunscombe*. Bristol; London: W. Pine, T. Cadell, M. Ward, etc.; J. Buckland, 1773.

Fawcett, John. *An Account of the Life, Ministry, and Writings of the Late Rev. John Fawcett, D. D.* London; Halifax: Baldwin, Cradock, and Joy; and P. K. Holden, 1818.

Finn, Nathan A. "The Renaissance in Andrew Fuller Studies: A Bibliographic Essay." *SBJT* 17.2 (Summer 2013) 44–61.

Flint, Thomas. "A Brief Narrative of the Life and Death of the Rev. Benjamin Francis, A. M." In *The Presence of Christ the Source of Eternal Bliss: A Funeral Discourse [. . .] Occasioned by the Death of the Rev. Benjamin Francis, A. M.*, by John Ryland, 33–76. Bristol, 1800.

Fuller, Andrew. *The Complete Works of Andrew Fuller*, edited by Michael A. G. Haykin. 17 vols. Berlin: de Gruyter, 2016–.

———. *The Complete Works of the Rev. Andrew Fuller with a Memoir of His Life by Andrew Gunton Fuller*. 3 vols. Edited by Joseph Belcher. Philadelphia: American Baptist Publication Society, 1845.

Fuller, Andrew, and John Ryland Jr. *The Qualifications and Encouragement of a Faithful Minister, Illustrated by the Character and Success of Barnabas. And, Paul's Charge to the Corinthians Respecting Their Treatment of Timothy Applied to the Conduct of Churches Toward Their Pastors*. London, 1787.

Furneaux, Philip. *A Sermon Preached at the Ordination of Mr. Samuel Wilton*. London: J. Buckland, and J. Payne, 1766.

Gill, John. *A Collection of Sermons and Tracts*. 2 vols. London: George Keith, 1773.

———. *A Complete Body of Doctrinal and Practical Divinity: or a System of Evangelical Truths, Deduced from the Sacred Scriptures*. 1839. Reprint, Paris, AR: Baptist Standard Bearer, 1989.

———. *Complete Body of Practical and Doctrinal Divinity: Being a System of Evangelical Truths, Deduced from the Sacred Scriptures*. Abridged by William Staughton. Philadelphia: Delaplaine and Hellings, 1810.

———. *An Exposition of the Old and New Testaments*. 9 vols. 1809–10. Reprint, Paris, AR: Baptist Standard Bearer, 2006.

Gill, John, and Samuel Wilson. *The Mutual Duty of Pastor and People, Represented in Two Discourses Preached at the Ordination of the Reverend George Braithwaite, M. A.* London: Aaron Ward, 1734.

Gordon, Grant. "The Call of Dr John Ryland Jr." *BQ* 34.5 (1992) 214–27.

———. "John Ryland, Jr. (1753–1825)." In *The British Particular Baptists, 1638–1910*, edited by Michael A. G. Haykin, 2:17–28. Springfield, MO: Particular Baptist, 2000.

Grant, Keith S. *Andrew Fuller and the Evangelical Renewal of Pastoral Theology*. SBHT 36. Milton Keynes, UK: Paternoster, 2013.

Greene, John. *Reminiscences of the Rev. Robert Hall, A.M. Late of Bristol, and Sketches of His Sermons Preached at Cambridge Prior to 1806*. London; Cambridge; Leicester; Bristol; Birmingham; Ipswich; Bury St. Edmonds: Westley and Davis; Deighton and Sons, and Johnson; Coombe; Bulgin; Wrightson and Webb; Piper; Lankester, 1832.

Gregory, Olinthus. "A Brief Memoir of the Rev. Robert Hall, A.M." In *The Works of the Rev. Robert Hall, A.M. with a Memoir of His Life, by Dr. Gregory; Reminiscences, by John Greene, Esq.; and His Character as a Preacher, by the Rev. John Foster*, edited by Olinthus Gregory and Joseph Belcher. 4 vols. New York: Harper & Brothers, 1849.

Hall, Robert. "Editor's Preface." In *Hymns Adapted to Public Worship, or Family Devotion: Now First Published, from the Manuscripts of the Late Rev. B. Beddome, A. M.*, by Benjamin Beddome, edited by Robert Hall, ix–xi. London, 1818.

———. "Recommendatory Preface." In *Hymns Adapted to Public Worship, or Family Devotion: Now First Published, from the Manuscripts of the Late Rev. B. Beddome, A. M.*, by Benjamin Beddome, edited by Robert Hall, v–viii. London, 1818.

Harman, Allan. "Matthew Henry's Move to Hackney in 1712." *Reformed Theological Review* 80.2 (Aug. 2021) 155–73.

Harris, Murray J. *The Second Epistle to the Corinthians: A Commentary on the Greek Text*. New International Greek Testament Commentary. Grand Rapids: Eerdmans, 2005.

Hayden, Roger. "Bristol Baptist Academy, 1720 to Present." *Dissenting Academies Online: Database and Encyclopedia*. Dr. Williams's Centre for Dissenting Studies, August 2011.

———. *Continuity and Change: Evangelical Calvinism Among Eighteenth-Century Baptist Ministers Trained at Bristol Academy, 1690–1791*. Chipping Norton, UK: Nigel Lynn, 2006.

———. "The Contribution of Bernard Foskett." In *Pilgrim Pathways: Essays in Baptist History in Honour of B. R. White*, edited by William H. Brackney et al., 189–206. Macon, GA: Mercer University Press, 1999.

———. "Evangelical Calvinism Among Eighteenth-Century British Baptists with Particular Reference to Bernard Foskett, Hugh and Caleb Evans and the Bristol Baptist Academy, 1690–1791." PhD diss., University of Keele, 1991.

Haykin, Michael A. G. "Baptists Reflecting on Adam and Eve in the 'Long' Eighteenth Century." *SBJT* 15.1 (2011) 92–99.

———. "Benjamin Beddome (1717–1795)." In *The British Particular Baptists, 1638–1910*, edited by Michael A. G. Haykin, 1:167–83. 1st ed. Springfield, MO: Particular Baptist, 1998.

———. "Benjamin Beddome (1717–1795)." In *The British Particular Baptists, 1638–1910*, edited by Michael A. G. Haykin and Terry Wolever, 4:258–73. Springfield, MO: Particular Baptist, 2018.

———. "Benjamin Beddome (1717–1795): His Life and His Hymns." In *Pulpit and People: Studies in Eighteenth-Century Baptist Life and Thought*, edited by John H. Y. Briggs, 93–111. SBHT 28. Eugene, OR: Wipf & Stock, 2009.

———. "Benjamin Beddome (1717–1795) of Bourton-on-the-Water." In *A Scriptural Exposition of the Baptist Catechism*, by Benjamin Beddome, i–x. 1776. Reprint, Birmingham, AL: Solid Ground Christian Books, 2006.

———. "Benjamin Beddome and the Bible." *Evangelical Times* 51.2 (Feb. 2017) 12, 15.

———. "Benjamin Francis (1734–1799)." In *The British Particular Baptists, 1638–1910*, edited by Michael A. G. Haykin, 2:17–28. Springfield, MO: Particular Baptist, 2000.

———. *"Blest Be the Tie That Binds": Remembering John Fawcett—His Life, His Times, His Hymn*. Louisville, KY: Andrew Fuller Center for Baptist Studies, 2017.

———. "British Particular Baptist Biography." In *The British Particular Baptists, 1638–1910*, edited by Michael A. G. Haykin and Terry Wolever, 1:15–19. Rev. ed. Springfield, MO: Particular Baptist, 2018.

———, ed. *The British Particular Baptists, 1638–1910*. Vol. 1. 1st ed. Springfield, MO: Particular Baptist, 1998.

———, ed. *The British Particular Baptists, 1638–1910*. Vol. 2. Springfield, MO: Particular Baptist, 2000.

———. "A Cloud of Witnesses—Benjamin Beddome (Part 1)." *Evangelical Times* (July 1, 2001). https://www.evangelical-times.org/a-cloud-of-witnesses-8/.

———. "A Cloud of Witnesses—Benjamin Beddome (Part 2)." *Evangelical Times* (Aug. 1, 2001). https://www.evangelical-times.org/a-cloud-of-witnesses-19/.

———. "A Cloud of Witnesses—Benjamin Beddome (Part 3)." *Evangelical Times* (Sept. 1, 2001). https://www.evangelical-times.org/a-cloud-of-witnesses-18/.

———. "'Drawn in Crimson Lines': Colour in the Hymnody of Benjamin Beddome." *Puritan Reformed Journal* 14.2 (July 2022) 60–64.

———. *From Reformation to Revival: The Story of British Evangelicalism with Particular Attention to the Particular Baptists, 1520s–1830s*. Occasional Publications 4. Louisville, KY: Andrew Fuller Center for Baptist Studies, 2017.

———. "'Glory to the Three Eternal': Benjamin Beddome and the Teaching of Trinitarian Theology." In *Glory to the Three Eternal: Tercentennial Essays on the Life and Writings of Benjamin Beddome (1718–1795)*, edited by Michael A. G. Haykin et al., 34–50. MBH 13. Eugene, OR: Pickwick, 2019.

———. "'Glory to the Three Eternal': Benjamin Beddome and the Teaching of Trinitarian Theology in the Eighteenth Century." *SBJT* 10.1 (Spring 2006) 72–85.

———. *Holy Spirit Now Descend: Thomas Davis and the Evangelical Revival in Georgian Berkshire*. Evangelical Lives 1. Brighton, UK: Ettrick, 2022.

———. "John Fawcett (1740–1817)." In *The British Particular Baptists, 1638–1910*, edited by Michael A. G. Haykin and Terry Wolever, 5:193–217. Springfield, MO: Particular Baptist, 2019.

———, ed. *The Life and Thought of John Gill (1697–1771): A Tercentennial Appreciation*. Studies in the History of Christian Thought 77. Leiden: Brill, 1997.

———. *The Missionary Fellowship of William Carey*. A Long Line of Godly Men Profiles. Orlando, FL: Reformation Trust, 2018.

———. "'Nursing Fathers and . . . Nursing Mothers to the Israel of God': Benjamin Beddome on Praying for Godly Rulers." *JAFS* 7 (Sept. 2023) 65–68.

———. *One Heart and One Soul: John Sutcliff of Olney, His Friends and His Times*. Darlington, UK: Evangelical, 1994.

———. "Particular Baptists." In *The Oxford Handbook of Early Evangelicalism*, edited by Jonathan Yeager, 254–72. Oxford: Oxford University Press, 2022.

———. "'Those Who Plead for Thee': English Particular Baptist Preaching in the Long Eighteenth Century." *EQ* 94.4 (Dec. 2023) 299–311.

Haykin, Michael A. G., and Victoria Haykin. *The Christian Lover: The Sweetness of Love and Marriage in the Letters of Believers*. Lake Mary, FL: Reformation Trust, 2009.

Haykin, Michael A. G., and Terry Wolever, eds. *The British Particular Baptists, 1638–1910*. Vol. 1. Rev. ed. Springfield, MO: Particular Baptist, 2018.

———, eds. *The British Particular Baptists, 1638–1910*. Vol. 4. Springfield, MO: Particular Baptist, 2018.

———, eds. *The British Particular Baptists, 1638–1910*. Vol. 5. Springfield, MO: Particular Baptist, 2019.

Haykin, Michael A. G., et al. *Being a Pastor: A Conversation with Andrew Fuller*. Darlington, UK: Evangelical, 2019.

Haykin, Michael A. G., et al., eds. *Glory to the Three Eternal: Tercentennial Essays on the Life and Writings of Benjamin Beddome (1718-1795)*. MBH 13. Eugene, OR: Pickwick, 2019.

Hester, G. "Baptist Worthies—Benjamin Beddome." *Baptist Magazine* 57 (July 1865) 441–46.

Holmes, Derrick. "The Early Years (1655–1740) of Bourton-on-the-Water Dissenters Who Later Constituted the Baptist Church, with Special Reference to the Ministry of the Reverend Benjamin Beddome A.M. 1740-1795." Certificate in education diss., St. Paul's College, 1969.

Hussey, Joseph. *God's Operations of Grace but No Offers of Grace*. N.p.: Supralapsarian, 2015.

Ivimey, Joseph. *A History of the English Baptists Comprising the Principal Events of the History of Protestant Dissenters, from the Revolution in 1668 till 1760; and of the London Baptist Churches, During That Period*. Vol. 3. London: B. J. Holdworth, 1823.

———. *A History of the English Baptists Comprising the Principal Events of the History of the Protestant Dissenters, during the Reign of Geo. III and of the Baptist Churches in London with Notices of Many of the Principal Churches in the Country During the Same Period*. Vol. 4. London: Isaac Taylor Hinton; Holdsworth & Ball, 1830.

Jackman, David. "The Hermeneutical Distinctives of Expository Preaching." In *Preach the Word: Essays on Expository Preaching in Honor of R. Kent Hughes*, edited by Leland Ryken and Todd A. Wilson, 9–21. Wheaton, IL: Crossway, 2007.

Jewson, Charles Boardman. *The Baptists in Norfolk*. London: Carey Kingsgate, 1957.

Julian, John, ed. "Beddome, Benjamin, M.A." In *A Dictionary of Hymnology*, 121–24. New York: Charles Scribner's Sons, 1892.

———, ed. *A Dictionary of Hymnology*. New York: Charles Scribner's Sons, 1892.

Kruse, Colin G. *2 Corinthians: An Introduction and Commentary*. Tyndale New Testament Commentary 8. Downers Grove, IL: InterVarsity, 2015.

Larsen, Timothy, et al., eds. *Biographical Dictionary of Evangelicals*. Downers Grove, IL: InterVarsity, 2003.

MacLeod, Angus Hamilton. "The Life and Teaching of Robert Hall, 1764–1831." Master's thesis, Durham University, 1957. http://etheses.dur.ac.uk/798/.

Manley, Ken. *"Redeeming Love Proclaim": John Rippon and the Baptists*. SBHT 12. Carlisle, UK: Paternoster, 2004.

Mann, Isaac. "Calendar of Letters, 1742–1831." *BQ* 6.2 (Apr. 1932) 83–85.

———. "Calendar of Letters, 1742–1831." *BQ* 6.4 (Oct. 1932) 173–86.

McGuckin, John A. *St. Gregory of Nazianzus: An Intellectual Biography*. Crestwood, NY: St. Vladimir's Seminary Press, 2001.

McKay, Stephen. "The Trinitarian Theology of Particular Baptists in England (1734–1795): Anne Dutton, Benjamin Beddome, Caleb Evans, and Samuel Stennett." Master's thesis, Australian College of Theology, 2019.

McNutt, Cody Heath. "The Ministry of Robert Hall, Jr.: The Preacher as Theological Exemplar and Cultural Celebrity." PhD diss., The Southern Baptist Theological Seminary, 2012.

Montgomery, Jason C. "Benjamin Beddome and the Modern Question: The Witness of His Sermons." In *Glory to the Three Eternal: Tercentennial Essays on the Life and Writings of Benjamin Beddome (1718–1795)*, edited by Michael A. G. Haykin et al., 142–71. MBH 13. Eugene, OR: Pickwick, 2019.

———. "Benjamin Beddome: The Fruitful Life and Evangelical Labor of a Forgotten Village Preacher." PhD diss., Southwestern Baptist Theological Seminary, 2018.

Morris, J. W. *Biographical Recollections of the Rev. Robert Hall, A. M.* London; Cambridge; Leicester; Bristol: George Wightman; Johnson; J. F. Winks and R. Tebbutt; Bulgin, 1833.

Naylor, Peter. *Calvinism, Communion, and the Baptists: A Study of English Calvinistic Baptists from the Late 1600s to the Early 1800s.* SBHT 7. Carlisle, UK: Paternoster, 2003.

Newman, William. *Rylandiana: Reminiscences Relating to the Rev. John Ryland, A.M.* London: George Wightman, 1835.

Newton, John. Collection CO199. Princeton University, Princeton, NJ. http://arks.princeton.edu/ark:/88435/dj52w4735.

———. "Tuesday 27 June 1775." Transcribed by Marylynn Rouse. The John Newton Project, Jan. 20, 2014. https://www.johnnewton.org/Articles/371303/The_John_Newton/new_menus/Hymns/OH_Book_1/OH_Book_1.aspx

———. "Wednesday 7 August 1776." Transcribed by Marylynn Rouse. The John Newton Project, Jan. 20, 2014. https://www.johnnewton.org/Articles/371159/The_John_Newton/new_menus/Hymns/OH_Book_1/OH_Book_1.aspx.

———. *Wise Counsel: John Newton's Letters to John Ryland, Jr.* Edited by Grant Gordon. Carlisle, PA: Banner of Truth Trust, 2009.

Norris, Frederick W., ed. "Introduction." In *Faith Gives Fullness to Reasoning: The Five Theological Orations of Gregory Nazianzen*, by Gregory of Nazianzus, translated by Lionel Wickham and Frederick Williams, 1–82. Supplements to Vigiliae Christianae 13. Leiden: Brill, 1990.

Nuttall, Geoffrey F. "Letters by Benjamin Francis." *Trafodion* (1983) 4–8.

Oliver, Robert W. *History of the English Calvinistic Baptists, 1771–1892: From John Gill to C. H. Spurgeon.* Edinburgh: Banner of Truth Trust, 2006.

———. "John Gill (1697–1771): His Life and Ministry." In *The Life and Thought of John Gill (1697–1771): A Tercentennial Appreciation*, edited by Michael A. G. Haykin, 7–50. Studies in the History of Christian Thought 77. Leiden: Brill, 1997.

Osborn, G. "An Introductory Address." In *The Duty of Ministers to Be Nursing Fathers to the Church; and the Duty of Churches to Regard Ministers as the Gift of Christ*, by John Ryland Jr. and Samuel Pearce, 5–9. London, 1796.

Owen, John. *The True Nature of a Gospel Church and Its Government.* London: William Marshall, 1689.

Percival, Henry R., ed. *The Seven Ecumenical Councils of the Undivided Church.* Vol. 14 of *NPNF*2. Edited by Philip Schaff and Henry Wace. New York: Charles Scribner's Sons, 1900.

Pickles, Stephen. *Cotswolds Pastor and Baptist Hymn Writer: The Life and Times of Benjamin Beddome.* Upham, UK: James Bourne Society, 2023.

Porter, Roy. *London: A Social History.* Cambridge, MA: Harvard University Press, 1994.

Ramsey, Daniel S. "'The Blessed Spirit': An Analysis of the Pneumatology of Benjamin Beddome as an Early Evangelical." PhD diss., The Southern Baptist Theological Seminary, 2017.

———. "The Pneumatology of Benjamin Beddome." In *Glory to the Three Eternal: Tercentennial Essays on the Life and Writings of Benjamin Beddome (1718–1795)*, edited by Michael A. G. Haykin et al., 89–117. MBH 13. Eugene, OR: Pickwick, 2019.

Research Centre "Cultures, Sociétés et Technologies de l'Information." "Demography." Georgian Cities, n.d. https://18thc-cities.sorbonne-universite.fr/-Demography-.html#1.

Reynolds, J. L. "Introduction." In *A Scriptural Exposition of the Baptist Catechism, by Way of Question and Answers*, by Benjamin Beddome, 3–27. Richmond, VA: Harold & Murray, 1849.

Richards, William, and Thomas Wright. "Questions Proposed by the Reverend Mr. William Richards; and the Answers Returned." In *A Sermon Preached at the Ordination of the Reverend Mr. Thomas Wright*, by Samuel Chandler, 3–16. London: J. Waugh, 1759.

Rippon, John. *The Baptist Annual Register, for 1790, 1791, 1792, and Part of 1793. Including Sketches of the State of Religion Among Different Denominations of Good Men at Home and Abroad*. London, 1793.

———. *The Baptist Annual Register, for 1794, 1795, 1796–1797, Including Sketches of the State of Religion Among Different Denominations of Good Men at Home and Abroad*. London, 1797.

———. *The Baptist Annual Register, for 1798, 1799, 1800, and Part of 1801, Including Sketches of the State of Religion Among Different Denominations of Good Men at Home and Abroad*. London, 1801.

———. *The Baptist Annual Register, for 1801 and 1802. Including Sketches of the State of Religion Among Different Denominations of Good Men at Home and Abroad*. London, 1802.

———. *A Brief Essay Towards an History of the Baptist Academy at Bristol; Read Before the Bristol Education Society, at Their Anniversary Meeting, in Broadmead, August 26th, 1795*. London, 1796.

———. *A Brief Memoir of the Life and Writings of the late Rev. John Gill, D.D.* 1838. Reprint, Harrisonburg, VA: Gano Books, 1992.

———. "Rev. Benjamin Beddome, A. M. Bourton-on-the-Water, Gloucestershire." In *The Baptist Annual Register, for 1794, 1795, 1796–1797, Including Sketches of the State of Religion Among Different Denominations of Good Men at Home and Abroad*, 314–26. London, 1797.

———. "The Rev. John Reynolds, A. M. London." In *The Baptist Annual Register, for 1794, 1795, 1796–1797*, 41–44. London, 1797.

———. "Sketch of a Sermon by the Late Rev. B. Beddome." In *The Baptist Annual Register for 1798, 1799, 1800, and Part of 1801, Including Sketches of the State of Religion Among Different Denominations of Good Men at Home and Abroad*, 415–21. London, 1801.

Ryken, Leland, and Todd A. Wilson, eds. *Preach the Word: Essays on Expository Preaching in Honor of R. Kent Hughes*. Wheaton, IL: Crossway, 2007.

Ryland, John, and James Hinton. *The Difficulties and Supports of a Gospel Minister; and the Duties Incumbent on a Christian Church*. Bristol: Harris and Bryan, 1801.

Ryland, John, and Samuel Pearce. *The Duty of Ministers to Be Nursing Fathers to the Church; and the Duty of Churches to Regard Ministers as the Gift of Christ*. London, 1796.

Sanchez, Paul A. *Spirituality of Love in Andrew Fuller's Ordination Sermons*. Occasional Publications 7. Louisville, KY: Andrew Fuller Center for Baptist Studies, 2018.

———. "'To Love the Souls of the People': Andrew Fuller and the Virtue of Love in Pastoral Ministry." *Bulletin of Ecclesial Theology* 9.1 (Sept. 2022) 85–99.

Schaeffer, Francis A. *No Little People*. 1974. Reprint, Wheaton, IL: Crossway, 2021.
Seki, Yuta. "Pastoral Usefulness: Retrieving Wisdom from the Letters of Benjamin Beddome." Paper presented at the annual meeting of the Evangelical Theological Society Ontario and Quebec, Toronto, October 12, 2024.
———. "Pastoral Usefulness: Retrieving Wisdom from the Letters of Benjamin Beddome." *JAFS* 10 (Spring 2025).
———. "A Resurgence of Benjamin Beddome Studies: A Bibliographic Essay." *JAFS* 8 (Spring 2024) 45–60.
Spurgeon, Charles H. *Lectures to My Students: A Selection from Addresses Delivered to the Students of the Pastor's College, Metropolitan Tabernacle*. London: Passmore and Alabaster, 1875.
Stennett, Joseph. "A Funeral Sermon, at the Internment of the Reverend Mr. Samuel Wilson." In *Sermons on Various Subjects and Occasions*, by Samuel Wilson, 1–14. London: G. Keith; J. Ward, 1753.
Stennett, Samuel, and John Thomas. *A Charge and Sermon [. . .] Delivered at the Ordination of the Rev. Mr. Caleb Evans*. 2nd ed. Bristol: S. Farley, 1767.
Stitzinger, James F. "The History of Expository Preaching." *Master's Seminary Journal* 3.1 (Spring 1992) 5–32.
Stokes, Williams. *The History of the Midland Association of Baptist Churches, from Its Rise in the Year 1655 to 1855*. London: R. Theobald, 1855.
Strivens, Robert. "Bernard Foskett (1658–1758)." In *The British Particular Baptists, 1638–1910*, edited by Michael A. G. Haykin and Terry Wolever, 4:87–103. Springfield, MO: Particular Baptist, 2018.
Swaine, Stephen Albert. *Faithful Men, or, Memorials of Bristol Baptist College, and Some of Its Most Distinguished Alumni*. London: Alexander & Shepheard, 1884.
Turner, Daniel. "Consolation in Spiritual Darkness: A Letter from Daniel Turner to Benjamin Beddome 1762." Edited by Gray Brady. *JAFS* 2 (Feb. 2021) 59–70.
———. *Consolation in Spiritual Darkness. A Letter from the Late Rev. Daniel Turner, M. A. of Abingdon, to the Rev. Benjamin Beddome, of Bourton*. London: Williams and Co., 1816.
———. "Spiritual Darkness." *Baptist Magazine* 7 (Jan. 1815) 8–14.
Underwood, A. C. *A History of the English Baptists*. London: Baptist Union Publication Dept. (Kingsgate), 1947.
Van Biema, David. "The New Calvinism." *Time*, Mar. 12, 2009. https://content.time.com/time/specials/packages/article/0,28804,1884779_1884782_1884760,00.html.
Wallin, Benjamin, and Samuel Stennett. *A Charge and Sermon [. . .] Delivered at the Ordination of the Rev. Mr. Abraham Booth*. London: G. Keith, J. Buckland, W. Harris, B. Tomkins, J. Gurney, 1769.
Watson, J. R. *The English Hymn: A Critical and Historical Study*. Oxford: Oxford University Press, 1997.
Watson, Thomas. *A Body of Practical Divinity, Containing of Above One Hundred Seventy Six Sermons on the Lesser Catechism Composed by the Reverend Assembly of the Divines at Westminster: With a Supplement of Some Sermons on Several Texts of Scripture*. London: Thomas Parkhurst, 1692.
Wheeler, Nigel. "Andrew Fuller's Ordination Sermons." *Eusebeia* 8 (Spring 2008) 169–82.

———. "'Eminent Spirituality and Eminent Usefulness': Andrew Fuller's (1754–1815) Pastoral Theology in His Ordination Sermons." PhD diss., University of Pretoria, 2009.

———. *The Pastoral Priorities of 18th Century Baptists: An Examination of Andrew Fuller's Ordination Sermons*. Peterborough, ON: H&E Academic, 2021.

Whitley, W. T. *A History of British Baptists*. 2nd ed. London: Kingsgate, 1932.

Wilson, Samuel. *Sermons on Various Subjects and Occasions*. London: G. Keith; J. Ward, 1753.

Wilton, Samuel, and Francis Spilsbury. "Mr. Wilton's Confession of Faith, and Answers to the Questions Proposed to Him." In *A Sermon Preached at the Ordination of Mr. Samuel Wilton*, by Philip Furneaux, 41–66. London: J. Buckland and J. Payne, 1766.

Wolever, Terry. "Samuel Wilson (1703–1750)." In *The British Particular Baptists, 1638–1910*, edited by Michael A. G. Haykin and Terry Wolever, 4:183–209. Springfield, MO: Particular Baptist, 2018.

Wrigley, E. A. "A Simple Model of London's Importance in Changing English Society and Economy 1650–1750." *Past and Present* 37 (1967) 44–70.

Xu, Huafang. "Communion with God and Comfortable Dependence on Him: Anne Dutton's Trinitarian Spirituality." PhD diss., The Southern Baptist Theological Seminary, 2018.

Yeager, Jonathan, ed. *The Oxford Handbook of Early Evangelicalism*. Oxford: Oxford University Press, 2022.

Yoo, Jeongmo. "Benjamin Beddome's Christology." In *Glory to the Three Eternal: Tercentennial Essays on the Life and Writings of Benjamin Beddome (1718–1795)*, edited by Michael A. G. Haykin et al., 51–88. MBH 13. Eugene, OR: Pickwick, 2019.

———. "The Bristol Academy and the Education of Ministers in Eighteenth-Century England (1758–1791)." In *Church and School in Early Modern Protestantism: Studies in Honor of Richard A. Muller on the Maturation of a Theological Tradition*, edited by Jordan J. Ballor et al., 749–63. Studies in the History of Christian Traditions 170. Leiden: Brill, 2013.

www.ingramcontent.com/pod-product-compliance
Lightning Source LLC
Chambersburg PA
CBHW070324230426
43663CB00011B/2212